FRANK
UNEDITED

Other Lotus Titles

Forthcoming Titles

FRANK
UNEDITED

The Best of Frank Simoes

With a Foreword by
Dom Moraes

LOTUS COLLECTION
ROLI BOOKS

Lotus Collection

This edition published in 2003
The Lotus Collection
An imprint of
Roli Books Pvt Ltd
M-75, G.K. II Market
New Delhi 110 048
Phones: ++91 (011) 2921 2271, 2921 2782
2921 0886, Fax: ++91 (011) 2921 7185
E-mail: roli@vsnl.com; Website: rolibooks.com

Also at
Varanasi, Agra, Jaipur and the Netherlands

ISBN: 81-7436-303-3
Rs. 395

Typeset in AGaramond by Roli Books Pvt Ltd
Printed at Tan Prints (India) Pvt. Ltd., Jhajjar, Haryana

For Radhika
In fulfilment of one of
Frank's special wishes

Contents

Acknowledgements

The Publishers wish to thank the following publications who have graciously given permission to reproduce the articles, columns and stories included in this book:

Afternoon Despatch & Courier; The Asian Age; Goa Today; Magna Publishing Co. Ltd; Mid-Day; Outlook; The Taj Magazine; The Times of India; Verve Magazine.

The chapter 'Three Thunder-boxes and a Mandolin' first appeared in *Glad Seasons in Goa,* and the chapter 'A Perfect Pair of Breasts' in *Uncertain Liaisons*, both originally published by Penguin Books India Pvt. Ltd.

Our grateful thanks to Christopher and Stuart D'Rozario who made this book happen.

To Gita Simoes, our thanks for entrusting us with the legacy of Frank Simoes' work, and for helping us so unstintingly with every detail of the book.

While every effort has been made to contact the copyright holders of all the articles, any omissions are regretted.

****

Frank Simoes and I knew each other for perhaps a quarter of a century. We had many things in common. We were both born in the city that is now unfortunately known as Mumbai, and both our families originated in Goa when it was still under Portuguese rule. Had we been English, we would also have flaunted the same old school tie, for we both went to St. Mary's High School in Mazagaon, though he was junior to me. I knew him well, and wish I had known him better. But when we were young men, he was busy carving out a very successful career in what was still called Bombay, and I was living in various foreign countries. When we did eventually meet, it was through an old Bombay institution, the cocktail circuit, first founded by the British.

I lived abroad for twenty years before, in 1980, I returned to the city where I had been born, Bombay. Some of its physical features had remained the same, though it had been allowed to become grossly overpopulated and was consequently far more squalid and filthy than it had previously been. The malefic presence of communal hatred was felt everywhere.

But there were still islands of culture in the city, though widely separated. Some belonged to Marathi artists who wore impassioned beards, others were inhabited by Gujarati writers and painters. They had existed throughout the history of Bombay and so too, like a band of Robinson Crusoes isolated by history, had a small population of westernized intellectuals. All these groups had existed in my father's youth, and each group had met regularly in one another's houses to talk over Scotch, or chaas or cups of very sweet tea: to each his own.

Thirty years later, when I returned to live in Bombay, the groups still remained. I had not believed in cultural cliques when I lived in Europe and America, but here they seemed to me a necessity. They brought together the few like-minded people in Bombay and made them friendly. Otherwise each of them would have been alone, and none would have felt part of society, for normal Indian society, like it or not, was not what they fitted into. They might be patriotic Indians, but their minds and personalities had been moulded by western culture and they could not help this. It was a historical accident caused by the British years.

The nature of elitist westernized society in the city had also changed to keep pace with the times. Thirty years earlier, people had dropped into their friends' houses of a Sunday morning for a beer, or on weekday evenings for some stronger beverage. They almost always came uninvited, and were always made welcome; and they almost always stayed on for lunch or dinner, as the case might be. Now these intimacies had almost entirely disappeared. The group of westernized friends still existed, but they rarely visited each other's homes. They met and talked at cocktail parties or dinners thrown by other people.

I have dwelt on this point at length because it represented the new Bombay or Mumbai in which Frank and I met. We were friends but not intimates as my father had been with his closer associates. But we belonged to a tradition started by our ancestors. I first met Frank at a cocktail party. He was a tall, loose-limbed man, with a boyish face under prematurely white hair. His face sometimes glowed with pleasure when he met a friend or heard a memorable witticism, but could also seem withdrawn into a dream that nobody else could enter.

At this first meeting, I did not know who he was. I was later told that he was one of the most successful advertising men in India. Born of an aristocratic Goan family that had lost its money, he was brilliant in school, particularly with the manipulation of words. He put this talent to use once he had left school. One of the stories about him concerns my father.

Like all talented young writers, Frank wanted to see his work printed. He continually submitted 'middles' – short articles that appear on the editorial page of *The Times of India* – to that paper. My father was then the editor. Frank sent forty-nine 'middles' to the *Times*. All were rejected. His fiftieth submission described how it had felt to have forty-nine turned down in a row, and it was published. Frank used to tell this story, which illustrated two aspects of his character: a resilient sense of humour, which he could use against himself, and a refusal to accept defeat.

He joined a large advertising firm as a copywriter and wrote some of the most brilliant copy ever known in the world of Indian advertising. His copy was inimitable and some of his lines are not only remembered but also still used years after he wrote them. He and the team he inspired, together with the Taj Group of Hotels, made Goa a landmark on the map of world tourism.

He told me wistfully that he would like to be 'a proper writer'. He used to show me articles and essays, some of which appear in this book, and I felt he had a natural talent.

Quite suddenly, or so it seemed, he decided to fulfil his life's ambition. He was not, in my judgement, an impetuous man, but he sold his highly profitable company, and built a beach house in Goa. With his wife Gita and their daughter, he lived partly there and partly in a Mumbai flat.

In addition to his immense body of work as a copywriter, he wrote a biography of the Goan industrialist Salgaocar, a man who also grew from small beginnings.

Frank wrote on many subjects and in the end, unlike most people, he fulfilled his ambition and wrote a book, *Glad Seasons in Goa* which concerns the building of his house and the gradual development of his friendship with the local inhabitants. As its title suggests, it is a light-hearted book, funny and carefree, and yet it is a very human document and promised much for the future. Frank was pleased by its success and started to write a novel which he told me was more serious than *Glad Seasons*. He seemed very dedicated to this, and reported on its progress whenever we met. At this time he seemed to me to look slightly less well than usual, and departed to London for a medical check up. These became more frequent as time passed. He also became more sombre, more concerned in his mind with suffering and death. At a noisy party we sat with him all evening, and all evening, above the music, he described in melancholy detail how his pet parrot was going blind, and how he was powerless to help or comfort it.

What saddened me almost to tears as he told us this was how Frank himself looked. He had lost an incredible amount of weight. His elegant clothes hung loose on his body. An image came to me of Frank as the parrot and his grieving, helpless audience watching his pain.

The last time we ever met our remarkable friend was at another party. As on the previous occasion, he was too weak to stand, and we sat with him. Gita had not been able to come, and the other groups in the room were engrossed in their own conversations. Frank said with an effort, 'You both know how much I love Goan food ... well, I'm not allowed to eat it. I'm not allowed to drink but still ...' He sipped a weak whiskey and water. 'When I'm better, I'll finish my novel.'

When a friend dies, one's first instinct is disbelief. It was different with Frank, because of how he had looked the last time I saw him. I grieved for many things that had gone with him. He had acted, as I said earlier in this piece, as a binding force between like-minded people in Mumbai, and thus carried on a tradition started by our ancestors before Bal Thackeray was born. He took pieces of the hearts of many people with him to wherever he went. And he took with him also a talent, which might have become unique and important, as *Glad Seasons in Goa* and the articles in this book make clear. Frank will not write any more, but those interested in literature should read what he left, enshrined in this book, to see what might have been.

Mumbai   DOM MORAES
July 2003

****

The Byculla Boy

The beatings were savage
beyond all comprehension,
delivered with the full
force of his considerable
strength, the sharp edge
of a wooden ruler and a
desperate urgency which
left him sweaty, spent
and satiated.

O Come All Ye Faithful

The season is joyfully upon us when memory soars with songs of praise. The years take flight to the first brilliant starburst of my childhood. Words, a certain cadence, phrases of exquisite melody, golden déjà vu in the gathering dusk. Voices clustering on the Pied Piper heels of a little man with a long pole who moved like a dancer among the gas lamps creating, with a deft hoist, twirl, flick of his magic wand, pools of glowing light which shimmered in the haze of dusk like fireflies. 'Hark the herald angels sing ...' the voices of Christmas harvested the mean streets, offering glorious festive song in exchange for a tithe.

Ah, the sweet benediction, the holy wonder, the unfolding joy of it all. This was a Christmas like no other before it. I was, at long last, a carol singer in the choir of St. Anne's church. The youngest, twelve years old and, without question, the smallest singer in that peerless group, but I made up in vigorous voice what I so clearly lacked in stature. 'Restrain your enthusiasm, young man,' the choir master had said at our final rehearsal, 'must you pursue that high C with such abandon?' An unwise comment, even *unworthy*, indicating nothing so much as the severe professional limitations of the person who made it. No matter. Let there be Peace on Earth and Goodwill to All Men, and I reined in the unruly C.

Lamplight washed our little group in tones of the palest gold and after a moment's silence, and a silent prayer, we sang in one impassioned voice. Now, as I write, entire passages of lyrics and music return, unbidden, and with them memories of a happier time and a kinder place: the innocence of youth, of unquestioning belief, when all the world was newly risen and burnished with goodness. 'O come all ye faithful, joyful and triumphant ...' we sang in utter surrender as if our lives had been fashioned thus far for this single majestic purpose.

There was a sudden, hushed tide to the neighbourhood: street sounds ceased; the electric crackle of the tramcars seemed muted; even the ever present and distant roar of a city in full voice was diminished. Faces alight with anticipation began to appear on balconies, at windows; voices called to others, 'The carol singers are here!' Entire families gathered about us as we sang, in a community of feeling, a shared reverence for this moment of myth and magic, these loving words, this great and holy Eve. We reached our finale, 'Silent night, holy night' and I felt I was on the brink of some wonderful revelation that would change my life forever.

'Fifteen minutes, that's all you have.' The choir master thrust the collection box into my less than eager hands. Was this, I thought darkly, the reason why I was chosen? And then I recalled the incomparable flourish I had bestowed on the last notes of 'We Three Kings'. All doubts dispelled, I knocked firmly on the first door I came upon, assumed an expression of dignified yet appealing entreaty, and said, 'Please give all you can for the Holy Family crib.' And not a family turned me down, God bless them! Three generations, crowded into a single room, and yet a coin would rattle into my box and voices, brimful with the spirit of this most generous of seasons, rang out, 'Merry Christmas, Merry Christmas!'

With full and grateful heart, I understood, for a crib was a wondrous creation, symbol of the most holy of miracles, eternal harbinger of resurrection, of the triumph of good over evil, informed with a mystical radiance and abiding redemption. And when the men in our family – my father and I – built our own crib the next day, why then, it would be a crib like no other before or since, a crib to exult over, a crib to inspire hosannahs, a crib which only a team of craftsmen as deft, as sensitive, as creative as my father and I could bring forth ... 'You have a talent for destruction,' my father said, eyebrows bristling, a clear sign of rising ire. Near tears, I gazed upon the ruins of what would have served as a perfectly reasonable backdrop to a manger had I not, searching for a hammer, stepped on it in order to avoid crushing underfoot a pink and white plaster angel with wings aloft. An exchange of demolition, I felt, sore at the injustice, which should have won applause. My father was not, alas, sympathetic. 'Let us begin again,' he said sternly.

But where? I wondered, and how could such chaos give birth to the crib of cribs? Slats of plywood, tins of paint, a silver star, dozens of plaster figures sprawled in undignified disarray every which way – the Magi on their camels, homespun herdsmen and the birds and beasts of the field, red and blue coils of electric wire strung with tiny coloured bulbs, silver dust, glittering spangles, nails, pliers, hammers and in and over, floating in wisps above, piled high all over the room: hay! I had been appointed hay collector and had applied myself to the task with a zeal and fervour that would not be denied. My father, just back from work and about to plunge into a restorative feni, murmured, 'Dear God,' and added, quite unnecessarily, 'Mind where you put your feet.' I composed a silent prayer to the Holy Ghost, that most powerful and mysterious aspect of the Trinity and then, miracle of miracles, a glorious crib arose out of the chaos.

In the foreground, hay, used with discretion (despite my fervent pleas for the broad, daring stroke) offered light gold counterpoint to the figures of Mary and Joseph. Off to one side, the Magi, robed in kingly majesty, observed the scene with wise, hooded eyes. Humble peasantry, holding firmly to the odd ewe and lamb, kept modestly to the shadows, awestruck at this act of divine creation. Hidden in nook and cranny, the lights shimmered on the spangles and silver dust. My father placed the star, crowning glory, above the crib. 'Mother,' I called and my sisters and mother emerged from the kitchen with the preoccupied air of women absorbed in the serious business of food for festivity. My mother kissed the feet of our heirloom infant Jesus, old ivory with a gold crown; each of us did so and the figure was placed with gentle reverence between Mary and Joseph. And my cup of joy flowed over.

To superlative craftsmen such as my father and I, after the brilliant architectural accomplishment of the crib, the Xmas tree was the work of a few swift moments. It glowed cheerfully in a corner, a real tree, as high as I was tall, with gaily wrapped parcels promising all sorts of splendid delights arranged at the base. Basking in the brilliance of my labour, I was suddenly teased by an irresistible bouquet of smells, demanding my immediate presence in the kitchen where, I suspected, the women of the house were likely to go hopelessly wrong without my ability to taste and pass judgement on the Christmas feast.

'Hands off,' – I ignored this remark from my younger sister and with the dignity of a man who has just created a crib, used a spoon to scoop out a generous dollop of almond fudge now at its most desirable stage of bubbling lava flow. 'It might just do,' I said kindly, but one couldn't be too careful and I sampled lightly as I went along. The *kulkuls* were moist and soft, sugared just so, lattices of *lettria* nestled in spun cobwebs of egg yolk. There were ten satisfactory layers to the *bebinca*, the fruitcake sat plumly at the centre of all this grandeur while in a copper pot the great Goan pork stew, *sorpotel*, steamed in a rich marination of exotic juices.

As the clock struck midnight, my family and I, and thousands of others, would celebrate High Mass under the stars, with glad heart and grand ceremony, and the spirit would move within us as the bishop raised his mitre and spoke the hallowed, golden words, 'I bring you glad tidings. On this day, in the town of Nazareth in Galilee, a child was born ...'

****

Survival

When does one learn to fight the good fight? The gods were brutal in their benevolence when my turn came about. At the age of nine I was cast into the school of hard knocks, compulsory tutorials for the survival of the hardiest in the mean gullies of Byculla in Mumbai. Etched in my memory now as a region of the mind, limned by the evasive shadows of dusk and the menace of nightfall, waywardly lit by gaslight.

There were wolves and there were sheep. The wolves quickly learned the ways of the predator; the sheep the ways of subterfuge, flight or submission. The sheep sought survival. The wolves prevailed. The streets served as rough classrooms, playing fields and when we grew into teenage gangs, battlegrounds. The first tests were trials of skill, strength and pain, disguised as games with no option of escape. Win or lose, the reward and punishment never changed: the winners exacted their physical pound of flesh; the losers suffered pain and torment in inverse proportion to their lack of skill and strength. But the mayhem in the games we played had specific purpose. They first established, then honed the prerequisites for survival: the intelligence to develop skills; the strength to apply them; the will to overcome all odds; and the ruthlessness to exact a terrible price, in full measure, which tradition imposed on the losers.

I earned my bloody spurs, literally, at gilli-danda. This was a game for two or more. It was as simple in the playing as it was brutal in the conclusion. The gilli was a four-inch length of hard, rounded wood, shaved to sharp cones at either end which, when laid on the ground, balanced uncertainly at the centre. The danda was just that, two feet in length, an inch thick, sandpapered for smoothness and grip. At the point on the ground where the game began, a scoop was dug out, the gilli laid across it, and if the toss of the coin was in your favour, you took first turn. Legs astraddle the scoop, danda held firmly in a clasped grip and positioned just below the gilli, you scooped with all of your strength and with luck, and not a little skill, sent it soaring well above your opponent's head a good thirty feet down the road. You then laid the danda across the scoop on the ground. Your opponent picked up the gilli and tried to hit the danda with it. If he did you exchanged roles and positions. If he failed, the real game began.

You went to where the gilli lay, carefully observed its angle, the elevation of the conical points, the obstacles on the road ahead. Then you held the danda at the base, hit the gilli sharply on its point and, as it rose, tried to hit it hard and true straight down the street. The crowd (gathered like genies out of nowhere) scoffed aloud at these fatuous preliminaries. When would the drama begin? But if you were poised above the gilli, at the arctic center of the moment of truth, heart thumping at the consequences, you had to study all at once the angle of the gilli, the balance, the elevation of the conical point, working out where best you should tap the point, at what speed, with what degree of strength to achieve a waist-high elevation. And when you struck the gilli for distance, you had to strike very hard, dead into the meat of the center; and very true, straight down the street, pivoting at the very last moment so that the full balance and weight of the body were behind the blow. And when you saw the gilli sailing away, taking wonderful flight at just the right height, sixty, seventy, eighty feet down the road, the glow of pleasure was as nothing to the gloating anticipation of victory. You went to where the gilli lay and repeated the performance twice, then snarled at the opponent, 'Your turn.' He would have to start where you did and you knew by the defeat and fear in his eyes, avoiding yours, and his reluctant shambles, that he was a loser.

As I was for two years.

The loser walked the distance, the winner striding by his side. Close on their heels the crowd bayed for blood. At the end of the winner's third strike, often two hundred metres or more from the starting point, the loser was made to turn. The winner did the honours. The danda was placed across the loser's lower back. His elbows were hooked over either end. If he wore socks, these were removed. The gilli was shoved hard into the right shoe between leather and ankle. Then he was made to hop, hop, all the way back to the starting point. If the danda slipped from his back, or the gilli popped out of the shoe, or he stumbled and both feet touched the ground, he was taken back to the starting point where the grisly punishment began all over again. Half way along the foot with the gilli usually began to bleed and as the first drops of blood broke through the skin and splattered into the dust, the crowd, now a mob, cheered lustily, screaming for more. The winner was glad to oblige. He whacked the loser across the bum with his danda at ever shorter intervals. The faster he hopped the deeper the gilli tore into the skin and the more he bled until the end of the line was reached and he crumpled into the dust.

I learned two lifelong lessons in those years. I had to ignore the pain and fear to reach the end of the line. And I had to learn to win the game to put the fear and pain forever behind me. When I began to win I showed as little mercy to the losers as had been shown to me, but I knew now why this had to be done. It was the only way losers could become winners.

I soon realized that I had merely passed kindergarten, with distinction perhaps, but I was nowhere near graduation from the high school of hard knocks. Masters in the art and science of survival flaunted their triumphs all about me. There was the Top Master, with a temper as awesome as his choice of abuse. Both commanded universal respect, but his talent was held in awe. He was the creator of our Red Badge of Courage, the fighting top. Conjured out of a block of rock-hard teak. Armed with the razor-sharp, sword-edged kapalhari spike. Perfectly balanced. Adorned with skull-and-crossbones and suchlike emblems of carnage. As distant from today's ornamental tops as a Samurai sword from a paper knife. It was made for a single purpose: to spin at lightning speed, strike and destroy. No easy weapon. It took years to master and made impossible demands on strength, aim, balance and deadly intent. There was only one game and it ended in the annihilation of the loser's top which was smashed to bits, in a frenzy of violence by the winners, taking turns, using their tops as clubs, dealing terrible retribution, until all that was left of the fallen warrior top were pieces of wood and a single indestructible kapalhari spike.

The Top Master knew all about annihilation and resurrection. Legs sheared off mid-thigh under a tramcar, he took to carpentry, mastered the art and made a four-wheel platform carved with images of Shiva on which he propelled himself all about the streets of Byculla on the strength of his arms. He had made the transcendental leap from cripple to creator and the honour and respect he enjoyed were hard won.

*

I was being prepared, had I but known it then, for my own trial by torment at a school run by European missionary priests where the motto might well have been, BEAT THE DEVIL OUT OF THE BOY. The teachers embraced this injunction with an ardent addiction untempered by any such nonsense as restraint or mercy. But, at the very least, there had to be punishable cause. With Adolph 'Pole Vaulter' Britto, the Latin master, long soured by lack of response, none was necessary. His class had shrunk to ten boys, twice a week, banished to an obscure alcove at the far end of the school. With just two years to go my parents insisted I enrol, under the misguided notion that Latin might make a priest of me yet where all else had failed. Fat chance!

Lord of his den, Britto wielded absolute power, a massive right arm and a heavy wooden ruler three feet long with a thin edge. Much later, when our duel had become a cause célébre, I got to know the enemy well. He was a Portuguese East Indian Eurasian which, in his case, was the best of the baddest of worlds. Short, stocky, with a bristling crew cut, a Hitler moustache, beady eyes magnified by pebble glasses and a peacock strut. And he was a sadist who took great pleasure in inflicting pain. When I began to understand a bit about such things, I realized that he was very likely homosexual, repressed and frustrated, given the bondage of his religious beliefs and the taboos of the time. The beatings were savage beyond all comprehension, delivered with the full force of his considerable strength, the sharp edge of the wooden ruler and a desperate urgency which left him sweaty, spent and satiated.

He had been with the school, man and boy, for fifty years, and was inordinately proud of the pole vault record he had set which remained unbroken to the day. An Achilles heel! 'Angel' Veriato, who sat with me at the back of the class, didn't quite turn cartwheels, but he looked sly and conspiratorial. Veriato was born ancient, wise in the ways of guile and deceit. He piled school texts at the edge of his desk and read dirty books behind them with studious concentration. Britto never walked the aisle: he stood at the blackboard, cane in hand, and barked a command, 'Veriato, conjugate.' Veriato stood up, stuttered and made a hash of it.

'You are not prepared.'

'No, sir.'

'Why not?' Tap, tap, the ruler went.

'I was practising all last evening, sir. The pole vault. Sports Day is a month away, sir. I can just about make nine.'

'I did ten-six, Veriato.'

'Your record will never be broken, sir,' Veriato said with great and sincere conviction.

'Sit down, Veriato. You don't have the brain for Latin. From now on you will tidy the classroom, clean the blackboard and replace the chalk.' The beady eyes fixed on me, 'Simoes, conjugate.'

Veriato, you turd. '*Hic et ubique*,' I translated, 'Here and everywhere ...' I stumbled. I fumbled. Appalled by Veriato's depravity, I couldn't remember a thing.

'You are not prepared.'

'No, sir.'

'Why not?'

'I don't like Latin, sir.' Where had the words come from? Too late. The die was cast. There was a doomsday edge to the air.

'Stupidity I can understand. Insolence must be punished.' The eyes glittered, 'Come here.'

I stood in the preferred position, the 'crucifix', at rigid attention, arms outstretched at shoulder height, elbows locked, palms upheld. I had been caned before but never with such wanton brutality.

When he was done – six 'cuts' on each hand – he threw the ruler on the desk, took a deep breath and while I struggled to contain the searing pain and, worse, the humiliation, he passed a two-year sentence: 'I shall set a special passage for you to conjugate for every class, and if you miss a single word, you will be caned.'

What would my crippled Top Master have done?

I was fourteen. I had survived poverty, deprivation and the pitiless streets. I would do what my Top Master would have done. I would not bend to the pain and I would wait for the day when I could strike back.

True to his word Britto caned me twice a week. True to mine, I did not flinch and never opened a Latin text again. The welts on my hands took permanent residence, assumed intriguing colours and swellings as time went on, and when my parents discovered them (it had become difficult to hold fork and knife) they gave both the welts and me short shrift. 'You deserve this,' Mother said. My father: 'Study your Latin and you won't be caned.' And that was that. But it was an altogether different matter in school. Word had spread and what began as a mild diversion for students and masters turned to speculation (why had the principal been kept in the dark? ... what prevented Britto from throwing me out of class? ... clear grounds here for expelling the boy. Why is he still in school?). Applause from my peers (bite his balls off ... stick it to the bastard, Frank) and, when I entered my final school year, our feud assumed classic proportions: irresistible force vs. immovable object.

Holidays were periods of reprieve. The welts hardened into thick, tough callouses and when the beatings began again, served as shock absorbers to the pain. The masters, now fully au fait with the situation and sympathetic to a degree (I was up in all other subjects), avoided eye contact. Except for the English master who cheered me on. He was a Welsh priest, a huge bear of a man, bald as an egg, with piercing blue eyes and a voice sandpapered by three packs of Marlboro a day. He had been a professional wrestler in Wales before being called to the cassock. English was my favourite subject and I excelled. He regaled the class with a running commentary on the state of my hands ('A lively pink with a touch of magenta ... magnificent ... A fresh development class, hillocks!') and I took great heart a month before my school finals when he peered at my palms and chuckled, 'You'll win the war yet. Soldier on, Simoes.'

Britto would no longer catch my eye when he caned me. I looked straight into his. Word was out in the school yard that I would never submit, and when he raised the cuts to eight and then ten on each hand, I knew that Britto had lost the cause. Or had he? On a crisp January morning, with a sly feral grin, he delivered the coup de grâce. 'You will present yourself at the Masters' restroom at lunch recess, Simoes. There you will be caned.' To this day I remember the shame I felt, the utter helplessness and despair. To be caned before all the masters was the final humiliation. My knees knocked in the long walk to the restroom. I tapped at the door. Britto in this I'm-one-of-the-lads voice: 'Come right in, boy.' Matter-of-fact. All in the day's work. The masters lounged about in easy chairs. Studied nonchalance. Only the English master threw me an encouraging glance. I took up the crucifix position. Britto rolled up his shirtsleeves with slow deliberation and went at it with a grunt. Six and six, then three and three more. At each thwack the masters shifted uncomfortably in their seats. Done, Britto said, 'Get out'. And the devil took me. I refused to move, arms straight out – where did the strength and purpose come from? I was a statue frozen in stone. Not a quiver. 'I said get out. You are expelled from my class.' Then the Top Master took me by the hand and led me to my finest moment. Loud and clear, as though at elocution, I replied, 'I thought you were going to cane me, sir. Why don't you begin?' Dead silence broken by a snigger from the Hindi master. Wild-eyed, a deep guttural scream torn from his being, Britto hurled the cane at me. I ducked. It flew over my head and smashed the glass pane of a cabinet. Britto screamed again and reached for my throat, fingers clawed. The English master leapt to his feet. For a man so big he moved with the speed of a cat, caught Britto by the collar and shook him. 'That will be enough, Adolph.' Then turned to me, 'Make yourself scarce, Simoes.' I needed no urging.

That very afternoon Britto made a formal written request to the principal. I should be expelled from the school forthwith. This was a fate worse than death. Without a Senior Cambridge school-leaving certificate I would sink without trace into the bleak streets of my childhood. With it, there was a sliver of hope for a future. I was called to the principal's office at noon. Six priests, in spotless white cassocks, sat in a dimly lit room panelled in dark oak. A hanging jury of medieval inquisitors. J'accuse! In the sibilant vowels and evasive consonants of Southern Europe, the principal pronounced judgement, 'You have survived, by a single vote.'

The English master's great rolling belly laugh thundered off the ceiling. He stood up, put a hand the size of a ham on my shoulder and delivered his own coup de grâce.

'Donkeys survive,' he said, 'men of honour prevail. Get on with your life, Frank.'

I did.

****

Grandfather's Sugar Pills

Aplacebo is a small white sugar pill that does nothing for you except make you well. In double-blind tests, two groups of patients, matched by age, sex, race, background and common affliction, are separated only in the manner of their treatment: one group gets a potent medication, the other a sugar pill. More often than not, the sugar pill works better than the drug.

My grandfather would not have been surprised. He was a Doctor of Medicine in the true spirit of the words, and it was an article of faith with him that the real process of healing began in the deepest recesses of the human psyche, far beyond the reach of the pills and potions of his time. He practised his art with a wayward democracy – among the rich ('I steal from them!') and the very poor whom he treated free and, of course, on me, his favourite grandchild. His appearance at my sickbed made me feel better at once: he made a grand entrance, all six feet of him, in immaculate white ducks and a sola topi blancoed to perfection, twirling a short cane with a nimble dexterity worthy of the music hall. His moustache and French goatee were trimmed to a neat jauntiness and his opening remark was full of good cheer: 'Gone and done it again, have we?' He maintained, with some truth, that whenever a new germ appeared in the neighbourhood, I'd find it, make friends and bring it back home.

If he was good with patients, he was superb with the language. He attended my birth and, according to my mother, passed thoughtful judgement: 'A trifle large in the head and there's a certain crumpled effect, but I suppose we shall have to make do.' At the age when little boys eat everything in sight, he enquired politely as

I reached for my fourth hard-boiled egg at breakfast, did I eat them or had I started a collection? He held firm and jaundiced views about the ability of the local Jesuits to educate his grandson and I can see him now, monocle in place, scrutinizing my monthly report, not – even at the most wildly optimistic assessment – an encouraging document. 'Padres!' he'd say coldly, investing the word with immeasurable scorn.

I had much cause for confusion until my grandfather took me in hand. As far as he was concerned, Bombay wasn't just an education. It was and quite properly so, an extension of his personality. Our odyssey began on a Sunday morning. I remember asking him where we were going. 'Three and a half million people must eat,' he replied cryptically. We caught a tramcar, got window seats upstairs and, with a shower of blue sparks flying every which way, like a huge perambulating firecracker, we trundled through Dongri, Behndi Bazar, Mohamedali Road, until we arrived at Crawford Market.

'Your education,' said my grandfather, 'begins here.'

If today, I can tell the freshness of a fish by peering under a gill, or the goodness of a ladyfinger by breaking off the tip, or never allow an indifferent mango to slip by unremarked, I give thanks to my grandfather's inspired scholarship. At the end of the grand tour, he bought me a gift, a young squirrel. 'You are now responsible for another life,' he said, well pleased with himself, 'it is an education in itself.'

Later, he taught me to cook: more correctly, my mother taught me to cook while my grandfather instructed from a distance, feet up on an armchair, in loud Portuguese, much in the manner of a master chef with acolytes. These lessons in haute cuisine left me with much more than a discerning palate. I grew up with the conviction that in life, as in cooking, a fundamental honesty in the application of first principles was essential. Even a fried egg had to be peppered just before eating and never in the kitchen. Perhaps with the untutored you could cheat and get away with it; you could never lie to yourself.

Latin conjugation held no fear for me at school. Who else in the whole world, apart from my grandfather and I, were privy to its

origin: the strange birth and mystical suckling of Romulus and
Remus and the empire that began with them among the seven hills
of Rome? He discussed the news with me after breakfast each
morning, seriously, as between one well-informed gentleman and
another, and I always left for school with the conviction that the
world would have been much better managed if placed in the care
of my grandfather and me.

Now he sat on my bed and played a little game. He gave me an
ancient stethoscope which I plugged into my ears. I placed the other
end on his chest. 'That's my spleen,' my grandfather said. Long
moments passed. I was, on solemn oath, never to repeat a diagnosis
and there was a time limit. Serious, absorbed, he placed me on a
gold pocket watch. In the past, I had run through chicken pox,
'flu, malaria, stomach ache and even, on one shameful occasion,
runny tummy. I had precisely two minutes left and absolutely no
inspiration when all at once my grandfather began to behave
strangely. He took off his sola topi, flung it aside, mopped his brow
vigorously, wiped his neck, patted his cheeks, huffed and puffed
and murmured in a voice weak and trembling with some instant,
debilitating illness, 'I feel faint, dear God, it's the heat, the heat …'
'A touch of the sun,' I shouted triumphantly, and a smile tugged at
the corners of his mouth, 'Let's have a look at you.'

His examination was careful, gentle and very thorough, and
when it was over he chuckled and poked me in the ribs. 'You'll live,
provided you follow instructions.' They came in two parts, the first
a bottle containing a vile brew which I had to consume four times
a day; the second was a magic talisman, a silver rupee new from the
mint; it shone and glittered with a thousand points of light, potent
with meaning and promise. 'Under your pillow,' said my grandfather,
'day and night, and you'll be right as rain, I promise.' He was never
flippant about the silver rupee. It was handed over with a sense of
ceremony, a certain reverence, and in that sacramental moment when
our eyes met and our hands touched, I knew with a certainty beyond
all reason that all would be well.

The silver rupee never failed me. I remember a critical night
when I was near delirious with fever and my bedclothes were damp
with the sweat of an illness that had gone on all week. There was a

bruised look to my mother's eyes and my grandfather, for once, was grave and silent. I was to be 'cupped' and the paraphernalia for this arcane and ancient ritual lay neatly to hand – six small wine glasses, slices of onion, pieces of camphor. I clasped the silver rupee tightly in my hand – round, hard and comforting. One by one, the slices of onion were placed on my chest, a bit of camphor at the center of each, the wine glasses were made ready, the candle was lit. Flame to camphor, a wine glass quickly upturned, a sudden vacuum and the inverted glass clung to my chest, mysterious vapours swirling within it. While the skin beneath rose, turning an angry red. Six sharp wasp-stings and it was over. I was made to lie still till the 'cupping' took. I got well, of course, but only my grandfather and I knew that the silver rupee had, once again, turned the trick.

*

Thirty years after my grandfather's death, the retina in my right eye tore: sparks, flashes, jagged forks of white-hot light, a celestial fireworks after which, I was told, the chances of permanent blindness were five out of ten. I sat in silence and terror, pupils dilated, vision blurred, while the surgeons argued my case. They reduced me to an object, to an eyeball, to a detached retina; the universe of my being had shrunk to torn and shattered blood vessels. They talked of options and procedures: they would puncture the eyeball; they would go into the eye with sharp knives, with laser beams, with liquid nitrogen.

They never used my name.

And nobody gave me a silver rupee.

****

Memories of a Bombay Boyhood

The threads that make up the tapestry of my life were woven on the ancient looms of generations gone before; textured by experience; given bright and darker colour by precept and example; patterned by the rhythm and flow of a great city. I am without question – often ruefully – Bombay's child. I was born in this city, shaped by its influences, grew to manhood during the most turbulent years of its history and, driven by its unforgiving tutelage, carved a career for myself out of what often seemed to be solid rock.

But then, I had an example that would brook no denial. In 1895 my grandfather studied medicine in Bombay. Every night he sat on a wooden bench in a park near Horniman Circle, reading borrowed texts by the light of a gas lamp into the wee hours; awesome application which would, eventually, ruin his sight, but not before conferring on him two singular distinctions: he would become a doctor who could genuinely heal and, in course of time, the first Goan Portuguese Consul General in British East Africa. Then, as now, titles were flourished, and my grandfather, in his declining years, never lost an opportunity of reminding us of his.

As soon as I was old enough to show some evidence of reciprocity, he appointed himself my mentor and guide. I was sorely in need of one. A very small brown Christian in a very large Indian city, lumbered with the legacy of Saraswat Brahmin Roman Catholic Goanness, I grew up with the convert's burden of confessionals and rosaries, masses for every conceivable occasion, candlelit processions by the dark of the moon; with Spanish Jesuits and Irish Brothers of Mercy (anything but!), French Sisters of the Poor and Indian

Dominican friars; with choir practices, the strictures of Lent and the Silence of the Retreat. I spoke Portuguese at home with my parents, Konkani to the help, English at school and pidgin Hindi on the streets.

Even while the maps in Geography class showed the world stained Imperial Red, British India was heaving a sad, last sigh. Father Beech, true Brit, taught me English. Father Dalton, a Welshman, introduced me to the clarinet, and when I made my debut in the school band, splendidly outfitted in a uniform of blue and gold, brass-buttoned and generously epauletted, we played *Colonel Bogey* and the *Stars and Stripes Forever*. Father Sanches – Spanish, naturally – caned me regularly and well for flunking Latin conjugation. A diminutive Maharashtrian taught me to draw. A grand Parsi reincarnation of Apollo provided physical instruction, 'in the proper international manner'. My Anglo-Indian friends at school spoke nostalgically of home, when they meant England, which they had never seen. I was baptized by a German Jesuit, given my first Communion by an Indian bishop and confirmed by an Italian cardinal visiting from the Holy See.

I never thought to ask about the temple bells.

Or the chanting of psalms at the brown-and-gold synagogue. Or the robed figure in the minaret calling the faithful to prayer. Jain monks, garbed in whispering saffron, walked the alleyways. Koli fisherwomen, smelling of fish and the sea, moved about with feline authority. At night a small black man sang for his supper. He sang *Danny Boy* and *Old Man River* through a cardboard megaphone. The next morning he was magnificently drunk. At dusk, a beggar boy climbed on to a ledge below the eaves of an ancient bungalow and played heart-rending melodies on a reed flute. From my balcony, I could see the domes of the mosque at Haji Ali. A muted pearl at dawn, the looming spires of Gloria church, the stolid red-brick conviction of the Nagpada synagogue, a pantheon of deities at the highest elevation of the Kali temple near Byculla Bridge, their colours harsh and vibrant as the clash of cymbals.

Meanwhile, my formal education was about to take a great leap forward. Father William Beech S.J., came into my life; it was never to be the same again. He would teach me English. So be it.

Our first encounter was less than encouraging. My mother was present. Much to my chagrin, she related an anecdote I felt was best forgotten. When I was a child and beginning to learn the meanings of words, she had shown me an aeroplane. 'Aeroplane,' she said. Overwhelmed by the joy of discovery, I shouted 'Elephant!' It was my first, though certainly not my last, attempt to. grapple with words and their meanings. Beech's reaction gave me cause for hope. 'You have a future Simoes,' he said, chuckling, 'in the higher metaphysics of the English language even elephants have been known to take wing.'

Two months ago, I sat at my typewriter. I had to write an advertising campaign to persuade people to visit Goa in the monsoon, a time in the territory that I and most Goans love best. Inspiration had fled. One insipid sentence was erased only to be followed by another. I sought refuge in a large palm feni, and under its mellowing influence, I remembered my first English lesson with William Beech. Forty-five boys sat, without murmur or movement, while he recited from Keats. His voice held all of the yearning of a flute's lament at dusk, 'O what can ail thee knight at arms/alone and palely loitering/the sedge has withered on the leaf/and no birds sing ...' And in a stillness of flooding wonder I perceived that all things bright, beautiful and eternal were within brave reach of the mortal word.

Beech possessed an unerring instinct for the right and the good, and the ultimate talent of the great teacher: he made me a gift of what he loved. With sure, deft, sensitive step, he led me on journeys of splendid discovery through the landscapes of English literature. I explored valleys of whimsy and laughter, wildernesses of loneliness and terror, sun-dappled groves of contemplation and serenity. It was, above all, a discovery of self: I had found my vocation; for the rest of my life there would be no other. But there was to be much despair along the way, broken bones, and not a little blood on the floor. Yet the bleakest hour was not without light: of all the advice he gave me, the most simple, unmarked by rhetoric, has been informed over the years with the greatest meaning: 'Learn your craft, but remember, good writing comes from the heart. If you don't feel passionately and honestly about what you write, you'll

end up a critic with tidy infinitives, and may God have mercy on
your soul.'

If the psychic reality of William Beech's life was not made mine,
perhaps my life would have taken a wholly different turn. If my
grandfather had not introduced me to Bombay's harbour, on the
sound theory that there's not much mischief a boy can get up to
with a ten thousand-ton cargo ship, would I have ever become a
deckhand on a Japanese freighter? I spoke no Japanese; the 55-man
crew spoke no English; we got along famously. The year I spent in
Europe after that, living off the land, was fertile soil: the language
took seed; memories sprang to life in printed word and published
article; in turn, they made a livelihood of sorts in London possible,
freelancing for an advertising agency.

Stray threads in a predetermind fabric. I will never know. My
grandfather would have given the doubt short shrift. For him, all of
life was sacred and purposeful: the hieroglyphics of an infant's brain
and the far-flung spirals of receding galaxies were written by a single
mighty hand. He died of cancer of the throat, lucid to the last, after
prolonged suffering, refusing all medication because he wished to
experience every nuance of death in the primal meaning of the term.
He died very poor, and I have yet to know a man richer in the gifts
of life.

****

My God Died Young

It was a Roman Catholic childhood, God-gilded, in the most inquisitorial traditions of that great religion, born from and tempered by the flickering illuminations of candle and chant, the muted responses of the family rosary at dusk, the bells of the Angelus echoing over twilight spires, the shrouded lamentations of Lent, and the eternal blood, suffering and heartbreak of Good Friday. Miracles were the order of the day: the Virgin Birth, the Resurrection, the unfathomable mysteries of the Holy Trinity: God the Father, the Son and the Holy Ghost were yet God One, Triumphant and Most Holy.

Satan was a fallen angel. Fire and brimstone formed the foul stuff of his breath. In a wink of a horny eye he transported little Goan boys who played with themselves to the tops of the highest palm trees where their eyes rolled in their sockets; they drooled without stop, and, fatally possessed, spoke vile gibberish. Good and evil were locked in time and space, in universal struggle, with my soul – my very own – held forfeit to the outcome. I grew up with martyrs to the cause, recreated (with all of the embarrassing rhetoric of the Renaissance) in plaster and wood and gilt; chained, hung, crucified; transfixed by spear, arrow or crown of thorns; depicted always in the moment of death, gazing heavenwards, praising the glory of the Lord even unto the last sigh.

But none of the ritual and pageantry, the pomp and circumstance, the high drama of conservative Roman Catholicism going about its formidable business, and my own intense, wide-eyed and uncritical participation (I could never open the Lives of the Saints without a frisson of awe), served to mask a terrible fact: I was desperately afraid of God.

In my case, the handmaidens of the Lord had been Spanish Jesuits and I grew up with the God of the Old Testament, the God of creation, justice and retribution, whose Word was made Flesh and would forever live amongst us. The God of Albuquerque and Torquemade, whose standard-bearers held aloft both cross and sword, offering salvation as the single alternative to slaughter. Omniscient, omnipresent, my God had shaken the Tribes of Israel, 'And God said unto Moses, I AM THAT I AM. And Moses hid his face; for he was afraid to look upon God.' I too averted my eyes from the face of God for I lived with dread, as the Children of Israel once had, ' ... let not God speak with us, lest we die.' My God had made his son man by immaculate conception and then demanded the ultimate sacrifice of him. Never mind that Jesus of Nazareth raised the dead, preached the Sermon on the Mount, healed the incurably ill and made the miracle of loaves and fishes.

He had said, 'Love one another.'

And he had died the death.

It did me no good at all when I was told that God had made me in his image and likeness; that God was good; that God was love; that if I lived a life in praise and worship of Him, forever would I stand in the glory of His light. It did me no good at all, for I had discovered the awful truth of the seven blind men and the sighted boy.

Seven grown men, bearded and blind, led by a boy who was my age. They came along every Friday morning at first light and I heard them well before they came into sight; they chanted a kind of plainsong, a haunting ululation which rose and fell to the beating of handbells. The first blind man had his left hand resting lightly on the right shoulder of the man next to him, and thus strung out across the pavement, they made a shuffling line, testing the ground with a tentative foot before taking the next step. The last man in the row held the boy's hand in his. A beautiful boy, sighted and solemn. He did not smile or sing, but moved slightly ahead of the line, drawing it forward. I was wrong about the bells. They were metal clappers, tiny cymbals, held in the right hand, all seven pitched on a different note so that they covered an octave between them.

The men sang wordlessly, and the sounds they made were extraordinarily sad and moving. The metal clappers offered counterpoint with more character, but here again restrained in an oddly muffled fashion, as though the metal had been deprived of some essential element of its being. A tin can hung from the wrist which held the bell and from time to time a passer-by would throw a coin in. I always watched, enthralled, till they passed out of sight.

I decided that the boy was good and noble. In my mind's eye, he cared and ministered to the needs of these cruelly afflicted old men – ran their errands, bought their meager provisions – encouraged by parents who were both mature and kind. I embellished this little fantasy as time went on, and never allowed reality to intrude: not the boy's split lip one week, or the way he favoured a foot the next, and one morning – I will never understand why – I decided to follow them. All was not well. The boy held his head down; his movements were listless and uncoordinated; at the Nagpada synagogue, he stumbled and fell. The blind man clasping his hand jerked him to his feet with a sudden ferocity and a string of oaths, then quickly pulled the boy's sleeve down over the wrist, but not before I noticed that there was a circle of blood along the bone, old blood, in a thick congealed ring, and that the hands which I thought were held so trustingly together were, in brutal fact, manacled and chained ....

I wept that night.

What sort of creator would play a dirty Machiavellian trick like that on a nice kid like me?

*

I had taken the first bleak steps into Green's 'cooling world and vacant universe'. An existential landscape without beginning or end, where Gods and demons alike were papier mâché figments in my mind, set aflame by the collusive anguish of the race: the truth of fang and claw, mindless hate and foetid death, roiling and steaming deep within the sulphurous caverns of the unconscious. The Grand Masters of this sere netherworld courted me with their siren songs. Aleister Crowley showed me the pentagram, the Mark of the Beast writhing on his brow. Nietzsche closed my fingers about the dripping blade. The ovens of Belsen spun their obscene hieroghpyhics on a blood-riven sky and the clotted ash settled like the sign of Cain on my heart and all humanity's. Thanatos danced on a mountain of skulls; Eros drowned in a cauldron of hate. I was stripped of faith; the flesh of my belief lay torn and festering. The vapours of the time dripped acid into the wounds: the Second World War had exposed the insanity of the species; Yeats' 'rough beast' howled at the full moon of our madness; six million Jews who had paid the price knew that God was a lampshade, a gold filling, a bar of soap. We, who survived, knew better. We worshipped at the black altar of thermonuclear death: the mushroom cloud became the unholy icon of our times.

Losing one's faith is not a sanguine experience. I scourged my conscience along the penitential alleyways of metaphysical proof, and the hollow ring of idiot laughter echoed down the corridors of time. O the comic daring, the deathly yearning, the sheer breathlessness of it all! The Greeks of the Forum; the Knights of the early and Middle Ages. Augustine, Aquinas and Anselm of Canterbury and a three-ring circus of other Apologists even unto the present mayhem. How they argued the conundrum: which came first, soulful egg or sacrilegious chicken? Merry-go-rounds of cant; bucketfulls of metaphysical popcorn; a clown's treasure of fool's gold.

Here we have Anselm in the eleventh century (a good and sincere man; so were they all) craftily dismantling the Chinese boxes of his mind and discovering the ontological proof (you better believe this!): If God did not exist, one may still conceive of a being precisely like God who does exist. But this being has gone one better than God, because in addition to possessing all of God's omnipotent powers, he exists, which makes him greater than God. Clearly, this is impossible. God being the greatest conceivable being, it is absurd that there could be a being greater than Him. Thus it is absurd to deny that God exists. Stuff and nonsense, says Aquinas, putting the boot in, knowledge of God can be gained through natural reason. Kant agrees, jumping with great elegance on the bandwagon. William Paley weighs in on the side of the angels with a neat analogy: a human artefact, a watch say, is designed for a purpose: to mark time. Observations of the universe show that it reflects adjustments of means to ends, irrefutable proof of an intelligent designer.

And how many angels could dance on the head of a pin? And why did Spinoza, spurning my dread, draw glittering fountains of hope from a cosmic wellspring at the dead center of my third eye? And could I stand the pain (worse, the sick humiliation) bent over a chair as he hit me on the bum with the straight edge of a ruler, this Man of God! With the full striking force of his arm, panting while he counted, 'Thirty-one, thirty-two, three ...' to the disciplinary fifty, panting and heaving like some monstrous beast in violent orgasm, because I had raised my hand in the Moral Instruction class and asked, 'Father, why is it wrong to masturbate?'

*

The decades were unkind to the God I had known, feared and lost. We had taken Voltaire's cynical epigram: 'If God did not exist, it would be necessary to invent him' to our greedy little hearts. Man had at last made God over in his image. And I saw Michelangelo's life-giving hand of God on the ceiling of the Sistine Chapel now holding an Uzi machine pistol, or a fistful of dollars, or the fragile psyches of flower children, or a syringeful of smack. The voice of thunder which smashed Jericho's walls now called the faithful to gestalt therapy; exhorted the multitudes from the ramparts of the Red Fort; belted red hot rock in Madison Square Garden while the groupies offered up the incense of mind-numbing hysteria; railed, from the tabernacle of the White House, against the Marxist anti-Christ (fair's fair: surely, from an equally valid point of view, the State as God). The ballistic missile was the burning bush of our age. Cults washed the mind Mongoloid clean and their God-figures strode the world in bulletproof limousines. God was Freud. No, he was Skinner. Lenin. Schumacher. Gandhi. John Lennon! He spoke in conflicting tongues: the Towers of Babel stood again. And no more was the cry heard in the land: 'Blessed are the meek for they shall inherit the earth.'

A Jesuit friend said to me at the time: 'If you feel God does not exist, why despair? If you feel He does but you have lost Him, you're well away. The real problem begins when you find Him.'

I retreated from this prophetic sophistry into literature and poetry: dangerous, metaphysical pastures, fraught with menace and magic: the beating of great musty wings; the quick scuffle, the scream cut off, in the tall grass; the slow hiss beneath the wet green rock; the dance of the peacock and the song of the thrush; the still dark enchantment of the reed-fringed lake; the sun-dappled glade and the eldritch voices, dulcet, beckoning. Appearances and reality blurred into illusion.

The great religious poets knew that reality was perception; perception knew no dimensions and was valid beyond time, space and causation. They *knew* in the biblical sense, in the soul of their being. Blake and Donne. Hopkins, Rossetti and Swinburne. They knew God as the ceaseless unfolding of mystery upon mystery. Stone, bird, beast, man, the wild and gentle elements, were ordered by cosmic harmonies, formed, perished, reformed within layers of infinite meaning, marking time to the ebb and flow of the heart's blood, given form in the hieroglyphics of dreams and the incantations and rituals of magic; known, finally, in the silent implosion of the moment of grace: 'Now God comes to thee, not as in the dawning of the day, not as in the bud of the spring, but as the sun at noon to illustrate all shadows, as the sheaves in harvest to fill all penuries, all occasions invite his mercies, and all times are his seasons.'

The artist is without choice. God-riven, he lives within, 'The Holy Word that walk'd among the ancient trees.'

I may cause offence with this statement, but it must be made. I believe that a great creative work – poem, sculpture, painting, novel or symphony – is as much an act of divinity as of art. It transcends time (Goya's lithographs of the Napoleonic wars in Spain, Picasso's *Boy leading a blind minotaur* have, perhaps, more meaning today to greater numbers of people than ever before); it is unaffected by cultural paradigm shifts (Beethoven's Sixth, Shakespeare's sonnets); and, if the equations of quantum mechanics are auguries, perhaps space and causality as well. A work of art is an act of birthing. We have many terms for this ineffable transition. Plato spoke of 'perfect forms', meta concepts for all things, which exist before the physical materialization. Quantum mechanics talks of 'probability fields' in the impeccable mathematics of that Carrollian discipline. Rupert Sheldrake and Lyall Watson are biologists who arrived, by very different paths, to the idea of 'formative causation'. The Old Testament tells us, with the brevity of Divine Revelation, 'And the Word was made Flesh.' Distilled to a single dazzling proposition: all things are prefigured: a swallow's flight, the birth of a star, the dance of the dolphins, the newborn infant's cry, the perfect sonnet … all are 'prefigured in the drift of stars'. Life is the raw clay seeking the Creator's templates.

'Where is God?'
'God is everywhere.'
— From a catechism for children.

*

In *Memories, Dreams, Reflections*, which is a summation of an extraordinary life's work in the realm of the mind, Carl Jung postulates a collective unconscious, repository of all the memories and experiences of the race, from the single cell born out of primordial broth to contemporary man. It is not a dormant or quiescent layer of psychic bedrock, but active and often volcanic. He regarded the individual human being much as he would a cell of the brain: cocooned in the vibrations of millions of transmissions and receptions between billions of nerve-endings, enshrining in a single mortal frame, the gamut of life, from the personal 'I' to all of past humanity. The collective unconscious explained, on a simple level, the processes of instinct, on subtler levels, the phenomena of synchronicity (Jung did not believe in coincidence) and parapsychology, and, on an even more fundamental plane, the peak or core religious experience, beyond description, transcendental.

Jung's was one – albeit singular – voice calling attention to a whole paradigm shift going on just below the level of the general horizon, a groundswell of change in the physical sciences which I (comfortably ensconced in the arts) discovered unevenly, bit by extraordinary bit. There were other, muted, clarion calls. A friend, Stanislav Grof, Resident Scholar at that haven for the open-hearted, the Esalen Institute in California's Big Sur, scientist and world authority on the psychedelic LSD, sent me his latest book *Realms of the Human Unconscious*, an account of eighteen years of controlled, clinical experiments with LSD, working with hundreds of subjects in Europe and the US.

As with Raymond Moody's meticulous recording of near-death experiences the world over, here too Grof came upon a common pool of psychic responses, inexplicable in terms of conventional understanding, surprisingly open to categorization, and with many startling correspondences with Jung's collective unconscious. The LSD experience followed a distinct statistical pattern: first, a disintegration of the barriers of sense responses (the voice of a rose, the scent of a painting, the colours of a symphony), then a swift and often tumultuous regression in time through physical states, beyond birth and foetal memory to ancestral, racial, evolutionary and past-incarnation experiences; later, a spatial expansion of consciousness to include primary and total identification with other persons, groups, plants and animals; and finally the 'core' experience again (always associated with great religious ecstasy): the Oneness of Life and All Creation.

The near-death (temporary 'clinical' death) experiences recorded by Moody in *Life After Life* and other researchers worldwide again point to a complex pattern of transition with many common elements (out-of-body experiences, tunnel passages, figures of shimmering light and compassion) and seem to reaffirm that human consciousness transcends (no one quite knows in what form) physical termination. With both LSD and near-death, there was permanent change: all existence was seen thereafter as reverential and sanctified, one and indivisible. The questions were unimportant, as were the answers. There was acceptance and serenity. I am that I am.

While Grof and Moody were examining the psyche in critical stages of transformation, revolutions were taking place in the physical and natural sciences. Physicists like Oppenheimer, Niels Bohr, Heisenberg and Capra, observing the nature of the atom's constituents, found they had to resort to the concepts and even the language of Eastern mysticism.

Niels Bohr: 'The great extension of our experience in recent years has brought to light the insufficiency of our simple mechanical conceptions and, as a consequence, has shaken the foundation on which the customary interpretation of observation was based.'

Sri Aurobindo: 'All things in fact begin to change their nature and appearance: one's whole experience of the world is radically different ... There is a new vast and deep way of experiencing, seeing, knowing, contacting things.'

In *The Tao of Physics* Fritjof Capra writes, '... modern physics leads us to a view of the world which is very similar to the views held by mystics of all ages and traditions.' In the mechanics of meditation and the soul of the atom, the cosmos is seen as, 'one inseparable reality – forever in motion, alive, organic; spiritual and material at the same time.' The essential substance of the atom and the universe is 'neither wave nor particle, neither still nor in motion, now fluid, now fixed, ever-changing ... there is only the dance.'

Biology, too, would never be the same again. New and seminal hypotheses (based again on empirical evidence meticulously gathered) were put forth by brave scientific spirits: Dr Lyall Watson, drawing on the experience of biology, anthropology and archaeology, developed the concept of meta-intelligence in such seminal works as *Supernature, The Romeo Error* and *Lifetide*. Biochemist Lewis Thomas, president of Sloan-Kettering Memorial Cancer Centre in New York and author of the national award winner, *The Lives of a Cell*, tells with the clarity of Montaigne, the wonder of a lyric poet and the reverence of a true believer, of the divine mysteries of biochemistry. Most recently, Rupert Sheldrake, Fellow of the Royal Society, in *A New Science of Life*, investigates the form and dimensions of meta-intelligence. They, and hundreds of scientists in disciplines as far removed as molecular biology and astrophysics, have pointed the way to a conclusion which may no longer be denied. Man is merely a part of the grand design. The Designer exists though his purposes are not known.

Here are three examples from thousands: Faith-healing or suggestion causes warts to disappear. Lewis Thomas writes about the complexity of this apparently simple act: first, various classes of lymphocytes (B cells and T cells, suppressor cells and killer cells) have to be sorted out; the right ones isolated and dispatched to the site to work on the task of tissue rejection; the blood supply to the wart shut off by chemical mediators selecting the right arterioles from thousands, 'some intelligence or other knows how to get rid of warts and this is a disquieting thought.' Watson reports on how isolated colonies of monkeys on deserted islands off the coast of Japan became fish-eaters. One of the islands was colonized by fishermen. The monkeys on that island, in imitation, began to catch and feed on small fish caught in the shallows. Simultaneously, monkey colonies on the other islands, separated by hundreds of miles of sea, began to fish in the shallows.

And here is my favourite Ultimate Statistic: the sex of an infant at birth is a random event, yet after each of the two World Wars (when we began to keep count of such things), with the wholesale depletion of the male population, the male/female ratios were seriously and threateningly disturbed. Then, over the next few years, the birth ratios changed, male births outstripped female until pre-war ratios were reached and the normal balance restored.

I had come full circle and while I could not claim 'to know the place for the first time', it was informed with a familiar and blessed sense of déja vu.

*

A few years ago I began a simple form of meditation. It was a propitious time. I was alone for a fortnight. I meditated twice a day, as I had been taught, sitting cross-legged, palm on palm, in a dark room with my eyes closed. It took a few minutes before my breath softened, the pulse-beat became slower and quieter. Childhood memories, long forgotten, returned. They were vivid and tactile and when they went away, a white glow took their place, stayed for a while and receded, and I settled into the stillness of a perfectly delightful paradox: I was aware as never before and yet I was aware of nothing, and this was profoundly right.

My wife Gita returned to Bombay unexpectedly one evening and found me meditating on the bedroom floor.

She said, 'Good God!'

And I thought, well said ....

****

The Lord of the Manor

Altamount Road lay steeply
ahead. Sisyphus, here
I come! I aged rapidly -
a good ten years with every
hundred yards - until,
terminally octogenarian,
I tottered to the doorstep
of 11 Chitrakoot

Meditation On A Bean Bag

I acquired the bean bag when I was twenty, with my first pay-check. I had never before felt the need to embellish my modest paying guest surroundings with an object of desire and the bean bag became an unwitting metaphor for time, place and lack of purpose. It was an extension of my being, mindlessly fluid and directionless, taking languid flight to all points of the compass as the mood moved us and redolent with the potential for whimsical change. I had no idea what went on inside the bean bag any more than I had about what went on inside myself. Neither of us had a point of focus; we created our universe as we went along, but I was inordinately proud of my bean bag's mercurial, polymorphous talents, particularly the way it combined form and function, seamlessly, the whole miraculously more compelling than the sum of the parts.

I did not know it then but my acquisition of the bean bag was the beginning of a personal quest to inform my immediate surroundings with a sense of self. The pivotal word here is personal. It led me many years later in Venice to purchase a signed limited edition print of a Salvador Dali painting which I could ill afford. *The Blue Unicorn* was for me, an aspiring writer, a shining testament of the power of the unfettered imagination to transcend the tyranny of the accepted paradigm. I began to understand as I grew older that none of us are of one piece but complex vortices of perception and experience involved in a metaphysical relationship with a mysterious kaleidoscopic environment. The harsh, primary compulsions of youth were gentled by the subtleties and ambiguities ôf a universe far, far more intricately and wondrously wrought than anything I could imagine. In terms of my personal surroundings I sought to make some of the magic my own.

I did not come gently to that good conclusion. I had grown up in the unforgiving culture of the Saraswat Brahmin Roman Catholic Goan. With cross, sword and Inquisitorial zeal the Portuguese laid down the crucifying doctrine of fascism, admitting of no doubt, offering certainty in return for unconditional surrender, acknowledging only the one true faith; all else was heathen, evil and doomed to the burning stake. A siege and slaughter mentality, reflected in the way they lived and built. Houses like fortifications with walls three feet thick; tiny arched windows barred with iron; dark heavy furniture which had no truck with physical indulgence – high-backed, perfectly perpendicular chairs which forced one to sit erect, hard-planked beds, chapels with narrow pews where the only tolerable position was on one's knees. Architecture, culture and religion conspired to create the inner darkness which kept Goa's lush and wanton fecundity at bay.

Fortunately for me I had been banished into the wilderness of Mumbai young enough to escape the generational shadow that still casts a blight on the green and pleasant land of my forefathers. Twenty years after I acquired my bean bag, I made the second most important acquisition of my life, a wild, untamed acre on a Goan beach, unsullied by man and surely touched in its savage, windswept beauty by the hand of God. In the gathering dusk, the late Sanju Walawalkar, a gifted and sensitive architect, my wife and I sat on a dune and tried to give meaning to inarticulate desire. Sanju had asked for and read every word I had ever written on Goa (exemplary fortitude!) and now she wished to know how we felt about each other and the future. No discussion here on architecture, design, spaces: views, elevations, materials; costs and contractors; just thoughtful words on a fair wind about the nature of being and fulfillment.

A year to the day Rockheart made us welcome. It seemed to rise as naturally and effortlessly as the palms, to have been there forever, organic as sun, sea and sand, indivisible from the elements, quintessentially Goan yet equally ours. At long last I had given back to the good Goan earth and to generations yet to come, in some small measure, the overflowing bounty I had received.

Last week at Rockheart I pondered on the vagaries of one's personal space. Across the next dune a fisherman friend of mine walks on hard cowdung floors, with open-faced, hand-dressed laterite brick walls under a sloping roof of coconut beams and Mangalore tile, and sleeps on a reed mat with his dog. He would have it no other way. Two miles as the gull flies another friend, Jimmy Gazdar, has realized the impossible dream, a magnificent Renaissance Italian palazzo on the side of a cliff set like a jewel in five acres of gardened brilliance which Renoir would have painted without pain. He would have it no other way. I am comfortable in both homes; I would not choose to live in them; but I honour Joaquim and Jimmy for following their star, as I have mine.

To each of us, our once and future bean bag.

****

They Call Me Mr Gita!

On that fine spring morning when we swore beautiful and eternal vows to each other, only one small wisp of cloud marred the perfection of a joyful azure horizon: I was sad because her surname – wed so melodiously to her given name – would now change forever. Gita Simoes. Not too bad though. The quick brevity of the first gave balance and poise to the langorous vowels and lazy sibilants of the second. We could have been less fortunate – Anuradha Alfonso, for instance, or – one shudders at the narrowness of most escapes – Saraswati Fernandes!

I made one quiet vow. Gita would be no traditional Indian wife, bound to hearth and home by iron bands. I would, in the finest of liberal traditions, encourage her to seek a singular identity. She would flourish in her own right, make her own happy journey to maturity and freedom. The girl had talent; she drew after a fashion, and painted. I would get her a studio with good natural light, encourage her to work towards an exhibition, guide and counsel her with all the generosity of spirit at my command. I could see it all, the opening, the accolades, the *Times* review, 'Gita Simoes, wife of the highly successful journalist and advertising man, Frank Simoes, shows great promise ... '

It is ten years to the day. I take the maid to the local bank to open an account. Not on; she must be introduced by an existing account holder. The clerk retreats into a maze of red tape. The maid dissolves into tears. I try logic, persuasion, flattery ... nothing works.

'My name is Frank Simoes,' I begin again, promising trouble in every clenched syllable, 'and I want to see your manager.' The clerk's eyes light up in friendly recognition. 'Wait a minute,' he says, 'any connection with Gita Simoes, the lady who designs the *Taj Magazine*? I saw her picture in the papers the other day. Isn't she … ' I cut him short. 'I'm her husband,' I say, thinking back ruefully to earlier, innocent days when I'd have said, 'She's my wife.' The clerk beams. The maid acquires a banker.

Mind you, it did not happen overnight. When the wife announced happily one evening that she had a job, 'helping out with the graphics at the Taj' one was pleased and indulgent and willing to give freely of oneself. She would need the timely piece of advice, the hard critical appraisal, the potent creative idea. One would rally around, of course, for there might even be here (no telling about these things) the beginning of a career of sorts. Ho hum. One morning, years later, I opened the *Times* and there, on Page 7, was the better half (that's right) smiling graciously as she received an award from an ancient party who beamed back at her with a zesty enthusiasm I did not appreciate at all. She had won the year's premium advertising award. But that was my profession! What was going on here?

Today, much and wisely married, I am inured to the trunk calls that shatter our day of rest. I manage my company, at best, erratically. While I swing between benign euphoria (my staff call me then, 'The Great White Hope') and superior temper tantrums ('Watch out for the Towering Inferno,' they whisper, much to my delight), my wife handles the graphic design affairs of a fivestar hotel group with endless patience and unruffled good humour. At Taj parties I walk five paces behind her, hands clasped behind my back, mustering a cold dignity, much in the manner of the Duke of Edinburgh, while tall, terrifically handsome men hug her and kiss her on the cheek. When I try that on their wives, I get hard looks. She works a nine-hour day and there she is, at the end of it, fresh as a daisy, ready for a night on the town while I am about ready for the cleaners. It does me no good at all when the phone rings at that very minute and a voice – a lowly tradesperson no doubt – says, 'Mr Gita, please may I speak to Mrs Gita.'

For all of you males out there, who care for your successful wives, a bit of advice. The main thing, of course, is to be gainfully occupied. Take up a hobby. Nothing as gross as golf, or as simple-minded as the guitar. Crochet now is something to think seriously about – as creative a hobby as you care to make it. There are practical benefits – you knit nice tea cosies, place mats and, with time, even whole tablecloths. Cooking too has much to be said for it. A word of caution here. Do not attempt a grand start, such as offered by the seductions of Craig Clairbourne's *New York Times Cook Book*. There is an admirable lady, who knows her onions, called Peggy Bracken. She has written a useful little gem, *The I Hate To Cook Book*. This is a beginner's manual of much worth for it makes simple and edible that which is essentially infinitely complex. I commend, as a first experiment, 'Stay-a-Bed Stew' or 'Hurry Curry'. You can't go wrong. But if cooking does not make you feel whole and complete, you can try – with no guarantees – potted plants. I am told by those who should know that, if you are worthy, and think kind thoughts at them at sunrise and last thing at night, you will develop a warm, sustaining relationship. Having had a nasty experience or two with cacti in my time, I am neutral to the idea.

There will, despite your best efforts, be dark moments. A macho bachelor friend may let drop the unkind term, 'house husband.' Do not be dismayed. John Lennon was proud to be one. You may be reduced to a quivering shambles by the simple business of renewing a ration card. At such times, think positive thoughts. This one cheers me up no end: behind every successful woman there is a good man.

****

Some Things Never Change

At the age of seven, I was blithely indifferent to girls. They were around, so they obviously had a place in the scheme of things — somewhere, say, between a rock and a bush, though certainly not as interesting: you could throw rocks about with stimulating results and you never knew what you might find under a bush. But girls seemed to serve no useful purpose whatsoever. Until one Sunday morning, outside St. Anne's Church after High Mass, when I discovered to my everlasting shame the lethal potential of the gentler sex.

> Primrose Hill is green
> Primrose Hill is yellow
> As I walked down Primrose Hill
> I met a pretty fellow

With that, recited breathlessly, and a manic gleam in her eye, she threw her arms about my neck and kissed me wetly. The monstrous child stank of peppermint and Johnson's Baby Soap and was a head taller than I. At seven I did not have the strength to stomp her into the ground. For weeks after that my friends would liven the dull moment with droll references to 'Primrose Hill' and 'pretty fellows' while falling about in unseemly mirth. Pitched battles and bloody noses saw honour restored.

Years later, I arrived at two conclusions about girls — love them or hate them, one couldn't live without them; and all my fellow males out there, harbouring illusions of chauvinist superiority, were wrong: *we* were the weaker sex. I have long since learned to put a brave face on it. I have been – and am – unabashedly, today – putty in the hands of the women in my life, willing, participative victim to what a psychologist friend (a woman, naturally) calls 'passive control'. This is a subtle and devious technique, as insidious as it is sublime, which seeks (even as you sink without trace for the third time) to inspire the joyful thought, 'What a way to go!' There is only one intelligent response: lie down and enjoy it.

Man and boy, I have been the object of masterly displays of the art. The hint of a suspicion of a tear; the lovingly reassuring promise, ' Of course we'll do it your way, darling', only to find, weeks later, that you have happily done it her way, not quite knowing when, how or why you have changed your mind; a soupcon of wistful tendresse as a memory is recalled of which you are, sadly, not a part; the soft, poignant tremor of the lips in response to your beastly behaviour (accepting and forgiving all), and then, that evening, the perfectly done roast chicken with roast potatoes … and I am soft clay to be fashioned into whatever compliant shape she fancies, all fat chuckles, good humour and ready to be put to bed without fuss.

This has been going on for quite some time now. Three years after the shameful Primrose Hill episode, the young person in question, now pleasing in strange and disturbing ways, held my hand on Mazagaon Hill and lead me up the garden path. It's been that way ever since, and bigger biceps don't help. Take the matter of Ooty. 'Mountains,' said the lady in my life, 'tea estates, fresh air, pine forests, colonial clubhouses and fireplaces …' 'What's wrong with Goa?' I asked, and there I was, three weeks later, quivering like a coconut palm in a high wind, having barely survived a nine-hour drive through wild countryside, monsoon gales, around terrifying precipices on crumbling roads, in a vintage Ambassador, driven by a suicidal maniac in a tearing hurry. And, as I had suspected, when you've seen one Toda, you've seen them all.

You would have thought that now, in life's midsummer, I should have learned from the error of my ways. But no, here I go again. She is – like all the women in my life – quite ravishing. Lithe as a young reed, doe-eyed, with a spring in her step and a smile to make strong men wilt. She insists on laughter wherever she goes, and she goes first class or nothing all the way. I confess to having spoiled her rotten. London, Las Palmas, Geneva, Paris, Singapore ... champagne flights, no less, fivestar caravanserais. Beluga and foie gras and chauffered limousines, and when she is poised on her toes, in a black bikini, at the edge of the Taj Holiday Village pool in Goa, and executes a perfect jack-knife, arrogant young males gasp and hurl glances of pure hatred at me, while I chuckle – yes – fatly!

She is the quintessential female: wilful, capricious, cozening, given, in the space of bewildering moments, to goodness and guile, loving kindness and arctic indifference; talented in ways which leave me wondering. We fight, make up, fight again ... her eyes glisten; I swear eternal sorrow; generously, she offers an olive branch ... 'She has him round her little finger,' say my friends enviously. Too true, and I'm not complaining.

Her name is Radhika; an entrancing six-year-old going on an iron-willed sixty; my daughter.

Will the battle between the sexes never cease?

****

My Dog's Best Friend

There is a misconception among my friends that I own a dog, a white mongrel bitch who answers to the name of Snowy. Nothing could be farther from the truth. Snowy owns me.

All my life I have been owned by dogs of various pedigrees and persuasions. The first dog to have me, albeit with reservation, was a bull terrier named Pop. He took me under his paw at an impressionable age, and became friend, guide and mentor while I explored the enthralling landscapes of dogdom. He was patient with my deficiencies: I would never learn to follow a scent, gnaw at a bone or terrify a cow; but a really intelligent dog could make something out of me. I was given a loose rein, with a nip here and a growl there to keep me in line whenever I was inclined to stray.

As I grew up, I was passed from dog to dog, so to say. There was Freda, a highly-strung dachshund of impeccable pedigree, given to violent histrionics when thwarted or denied; Freda educated me on the ways of aristocracy. Rauf, a huge mongrel who liked to pretend he was a wolf, led me to believe that all uniforms were essentially fascist: he attacked postmen and policemen on sight. Alfredo was the most notorious of the lot, a prodigious lover who sired progeny all about the neighbourhood. It was an article of faith with him that love transcends all, with the possible exception of a nice piece of liver.

I am now – as any dog who's known me will happily tell you – lovely to have about the house. I have even managed to pick up a few tricks. If a ball is put at my feet I throw it willingly and as often as called for. I will, on command, stroke backs and tickle stomachs. When asked, I supply a fresh liver biscuit instantly. I am a very good man to take for a walk and I understand the value of lampposts.

Snowy came into my life quite by chance. One witching, moon-bright night on Anjuna Beach in Goa, temporarily dogless, I was approached by an English hippie, a forlorn waif of a girl with a white puppy in her arms. She had found the dog on the beach, abandoned, bruised and bloody and would we please give it a home? Snowy opened a wary eye, recognized me at once, grinned in the sloppy manner of a puppy who's on to a good thing and laid a small tentative paw in the palm of my hand. The rest, as they say, is history.

Snowy's lineage was a mystery. At the age of two, she raced like a greyhound across the hallowed lawns of the Willingdon, teaching me to jog. This was clearly no mean Goan beast, but an animal of superior, if not noble pedigree. A retired colonel followed her progress keenly, and offered a military opinion, 'Nice whippet you have there.' And whippet she became until one fateful morning at the vet's when she got into an argument with a French poodle over the seating arrangement. The vet said to me, 'You want to watch that Rampur hound of yours. Dangerous breed.' A Rampur hound owned me! And I will never forget the dark moment when Snowy, on nipping a neighbour's servant, was referred to scathingly as '… that damned mongrel.' I crawled, hurt beyond words, into the study for the day and only emerged when Snowy coaxed me out with the latest issue of *Time*.

There are happier memories: the comeuppance of the Dog from Dallas comes cheerfully to mind. His American owners showed scant respect for the conventions we all took as read, and allowed the dog to roam the neighbourhood alone. A burly Caucasian beast, with no manners, he raised a contemptuous leg at the gulmohur in our garden and sneered each time he saw Snowy until, one splendid evening, in the glorious spirit of her Rampur forbears, Snowy engaged the Dog from Dallas in bloody battle. The gardeners stopped working to look on. Neighbours appeared as if by magic. This was no mere dogfight. The national honour was at stake. No quarter was asked for; none given. A rousing cheer broke out: Snowy had drawn first blood. The Dog from Dallas had a bloody ear. Within minutes, spirit broken, he charged headlong down the road, Snowy in hot pursuit.

That evening the doorbell rang. I opened it and swallowed. Retribution loomed over me in the shape of a huge, crew cut prime American male, from the deep south yet. He did not look friendly. 'You-all gotta hound dawg?' 'That's right,' I said. 'Your dawg beat up on my dawg, mister, beat up on him bad. I wanna ...' At that moment Snowy stepped daintily into the drawing room. Her brown eyes were soft and gentle. She wagged her tail, wiggled her hips, crinkled her nose at the American and made small happy sounds. He stared in utter disbelief, then grinned sheepishly, 'Aw, gee ... sorry fella. Have a good day.'

Now that Snowy is in the family way, I am compiling a list of texts for puppies who wish to grow up to be wise dogs. 'Cats and Other Nice Things to Eat' heads the list. 'Fangs a Lot' instructs on the fine art of intimidation, begins with 'A Hint of a Suspicion of a Growl', proceeds to meatier stuff, 'How to Raise Your Hackles Without Really Trying' and, when all else fails, encourages direct action, 'When You Really Mean Business, Bite!' 'Paw No More ...' is an inspirational text on the life of luxury. The chapter on food, 'I Have a Bone to Pick With You' is full of such gems as 'Liv-er Little' and offers guidelines for other delicate manoeuvres ('Avoiding Vegetables Without Ruffling Feelings', 'Make Your Master Share His Mutton') designed to ensure that the inner dog is provided for with love, care and sustenance.

It will, by now, be clear to the keen reader that I am a dog's best friend. If, by chance, you happen to come upon a tall, slim, elegant (heel boy!) diffident, awkward, distraught figure, trotting at the end of a leash, being led by an elegant Rampur hound which may yet be a whippet but never a mongrel, take heed: you are looking at a man who will always be owned by a dog. He has been superbly trained. He responds with alacrity to the most subtle demands of the leash. He knows where all of the choicest smells lie.

He has not, thus far, been seen to raise his leg at a lamppost but one never knows.

****

Get Those Biceps Bouncin', baby!

When I was forty and foolish enough to believe in such things, I took stock of my physical assets and was not impressed. Bad enough that I had to bend forward like one of those pendulum dolls to get a brief glimpse of my toes. Worse yet, gravity was making itself alarmingly felt: I was beginning to resemble a pear on the threshold of self-realization. 'You have a high waist,' said the friendly neighbourhood mortician who moonlighted as my allopath on his off days, 'and a l-o-n-g abdominal spread. If you must live high off the hog don't be surprised if you begin to look like one.' 'I've just turned forty doctor, do you think it's age?' I enquired nervously while a quartet of apocalyptic horses neighed derisively at my rear. 'Happens to all of us,' said my mortician adviser, 'life may begin at forty but everything else starts to wear out, fall out or spread out.' Plagiarizer! Beryl Pfizer said that first. But I kept mum. It just doesn't do to get on the wrong side of your doctor. 'Putting it another way,' he continued cheerfully, now off and running, 'you're clearly on the wrong side of forty if you feel like the morning after the night before and you haven't been anywhere.'

Very funny. But I got the message. Those were the days when I still believed in doctors. 'Exercise,' he said, 'and lay off the fat.' And stung me for a cool handful of big ones when my wife been saying just that for years. Free. So I began to jog by morn's early light. If you were to catch sight of me at the crack of dawn on the crest of Cumballa Hill you were in for a stirring display of get up and gung ho. Vibrantly healthy, a keen and athletic seventeen, in sneakers and a track suit custom-made for incipient pear shapes, I flew on winged feet down the hill and along Carmichael Road. By the time I crossed over at Mahalaxmi and swung into Warden Road, the casual observer would allow that, for a man who would never see thirty again, I was doing very nicely indeed. I began to hurt at Scandal Point. At Kemp's Corner, little old ladies could be seen following my progress with alarm while tut-tutting at such irresponsible behaviour. Should a man in his fifties, I can still hear them say, carry on so? Too true. Altamount Road lay steeply ahead. Sisyphus, here I come! I aged rapidly – a good ten years with every hundred yards – until, terminally octogenarian, I tottered to the doorstep of 11 Chitrakoot only to have my cocker spaniel Snoopy, the Dog Who Knows No Sympathy, hand me his leash and order me out for his morning constitutional.

Did I lose weight? No. Did I eat less? Fat chance. All that exercise caused the stomach to get bigger and hungrier. Nature abhors a vacuum. I pigged. Did I feel like Stallone the Rock just before he demolishes the bad guys? Ho hum. *He* didn't have to cope with cracked joints, knotted calves, splintered shins, twisted tendons, crumbling arches and double vision: in short, I felt like an architectural ruin waiting, in fear and trembling, for a demolition order from the Bombay Municipal Corporation.

Now on the benevolent side of fifty, I recall my youthful shenanigans with a touch of wry nostalgia. Not that I have abandoned physical exercise. I'll have you know that it spruces up the muscles, clears the vision, blows the cobwebs away, gets the hormones buzzing and the liver sprightly as a spring lamb's. Every other morning, at the civilized hour of nine, Cumballa Hill sees a new and youthful me. No vulgar galloping about the landscape, but a swift and graceful walk/trot down the hill, assisted gently by the force of gravity and on to the swimming pool at the club where I float on my back in the deep end and count the leaves on a venerable banyan tree (I can never remember where I left off at last count and have to begin at the beginning every time I begin). This is a Zen Buddhist technique which opens the third eye and shields the inner ear from the raucous cacophony of all those disgracefully gauche temporary members who disport noisily at the shallow end. Another bonus to floating: it boosts your sense of superiority no end. Here are the thirty-lengthers hyperventilating alarmingly as they reach twenty-five; there the sprinters swallowing pintfuls of pool; anon the learners, water leaking from every orifice, now up, now under, splashing and lashing with furious abandon. Half an hour of delightful, waterbed reverie and I am ready to replace the carbohydrate and protein lost in all this strenuous exertion. Three generously endowed ham and cheese rolls later, do I jog up the hill home? Heaven forbid. With age comes wisdom. Muthu picks me up in the Peugeot and I wallow in sybaritic French upholstery on featherbed French suspension till I get to Chitrakoot, a good morning's workout well accomplished.

For the benefit of all you ditherers out there I have designed (though not yet patented, procrastination being one of the more enjoyable autumnal virtues) a set of exercises guaranteed to tone you up from top to toe. All they require is attention while you go about those other daily activities so easeful to body and spirit and which you must never, under pain of all kinds of nastiness, ever give up. They can be done anywhere, as the blurbs say, at any time, without anyone noticing. Pain, sweat and creak-free. Just the ticket for fifty-plus slouchers who hanker after youth's lost and lissome silhouette.

Here are the first of a series of exercises which I hope will enliven this column from time to time. We begin modestly with the wrist and fingers and then proceed to the arms. Best performed an hour and a half before lunch and a good two hours before dinner. Essential hardware: a Waterford crystal whisky tumbler and a bottle of good Scotch (the heft and weight of the glass is of critical importance; so is the Scotch. If, post-fifty, you are not able to afford Scotch, the size and suppleness of your biceps are the least of your worries; consult your accountant at once!). Also crucial to this exercise is a 60 ml measure, one of those hemispherical, hand-tooled silver jobs that yearn to be filled, with sacramental care, to the quivering, osmotic brimful. You know what I mean. Right up to just below the top, then drop by careful drop, till the Scotch rises above the rim, quivers like a jelly and threatens to overflow at the barest hint of heavy breathing. Then, ever so gently, take the Waterford tumbler in your right hand, incline the lip at an acute angle just below the edge of the measure. With thumb and forefinger swiftly (do not despair if you splash a bit; with time you will perform this feat with the dexterity of a bartender) upturn the contents of the measure into the glass. It is essential that you perform this manoeuvre at least thrice before lunch and four times before dinner. Physical therapists worldwide have gone on record to declare that no other exercise serves the tendons of the fingers and wrists better. Over time you develop a grip of micrometric delicacy and smooth, silky strength. Note that the rest of the body (with the exception of the eyeballs which tend, as you start on the exercise, to agitate nervously this way and that) remains perfectly still. This, as we shall see, is the guiding philosophy behind the series: only one muscle group at a time please.

Adhering unswervingly to this principle, the next exercise is simple and exclusive to the arm muscles from shoulder to wrist, with a bonus thrown in: your oesophagus gets a gentle workout as well. You will need three indispensable aids – an overstuffed sofa, one of those English country house affairs where you are tenderly embraced back and rear; a commodious footstool at the exact height of the seat of the sofa; an occasional table at your right and, if you are to get this absolutely correct and exercise both arms without bias, one again to your left. Proceed as follows: lower your rear elevation into the sofa, raise your feet and cross them on the footstool, wiggle a bit till you sink in. Raise the glass to your lips and take a decent mouthful. Swirl this about the tonsils a few times (excellent for the muscles of neck and throat). Swallow gently as your delighted oesophagus begins to undulate with exuberance and brio. Allow five minutes between sips at least. I have had complaints that this is fascist control at its most brutal and that it becomes near-impossible to fulfill such an unreasonable requirement as an hour comes to a close, you embark on a third refill, and the urge to get in as much exercise as quickly as possible gets the better of you. Remember, there is an isometric principle at work here. It calls for control (the same slow, measured speed every time you raise glass to lip); resistance, as the weight of the Waterford tests biceps, triceps and forearm; repetition between short periods of deep rest (no less than five minutes between gulps, you promised!); and meditation in tranquility as you enjoy the deep, satisfying glow that only exercise bestows, ponder the delights of the lunch to come, and raise a toast to the immortal Bard, no mean mover and shaker himself, 'And now in age I bud again …'

****

The Persuader

Practise wrath before the
mirror each morning. Snarl
and learn to smoke cigars.
Reduce all the confidence
you see around you to
a small heap of ashes.
With clients, be nice.

An Exchange of Cables - 1

The fax machine has been the death of the little white lie. Cables may no longer be lost in transit; letters refuse to go mysteriously astray; important documents will never again be misplaced in the mail. This exchange of cables with the Vice President, Client Servicing, of my advertising agency in Bombay, took place 10 B.F. (Before Fax) when all manner of evasion was possible. The time I spent in Goa, first searching for the perfect acre by the sea, then enjoying the fruits of my labour, was considerably enlivened by an encabled dialogue. While the exchanges were somewhat one-sided (I had the advantage of distance and ownership), a few are worth reproducing. Here is an example:

TO FS CANDOLIM GOA
FROM VP CS BOMBAY
 YOU SAID YOU'D BE AWAY FOUR DAYS ITS BEEN TEN STOP CREATURE FROM BLACK LAGOON HENCEFORTH ABBREVIATED TO CBLF FOR REASONS OF ECONOMY FURIOUS STOP I AM CHAIRMAN OF YOUR SECOND LARGEST CLIENT ORGANIZATION HE HISSED AT LAST MEETING I WILL NOT BE FOBBED OFF WITH PUSSYFOOTING JUNIORS STOP HIS EXACT WORDS STOP RETURN IMMEDIATELY STOP ANY DAY NOW MEN IN WHITE COATS WILL ARRIVE AT FUNNY FARM AND TAKE ME AWAY

TO FS CANDOLIM GOA
FROM VP CS BOMBAY
    CBLF THREATENS TO CALL IN OTHER AGENCIES FOR QUOTE PRELIMINARY DISCUSSIONS UNQUOTE THE SWINE STOP RATFINKS FROM JWT MCCANNS BBDO CONSPIRING AND CONNIVING OVER FIVESTAR BINGES WITH CBLF AND CRONIES STOP SAATCHIS CEO IS FIRST COUSIN TO CBLFS SECOND WIFE THEY PLAY GOLF EVERY SUNDAY FOR GODS SAKE (!) AND HE ALWAYS LETS CBLF WIN STOP DO YOU REALIZE THE DANGER WE ARE IN

TO FS CANDOLIM GOA
FROM VP CS BOMBAY
    FUNNY FARM DISTRAUGHT STOP CREATIVE GROUP MUTTERING DARKLY AND PLUCKING INVISIBLE STRAWS FROM ITS HAIR STOP EVERYBODY LOATHES CBLF ONLY TWO FEEBLE-MINDED CAMPAIGN CONCEPTS PRODUCED IN PAST FORTNIGHT BOTH REJECTED WITH TERMINAL PREJUDICE BY CBLF STOP WHAT AM I TO DO STOP ADVISE URGENTEST

TO FS CANDOLIM GOA
FROM VP CS BOMBAY
    WILL SCATHING INDICTMENT MAKE YOU SEE THE LIGHT STOP JUNIOR COPYWRITER PENNED DOGGEREL IN YOUR HONOUR TITLED THE OLD CROCK AND THE SEA STOP THE PREVENTION OF IMMORALITY ACT IN PUBLIC PLACES PREVENTS FURTHER QUOTATION STOP SHAME AND FIE WHEN ARE YOU COMING BACK STOP I AM TERMINALLY ANGUISHED AND MAY RESORT TO DESPERATE MEASURES

TO VP CS BOMBAY
FROM FS CANDOLIM GOA
    I AM SERIOUSLY CONCERNED ABOUT LACK OF CONTACT FROM BOMBAY STOP I HAVE BEEN IN GOA TEN DAYS YOU HAVE MY ADDRESS STOP NOT A WORD FROM YOU GUYS STOP WHERE IS YOUR SENSE OF RESPONSIBILITY STOP WHAT NEWS OF CBLFS CAMPAIGN STOP HAVE YOU COLLECTED OUTSTANDINGS FOR

JULY STOP ENOUGH OF THIS PFAFFING AROUND YOU TWITS STOP
EARLIER HIGH REGARD FOR YOU LOUTS IN DANGER OF
CRUMBLING STOP RESPOND SWIFTEST

TO FS CANDOLIM GOA
FROM VP CS BOMBAY
    CUT THE CRAP FRANK YOU WILL TAKE THE FIRST PLANE BACK
OR ELSE

    I did.

                        ****

The Personal Narrative

The following is a brief for a book on Frank Simoes' life
in advertising. The book, sadly, never got written, but the synopsis is as fine
an example as one can find on How to Sell a Book to a Publisher and
proves, yet again, Frank's brilliance as an ad man.

In the early Sixties, when I gatecrashed the advertising party, it was a profession exclusively staffed at executive and management levels by boxwallahs (exceptions were made for copywriters and art directors: it was the received wisdom that 'creatives' were long-haired, unwashed, dangerous, often mad and quite beyond the civilized pale). Client contact was maintained by pukka brown English persons drawn from the twittering classes, educated at the very best Indian public schools and the established Oxbridge universities. Wharton and Harvard were vulgar American kindergartens. Xavier's and Stephen's accepted under duress. However, the right family background (which clubs did the parents belong to?) was considered vastly more important than the right educational qualifications or the lack of them. Beginning with an hilarious interview with a very propah English managing director – and harking back a bit from there – one of the initial chapters explains how it came to pass that a Byculla Bum (as downmarket from the uppercrust Byculla Boy as you could hope to get) in his twenties, without an education, conned a crusty former Colonel of the Coldstream Guards as sexually bent as a corkscrew, Indian CEO of the largest, most conservative advertising agency in the Commonwealth, into making him an offer which he promptly accepted.

Wet behind the ears:

The initiation rites. Painful and bewildering and, from time to time, positively shameful. I discover that my black trousers (drain-pipe; Byculla hi-fashion at its cutting best!) white nylon shirt and bright green tie are not considered the epitome of sartorial finesse in the advertising business. My accent is in urgent need of demolition and recreation; my haircut is a joke; my granny glasses with the gold rims, without question, an ancient family heirloom. I am the only male copy trainee in a department of five female copywriters and a gay female copy chief. Suppressing my natural priapic instincts takes its toll. All that estrogen in so small a space leaves me shuffling about pale and wan. Until Mani Aiyer comes along (See article '2000 Grateful Words ... '). Mani takes me under a learned and sympathetic wing. We become friends, colleagues and, over the next ten years, prime plotters-in-arms, adventuring together in London, Calcutta and other agency hot spots, from our days as trainees to our final elevation to company directors. He features prominently in the book. Even more gratifying, I am taken in hand, in a manner of speaking, by a sexy young bimbet in client servicing (who comes from the right part of town but enjoys slumming). She introduces me to uppers and downers, fast cars, exotic liquid pick-me-ups and the creative uses of large, soft pillows (as if I didn't know!). A powerful account director is hopelessly enamoured of her and I enter joyfully into My First Big Feud and discover – contrary to all doomsday predication – that I possess a natural and wickedly honed talent for intrigue and strife. But I remain not so much naive as from a different planet. When I am invited to a gay party (a set piece) – you couldn't move a foot in the agency without brushing yet another limp wrist from your rear – my first question, to the utter horror of the all-male (?) gathering is, 'Hey where are the babes?' I do not make friends and influence people, but I have my moments.

I meet Bal Mundkar (later the creator of Ulka), at the time a senior account director mesmerisingly successful and a sexual

Olympic athlete. He eats three of my five lunchtime sandwiches every other day while lecturing me on girls, gizmos, getting-it-all and, infrequently, the advertising business. I grapple with the crass commercial world engaged in the greater glory of soaps, toothpastes, shirts, jams, chocolates etc., and, while dumbstruck at my lack of any sort of ability, I am even more appalled by the fact that everybody around me seems to know even less than I do about writing advertising copy. I am surrounded by mystery. Who is Kersey Katrak, owner of Mass Communication and Marketing? And why is he feared and loathed by all in the business? Why is Ding Dong Bell, the agency's British CEO always tête-à-tête with nubile young executive things of the wrong gender? Why does the latest white import, Margaret Duff Challan, the agency's marketing guru, fifty if a day, with a faint moustache which refuses to be suppressed by cosmetic bleach, stalk me with such determination down the agency's darker corridors? I am – soon – shudder! – to find out! Why is it that the very best people in advertising follow other first professions – Gerson da Cunha, Zul Vellani and Alyque Padamsee in theatre? Arun Kholatkar in fine art? Mickey Patel in satirical cartooning? Kersey Katrak in playwriting and poetry? Shyam Benegal taking off every other year to make feature films? Ding Dong Bell in pederasty. Bal Mundkar in unbridled priapism? And why are voices lowered worshipfully when the name Subhas Ghosal comes up?

But I learn fast. Bhagwan Wadhwani, a client and soon to become a close friend (he too features strongly in the book) teaches me the sterling worth of the three Bs – Booze, Broads and Big Bucks, the 'most potent stress relievers know to man', not necessarily in that order of priority. The 'model as nymphomaniac' is brutally laid to rest. I discover, to my cost, that lowly copy trainees do not get to tumble in the hay with lissome models (only ape-like photographers with knuckles brushing the floor enjoy the privilege). But I am not abandoned by the kindness of strangers. Mitter Bedi, pioneering photographer, apprentices me to his trade with enormous kindness and patience; a diminutive Tamilian who spits in every eye takes my media education in hand; Katrak casts a benevolent eye in my direction; Arun Kholatkar, with icy contempt for his profession, begins my kindergarden tuition. I read 25,000,000 books on advertising and am even more confused than when I began. No one knows how a great campaign comes into existence. I pick up the buzzwords and throw them about with careless indiscrimination: creative strategy, copy platform, critical path analyses, market penetration, extrapolative samples, pilot tests ... They are of no help at all when I find myself marooned in a flood of biblical proportions in a train one hundred and fifty miles from Calcutta with a campaign I have to present to the board of directors of Smith Stanistreet, a pharmaceutical company of impeccable lineage – hoary, venerable, white East India thugs. I am greeted as hero and made to recount, in stirring detail, every last second of my adventure. The campaign is examined cursorily, accepted, set aside and I am invited for lunch (to continue my Boys' Own account) to the Bengal Club. I return a hero, with flattering encomiums, with my head twice its normal size and a promotion to senior copywriter handling my own accounts. I promptly embark on six separate and major feuds with the account directors handling these accounts. One of them has the temerity to red pencil my copy. I send it back with a curt note which begins, 'When will you learn to read without moving your lips?' Battle lines are drawn; plots and counterplots launched; no work gets done. Ding Dong rushes hither and thither trying to make peace, his nubile young things languishing for lack of attention. I begin to sense victory when the account directors join forces and threaten mass resignation if I am not sent packing forthwith. My copy chief and creative director throw me to the wolves. Ding Dong regards me with a sad and wistful eye. He knows I am not massagable. 'The management has decided,' he says, 'to transfer you to the Calcutta office as copy chief'. I am being kicked upstairs! Strange are the ways of the advertising business.

Bonking in Bongland

I pack my bag and ancient red Underwood portable and depart for the land of Tagore, Sundarban tigers and – stretching my knowledge of Bengal to its limits, and ever hopeful – seductive Sharmilas. My first fortnight does not augur well for the future. Campbell Bannerman, the Scotsman who runs Bensons in Calcutta, lives up to his countrymen's reputation for severe thrift and I find myself incarcerated in a cell with a cold shower in a flea-infested doss house on Calcutta's notorious Freeschool Street. All thoughts of a grand advertising career evaporate as I wear out yards of shoe leather seeking permanent accommodation. Enter, on the second floor of Karnani Mansion (chuckle, chuckle, yes, *that* Karnani Mansion), the Lavrovs, an ancient White Russian couple who, among the flotsam and jetsam of the Second World War, find themselves cast ashore in the city of dreadful Marwaris. They have a cubicle and shower to spare. I am interviewed by Lavrov and insist at once, as an author of great potential soon to be realized, on a desk to accommodate my heirloom Underwood. Lavrov ignores this pifflage. What, he wants to know, do I know about Russia? 'Isaac Babel,' I answer proudly, hinting at vast reservoirs of non-existent Russian expertise. Safer to stay with the one Babel I have read. I give Lavrov the benefit of a lengthy review: how a Russian Jew, to escape alive from yet another pogram, lies about his lineage and enlists in a Cossack cavalry regiment – as savage, bloody-thirsty, criminal and psychotic a bunch of Jew-hating killers as ever laid waste to the Russian steppes since Genghis Khan made the rivers run crimson. Lavrov and his wife roar with laughter and fall off their chairs. 'I was a Cossack colonel,' says Lavrov. 'I would lof for you to haf the room,' says Mrs Lavrov. One of their number of dwindling émigrés has died a week earlier from a lethal enthusiasm for cheap Indian vodka and I am invited to the wake the next evening. I rush back to the office to break the good news.

Bannerman heaves a sigh of relief and plunges, with unseemly haste and lack of tact, into the second most important item on his Agenda for Simoes. My reputation has preceded me. Humming and hawing, and rather red in the face, Bannerman warns me of the deep-rooted modesty of Bengal's maidens, of their chaste and unshakeable virtue, of their unassailable virginity ('No sexual hanky-panky here, Simoes') and of the mortal physical danger from homicidally inclined male relatives if one plays fast and loose with the local lasses. I reflect on this a fortnight later while in my office at lunch break entwined forelock to footnote in an embrace of Anacondian virtuosity by a young lady named Chatterjee. She is my secretary and our collaboration is rudely disturbed by the

the East End, who will soon own the universe, and no mean mover
and shaker himself when it comes to slinky young things of the
right shape and gender. He brushes Bannerman off and sends me a
'For Your Eyes Only' cable, 'Try not to shit on your own doorstep.
It creates a stink!' Encouraged no end, I take my secretary and her
duties seriously in hand. But Calcutta is destined to change me.
My education – in advertising and the great university of life –
really begins. At the head office in Bombay I was never without
recourse to my peers, few as they were; I had never lived alone or,
for that matter, in another city. In no time at all in Calcutta, I
realize why the two Brit expatriates – Bannerman and Wiltshire –
have been banished to the Colonies: they know nothing about
advertising; indeed, they would be hard put to sell the services of a
well provisioned brothel to an Iraqi battalion sequestered in the
desert. But they possess other qualifications perfectly matched to
our clients' (exclusively British, exclusively white, exclusively
boxwallah) expectations. Bannerman's father had retired as chairman
of one of Calcutta's oldest trading houses and was well, if not fondly,
remembered. Among his other achievements: president of the
Tollygunge Club (near all-white except for a handful of token natives
with the right background and accent); president of the Turf
Association, the Royal Golf Tournament, an OBE and de facto Big
White Chief of the expatriate Brit community. David Wiltshire's
credentials were better still. Eton, King's College and The Royal
Fusiliers from which he had decamped, (having discovered that
soldiering was not without its discomforts despite the extracurricular
sympathy of his commanding officer's wife) for the infinitely more
lucrative, vastly more sybaritic pastures of the advertising business.
Bannerman was a stuffed shirt and a prize nerd. Wiltshire was a
good egg. Both were perfectly happy to let Arun and me get on
with providing the advertising. There was a small problem: I hadn't
a clue as to where to begin. Jenson & Nicholson and Smith
Stanistreet were our biggest clients. As far as Stanistreet were
concerned there was some slight hope for the country after my brave,

surprising, exemplary etc., battle with flood and famine to bring home their bacon. To Jenson & Nicholson I was an unknown quantity and so far as they were concerned it would be nice if I remained that way. To complicate matters we had to staff up locally. And Bannerman and Wiltshire's idea of interviewing was to send hundreds of applications to us asking for a reasonable shortlist of two or three. (Please pre interview in multiples of ten!). Joy was further unconfined by the fact that Bensons had reopened in Calcutta after an ignominious five-year closure brought about by the open rebellion and sensible defection of such future luminaries as Satyajit Ray, Subroto Sen Gupta, Tara Sinha and a galaxy of lesser stars. They had started their own partnership shop, Clarion Advertising, and had begun promisingly by stealing all of Benson's Calcutta clients. The new Clarion management regarded Bannerman and Wiltshire with barely concealed disdain and us non-Bengali (insult!) imports as traitorous quislings to the cause of Indian Independence.

It is not the best of times. Bannerman chairs (he never holds or calls) an executive meeting, which consists of Bannerman and Wiltshire on the best chairs and Arun and myself on hard stools (the office has still to be furnished; Bannerman's utterly delicious Scots wife is in charge – however did he manage that! – she comes to the office daily and we hope that the furnishing will extend to the next century). Bannerman warns us of the dangers we face from the ill will, nay, the dire machinations, of the ex-Bensonites and exhorts us to 'put up a good show'. The meeting is dismissed. They depart for extended Bengal Club lunches and I seek instant solace in my secretary's efficient discharge of her duties, reflecting over the remains of a kathi kabab from Nizam's and other debris, that Masters & Johnson would have a field day over the intriguing state of my large – very large, I had insisted on that – teak desk.

I am, willy-nilly, force-fed into an advertising education. Jenson & Nicholson have been spending astronomical sums of money advertising paints to uppercrust South Calcutta matrons. Arun and I, fired by investigative zeal, spend three weeks trudging from one palatial dwelling to another (five hundred in all) only to discover, to our consternation, that not a single housewife knows where the paint on her walls comes from. Seventy-five per cent of the sample has never heard of J&N; twenty-five per cent believes the company makes Lux toilet soap; the rest are undecided between cosmetics, a popular laxative and packaged tea. Further keen sleuthing uncovers the hideous truth: J&N sells to the trade via wholesalers (whom they despise); the trade sells to unscrupulous contractors who dilute J&N paints by the bucketsful and plaster the walls of South Calcutta with the result. We report back to our Masters who, ever mindful of J&N's impressive turnover with the agency, tut-tut over our lack of hard core experience and inability to interpret survey results. We are ordered to proceed with the creation of brilliant advertising. I learn an important lesson: agencies never, but never, upset lucrative apple carts. J&N gets the advertising they so richly deserve – original, inventive, crackling with brio, different, highly visible and wholly irrelevant.

We pretty much have our own way at the agency after that. The few clients the agency services are perfectly happy to accept a set of pretty pictures and clever words in a scant hour's meeting for release the rest of the year. Bannerman and Wiltshire are perfectly happy to exchange serious marketing views with clients at the Bengal and Tollygunge Clubs and Firpo's Round Table. New business acquisition is not so much slow as whimsical when not arthritic. Never was the old saw, 'the triumph of hope over experience' exercised with such Proustian celebration of minor detail by our dedicated management duo. Bannerman arrives one Monday morning at the office flushed with excitement. He barges into my office, keeping a wide and nervous margin between himself and Ms Chatterjee, throws her a quick, 'Could Mr Simoes and I have a minute alone please' and then, pausing a moment or two for dramatic effect, rattles off breathlessly, 'Made an important contact at the pool last afternoon. James Brown, chairman of Walker Eastern, largest in the business. Get on to Bombay at once and have some desk research done.' 'Will do,' I say cheerfully. Action at last! 'When do we present a campaign?' 'Well, actually, I haven't been introduced to him but I know a chap at Grindlays who knows … ' Wiltshire doesn't even bother. He writes long and impassioned letters to members of the Bengal Society of Advertisers, paying excruciating attention to the

character of the client, the nature of the product or service, the
track record (how many agencies have been sacked, and how quickly?
Does the sod pay his bills on time?) and brings each pristine effort
for discussion with me. A discussion may last three-quarters of a
day and the original draft of five hundred words endlessly rewritten
over the next couple of weeks. (Did Trollope, I reflect in an idle
moment, labour thus?)

Wiltshire's epistolary efforts have been relentlessly pursued now
for months. Bannerman finds them praiseworthy in the extreme.
The year is well on its way to consummation when Wally Olins
phones for me at lunchtime (drat!). 'Do we have any new business
in the pipeline?' 'No'. 'What on earth are you and Kholatkar doing
there?' 'Well ... ' 'Well me no wells. Do you know how much you
clowns cost the company?' Silence, I decide, is the better part of
discretion. 'Can't have you wasting your time out in the boondocks.
How would you two like to return to Bombay as copy chief and
executive art director?' Right on!

Well, not quite. Professionally I had been booted upstairs yet
again. (Kholatkar, 'Good God. So far you were merely insufferable,
now ... '; Bannerman, a trifle uneasily – who will put the clever
words and pretty pictures together? 'It is a rather serious promotion.
You'd better put your best foot forward. But not before we find
suitable replacements. David and I shall insist on that. Head office
must have some consideration for the pressures etc., etc.,' I am read
the riot act yet again. My behaviour this past year hasn't quite set a
shining example. No great harm done. Calcutta is a small office.
Bombay, however ...)

I reflect in all fairness that Bannerman has a point or two. I
haven't so much burnt the candle at both ends as consumed the
entire production of a small factory. In the process (in the company
of recently acquired soulmates, Bengali to a man and a lass or two)
I narrowly avoid arrest in an escapade of drunken revelry outside
Nizam's on Freeschool Street; I take to bodybuilding, heaving weights
every evening at a gym at Sonagachi only to discover, to my pleasant
surprise, the true nature of the neighbourhood, and that my fellow
iron-pumpers are pimps, gangsters and other ne'er-do-wells, and
that the veiled lovely young things at darkened windows are not, as

I had regretfully imagined, chaste Bengali maidens in chastity belts. After a party, I crash the office car along Chowringhee in the wee hours and spend twenty minutes tottering about the wreckage looking for my glasses, without which I am blinder than the proverbial bat, only to find them undamaged, lying smugly in the centre of the road, thirty metres away. A police van arrives at the scene of the crime. The SI is wholly unsympathetic and I am hauled off to the local station to file a report. I get home at three. Dear Mrs Lavrov has been waiting up (I am now her long-lost Cossackian changeling). She takes one look at me, screams and faints dead away into the arms of an irate, mad-eyed husband who almost passes away himself. I seek explanations only to find my shirt sticking unpleasantly to my chest. It is soaked in blood. Mine! I have broken three ribs: one has punctured the skin and sticks out nastily, quivering every time I breathe like some monstrous life form in *Alien*. Three weeks mending in a hospital, where I make every effort to mend as slowly as possible, having been smitten as never before (yet again!) by an Anglo-Indian nurse. She has all the virtues of Florence Nightingale and a much nicer body. The day I leave I swear eternal love and devotion and proclaim sterling, honorable intentions. A month later, by dawn's early light, I slide off her front porch in New Alipore pursued by dialogue, dauntingly familiar, surreptitiously overheard:

Father	:	Have you any idea what time it is?
Florence Nightingale	:	But Dad …
Father	:	Two in the morning!
Florence Nightingale	:	What's wrong with two in the morning? We're serious about each other.
Father	:	Then why are you in such a disgraceful state?
Florence Nightingale	:	I'm all of twenty-four, Dad. (A steely, gritty tone which augurs ill. I have not heard it before.)
Father	:	Well, he's all of twenty-five. And no young man knows his mind at twenty five.

Florence Nightingale	:	He's doing marvellously at his job. And I've always fancied living in Bombay.
		(Hey, what's all this about?)
Father	:	I'll lay a bet you never will!

I flee into mountain fastnesses, more correctly, Calcutta's Lake District, in the company of a gentle giant, Shanti Banerjie, our new art director. He is an ancient party (forty if a day), a solid citizen, (permanently married) and a true-blue Bong of the old school, till recently state rowing champion at single sculls. He takes my real Bengali education in hand, introduces me to the ineffable joys of misti doi, hilsa and coffee clubs. We row together on the lakes. Like a flower opening petals to a bee, Calcutta gives generously of her manifold gifts. Poetry readings at Professor P. Lal, Satyajit Ray's first films. No one will ever know if I shed a silent tear at *Pather Panchali*. I get to become a rabid Mohammedan Sporting fan. I take river trips of incandescent beauty along the Hooghly's northern reaches in the company of Shanti and dusky maidens with bewitching eyes, and hair flowing like black lava down to the waist, alas, firmly chaperoned and impregnably virtuous unto the plighting of the wedding troth. I discover old Parsi Calcutta through the kindness of a stranger I meet quite by chance in a second-hand bookstore in Lindsay Street. Her father introduces me to the wonders of Bach's *Fugue in D Minor*. Her cousin and I find ourselves one magical December afternoon under Asia's largest and oldest banyan tree in the Botanical Gardens. She is just out of college and poised, unknowing as a young bud on the threshold of brave new futures. 'What,' I ask, 'do you enjoy most?' 'Writing,' she says and produces evidence of phenomenal inadequacy scrawled in an exercise book in her handbag. I lecture her (naturally, as a seasoned journalist of many years' stature) on the perils and pitfalls of Indian journalism. She is encouraged no end. Bachi Karkaria is on her way!

So am I, with not a little heartburn. Brace yourself Bombay. Here I come!

Bombay: the best of times; the worst of times

I do not arrive in Bombay in auspicious circumstances. I have been recalled to replace the female copy chief who has committed suicide by overdosing on barbiturates. To a person, the head office executive committee is against my appointment. Uneasy memories of earlier battles return. The opposition is formidable. Olins even more so. I am the best person for the job, he says, and that's the end of that. He is equally brief with me: 'If there's blood on the floor Simoes, you'll be made to clean up'. I assess the situation. I have five female copywriters of varying degrees of talent and other persuasions. This imbalance must be corrected at once. I take on a sixth female copywriter of utterly ravishing potential. She is the heiress to a royal family fortune from a South Indian principality, an acclaimed poetess (her favourite volume which she is never without, Donne's *Love Sonnets* – hurrah!). Her father has taken his princely skills into crass commerce, done extraordinarily well at it, and chairs a clutch of fat-cat companies. Her mother is a society hostess whose literary soirees are the talk of the town. With credentials like these (and the unstinted support of her brilliant copy chief) how can she fail to succeed? I intend to make every effort to ensure that she will. So, unfortunately, does a coven of drooling senior execs. I am unfazed. They shall be stymied. I have (ha, ha) first and immediate access. But will I have the time?

Bombay is light years ahead of Calcutta professionally. Bensons are by far the largest (and, under Olins, relentless rugger-scrum leadership) the most aggressive company in an industry not noted, shall we say, for its lassitude. We have a roster of clients as long as my arm. Olins idea of a good week's work is to add two or three to the list. Existing incumbents have to be serviced with lightning quick brilliance, or else; the brilliance, never flagging, must burst forth each day from the creative department. The buck stops where I sit and Olins, who leaves no turd unstoned for the greater good of the agency, makes me directly responsible for the creative output of the Calcutta branch. All their major campaigns must be cleared by – and if necessary – redone in Bombay. I count my blessings: three of the nine senior client servicing executives are staunch supporters (the rest committed enemies); these are Mani Aiyer, Nari Hira and Michael Brown, a Billy Bunterish, 300-pound Oxbridge intellectual and bon vivant married for a second time to a gorgeous Keralite half his age. I also have the unstinted loyalty of copywriters and art directors with the single exception of a Cassius lookalike, Arnie Reynolds, who bears watching and, as I am soon to discover, with good reason.

I plunge into the fray. Boon companions join me en route: Kabir Bedi, as film and TV executive; Shyam Benegal, who works for a rival agency, moonlights for us. Mitter Bedi, Ashvin Gatha, Kishore Parekh and other frontline photographers (soon to make their reputations internationally) aid and abet. A covey of gorgeous models encourage campaign creation and happy hours are spent assessing their suitability for Maidenform bras, Jantzen swimwear and suchlike. This is one area where clients and agency correspond with unbridled enthusiasm – opposing points of view are unscrambled within the creative department with the simplicity of genius, into boob- and bum-fanciers, with marginal aberrations for eye and hair-flippers and fringe lunatics who seek 'personality' above all else. This is the easy part. The rest is very hard work indeed, of an unimaginably difficult order. Bombay – and Western India – is the commercial hub of the country. Competition among products and services is fierce. Government regulations are thin on the ground and, for the most part non-existent or – with a wink and a nod – suspectible to bribery. All is cut-and-thrust in the marketplace, no holds barred, the weakest to the wolves and to the victor the fattest profit margins. Advertising is the cutting edge. And I – and the creative department – function at the cutting edge of advertising.

There are no short cuts to learning my trade. It is a hard grind all the way. It makes no difference if I have to sell a fivestar hotel's services or a pumping set to farmers, Maidenform bras to Gujubens in Gujarat or pep-up pills to hypertensive executives. It's solid graft from Day One. And I discover the first principle in campaign creation: the more you know the less likely are you to come up with a lemon. So I bone up on the product, the competition, the consumers, the pricing, the advertising (ours and theirs), the way the rest of the world does it, research reports as fat as my arm. I try the product out myself and when I am poorly equipped for this exercise (Maidenform!) get my female copywriters to bare for the good of the business. By now, I have been force-fed into a state of confused catatonia. The moment of truth arrives one morning when I sit before a blank sheet of foolscap on my Underwood and produce garbage. This goes on for a week. I have accumulated reams of rubbish, plumbing ever greater depths of worthlessness. I snarl and spit in every eye. I seek bloody and bruising confrontations with my account directorial enemies at the mildest of opportunities. The creative group hold their breath in my presence, tiptoe in and out of my office; hush and whisper at every turn; even my poetess gets short shrift. I go to bed one night surrounded by the wreckage of my sex life and leap out of bed at three in the morning (that wonderful hour!) with the Creative Idea fully and gloriously born. I do not know – and never will – how the process works. But I am not about to look a gift horse.

This is the easy part. It takes a fortnight to put the campaign together in-house. The first eyeball to eyeball confrontation takes place. My enemies have been sharpening long knives and these are concealed up sleeves and other unmentionable orifices at the Plans Board Meeting Presentation, a review of our campaign by Olins, two other members of the board, the account director who handles the client (smirking evilly), the technical departmental heads and the creative executives who have worked on the campaign. All hell breaks loose in the nicest possible way. (The account director: 'Not a bad first effort, However ...' supported by a director who knows in his gut – and how right he is! – that I am bad news: 'Freitas has a point ...'; Olins, studiedly neutral, saying not a word, testing his protégé, thinking no doubt, 'Does the boy have the balls for it?') Does he, indeed! I have busted balls in Byculla from the day I began to toddle. Joyfully I plunge into the fray. The fur begins to fly. There is blood on the floor. Not mine. Now for one, now for the other, Olins urges us to battle on. My creative cohorts attack from either flank. Out-manoeuvred, out-numbered, the director swiftly retreats to a neutral corner. The gay account director loses stomach for any further combat. Olins, grinning cheerfully, takes sides, 'Let's go with it.' We have won the day!

Or have we? This, as everyone around the table knows, is only a preliminary skirmish, a dress rehearsal so to speak for the Day of Days, when the agency makes a formal presentation to The Client. 'This would be a great business,' 'Billy Bunter' Brown had said to me over our first companionable bottle of Black Label, 'if we could get rid of the clients.' Never was a truer word spoken. Once in ten years or so, an agency may acquire a pearl of a client. A relaxed, friendly character, with no axe to grind, helpful in the extreme, knowledgeable, running an efficient but not paranoid shop, and keen to work in happy, symbiotic tandem with the agency for a common cause. It's an attitude which works wonders. Happy as larks at breakfast after a drought, the agency responds with glad cries and produces its very best year-in, year-out. Bhagwan Wadhwani is one such. Despite the growls, the Bronx/Sicilian drawl, and the mock-terror tactics, he is a good egg. Presentations are made after office hours, over a bottle or two of the best, and no matter how many agency personnel have ganged up on him, he is always alone and pleasingly direct – 'Skip da garbage' – throwing aside all the neatly bound folders – 'show me da ads.' Ten minutes of deep thought, then the slow, breaking smile, the bushy eyebrows wiggling approval and we are home and dry. Wadhwani, sadly, is in a minority of one. Our other clients run the gamut – from Pure Evil, thorough Pain in the Arse, Sudden Death, Slow Poison, Murder by Degree, Affliction by Attrition to Chaos by Committee. The last is the worst. Huge, unwieldly companies (with huge advertising budgets) managed by a dozen or so huge, unwieldy committees each mortally afraid of the one above it; even so, each must justify its miserable existence. The agency battles with the wind. Presentations drag on over months; are reworked and represented time and again as each seeks to justify its existence; are reduced to anemic shadows of the original, are presented eventually as unrecognizable, bastard changelings to the final committee, the Holy Inner Circle and the Chairman as God. 'I have better things to do,' the chairman says icily, 'than review this rubbish.' Hearts freeze. The agency is put on notice. Olins tries to save the day. 'We have made six presentations over the past three months,' he says firmly, 'to five committees and the dog's breakfast you see before you is the result.' The chairman raises an eyebrow, and says not a word. Olins has the bit between his teeth. 'May we present our original campaign to you?' The chairman turns to an aide. 'Give them a date,' he says. We have saved the day, but what of the war?

I discover Murphy's Law: if something can go wrong, it will, and the Peter Principle – work pressures accelerate in direct proportion to the number of people employed. But there is a bizarre selectivity at play which I will never understand. The larger, the more difficult the client, the more potent and ungovernable do Murphy's Law and the Peter Principle become. Thus, the client servicing group working on our largest – and most richly hated – client has spun off all sorts of unlikely tentacles: merchandising and marketing experts, motivational and media researchers, two account directors, account executives by the freightload and scores of nameless dogsbodies who rush about, pale-faced and paranoid, and are axed with metronomic regularity. And all the while, year-in year-out, the advertising looks as if it has been cloned – with even less inspiration – from the previous year's campaign. And there's Wadhwani and one or two other clients, serviced by a man and a dog, and a copywriter and art director, who get the advertising they deserve: brilliant, frothing over with gung-ho, get-up-and-go, forging to unassailable market leadership and laughing all the way to the banks.

The pressures begin to get to me. I work a twelve-hour day, six days a week and collapse, a total wreck on the seventh. The love of my life, disconsolate at the inability of Donne and Marvell to arouse consummative responses, introduces me to half of a little white pill. Wham. Shaam. Bingo. I fly on the wings of methedrine and begin to function with a swift, mad felicity which evokes raptures of breathless verse and reams of glorious advertising copy. It also leads to a thirty-pound weight loss, which I can ill afford, perpetual insomnia (which fifteen cups of black coffee a day do little to help) and The Curse – which all of the medical marvels of the day fail to alleviate: cluster migraine attacks. These come on without warning and with no regard to time, place or occasion. First, a general, almost psychic, discomfort, then a tingling above the right eye, along the right temple, blurred vision, dancing, twitching nerves along the neck and at the femoral artery, followed by profuse sweating and, swift as a blink, unbelieveable agony for an hour. I cannot speak, move, open my eyes. When I attempt to walk my knees buckle. The universe, reduced to white-hot agony, implodes in the right side of my brain. An hour later I fall into a deep, utterly exhausting sleep from which I shall never awake unless I find the strength to reach out for the dark brown bottle with the magical white pill.

My enemies within the agency and among one or two client organizations are overjoyed. The gay account director lets drop casually and with feigned sympathy, 'Frank had one of his attacks, poor chap, at the Duncans review. Very decent of the client. Had him rushed off home in a taxi. The campaign will be delayed yet again. Can't be helped I suppose. I do wish he'd look after himself.' A commendable attitude, one would think, but not when ventilated at a board meeting to review client servicing. But this is just for starters. Arnie Reynolds, the Cassius in drag, escorts me home one day (I can't make it on my own to a taxi) and then recounts to all who care to listen (just about everybody) every last twitching, gasping detail of my attack. A client I have mortally offended for insisting that he is wrong and we are right (Olins backs me up to the hilt) writes in asking for a replacement of the creative team. My copywriting angel disguised as muse droops like a flower forever deprived of sunshine. (And well she might!). The methedrine half-pill has long since become two pills and will, in the not so distant future, become a double dose. Olins calls me in one morning and says, without preamble, 'Against better judgement – including my own – I have decided to second you to the London office for six months.'

I raise a weary eyebrow, 'Training?'

'No,' – Olins grins – 'R&R. Warm beer, long johns, fat thighs, pork pies and Soho strip joints where all the great campaign ideas are born. And try not to learn anything. I don't want your career ruined!' I rush off to break the good news to the angelic one. We decide to play truant at once, and make off separately with a good deal of nonchalance which fools nobody, to our favourite trysting spot, the old, disused British cemetery tucked away in the nether regions of Colaba well beyond the army cantonment and barracks.

There, nestling comfortably among the tombstones, approving cherubim and crosses leaning askance, lost to all else, we court the muse. Glory be! Inspiration takes wing. The earth trembles, quivers, moves! I raise my eyes. A pair of angry army boots, itching to fly, quivers a foot before me. Carefully, I swivel my gaze this way and that. Army boots all over the place. Steel-tipped lathis tapping the ground with salacious menace. We are well and truly in the hot and sticky. An open jeep stands at the road. Six jawans escort us to it. We are made to stand in the back, the jawans barring all attempts at flight. Marvell bowdlerized, comes vagrantly to mind, from the general directions of the tombstones:

> The grave's a fine and quiet place.
> Why then this noisome, risqué embrace?

The taunts of the rude and scoffing multitude which gathers like magic at the scene of a crime fades, to be replaced by brooding terror as our pleas, queries, cries of anguish, are met with a gallows-at-dawn silence. We are taken to a colonel's office. He is the soul of crisp, military courtesy. And not without a sense of humour.

Our protests doth avail us naught. (Marvell chuckles yet in the wings).

'You were,' the colonel says mildly, 'behaving, shall we say, not quite correctly, in a residential area of a military camp.'

My poetess saves the day. In a voice dripping honey, she bares gleaming fangs.

'Could I have a word with General Shinde?' she asks.

The colonel stiffens.

'He's a friend of my father's.' A girl of splendid attributes. I knew it! The moment I took her on.

The colonel's military moustache quivers then settles into an amiable decision.

'Zealous lot, these jawans,' he says. 'No real harm done I suppose. Have I met your father?'

A name is dropped. The colonel sits to attention, opens a drawer, takes out a sheet of paper, scribbles on it with a ballpoint, dates it, slides it across to my loved one.

'Just a waiver,' he says apologetically, 'that my boys haven't caused you any offence.'

I reach out to sign it.

'Not you,' the colonel says.

He thanks us, shakes our hand, insists that the Jeep escort us to a taxi at Cuffe Parade, safely and solidly civilian. We sit in the front with the driver. I sigh. 'And to think,' I say – fool! – not giving it a thought, 'that I might never have made it to London.'

The soft yielding shoulder against mine stiffens and moves away. The scales have fallen from blazing violet eyes.

'Don't bother to write,' she says, 'and please try and break a leg.' I remember Alipore, other Nightingales ... Once more, I reflect, with feeling!

Mani Aiyer has preceded me to London by a fortnight. I check into my hotel. This is quite splendid. (Bensons treated visitors from the far-flung outposts of empire with paternal generosity. Our brown friends from across the ocean ... that sort of thing!) There is a cryptic message for me at the reception. 'I'll be in touch tomorrow. Don't – I repeat – do not contact me.' It is signed with the familiar, scrawled initial M. I get to the office and am seconded to a senior account director, Maurice Crane, a country boy from Seven Oaks, Kent, straight out of a Shropshire Lad, who has taken the big bad city by the horns and eight years, two wives, two Ferraris later, is merrily at the top of the pile. How on earth did he get there? He seems to do no work at all. Another cryptic note arrives at my desk from Mani. 'Meet me at the first floor library at one p.m. – M.'

In two weeks Mani had the place taped: the good eggs; the villains; who stood where in the pecking order; which of the secretaries were sympathetically inclined; ways and means to circumvent the system without the system ever getting to know about it; how the power structure worked, where the pressure points lay; the best neighbourhood pubs; the sheer iniquity of the licensing hours at pubs; what not to do at Soho which, by clever management planning, lay so conveniently to hand (I needn't have worried; Maurice Crane's idea of a training session was a three-hour lunch at an upmarket strip club); ah, yes, and if I ever wanted to learn something, where to go and who to talk to. But I was never, under the most trying of circumstances, to let on that I knew more than the person appointed to teach me. 'Ignorance,' Mani said, 'yearning to be set free. That's the ticket. For six months you are the white man's burden. Be grateful – loud and clear – at every opportunity.' He was so right. Subtle, underrated flattery got you places. A child-like eagerness to please. Wide-eyed attentiveness. But unbridled ambition, aggressive zeal and speed of any kind were to be avoided at all costs. 'Led to Wally Olins doom,' Mani confided later, 'banished to Bombay for being too keen.'

Quick learner that I am, I weasel my way through the system; doing as little as possible and, following Olins' injunction to the letter, pursuing rest and recreation with unflagging vigour. In this I am variously assisted by Maurice Crane and Soho's bottomless potential, an Irish nurse named Nancy Gormley who takes me off over the long Bank Holiday to her village in central Ireland, Bally James Duff, where I am the first Indian ever encountered (a set piece in the book). She introduces me to Black Velvets and the insatiable enthusiasm that overcomes deeply religious Irish maidens when they descend on London. My literary aspirations (I remain a great pretender with the manuscript of a first novel) are rendered asunder by an agent, Carl Routlege, but his wife Fay, in the interests of assisting budding talent, discusses literature and other pursuits with me while Carl is away at a writers' conference. I am invigorated no end. With Fay at my side, can literary fame be far behind? Maurice, ever the bon vivant, tries his best – and succeeds – in making a wine and nosh snob out of me. Neither of us know it but he has planted the seeds of endless years of marital strife! He is in the process of drafting my performance report and discusses bits and pieces of it with me at our favourite Soho watering hole over lunches of awesome length and variety (a Craneism after four Bloody Marys and three bottles of Beaujolais: 'In the dark the strippers come and go, who cares a hoot for Michelangelo!'). The report, while pleasing in the extreme, Maurice opines, lacks 'substantial achievement'. 'You shall write an advertising campaign,' Maurice says, eyes alight at the brilliance of the idea, 'for H. Samuel and Son, jewellers, my best clients and the greediest Jews after Shylock.' The campaign works like a dream and, despite H. Samuel's robust efforts to have my London tenure extended indefinitely, I return, bidding not farewell, but au revoir to this delightful mother-lode of Colonial excess ....

My report has arrived two weeks earlier. Olins is amused. 'You are destined,' he says, 'for great things. London says so. Who am I to deny you a meteoric future.' I am to remain copy chief for another six months (embarrassing this; my poetess is engaged – arranged by their parents – to an upperclass twit with no jaw) before being kicked upstairs to account director reporting directly to Olins and the board. 'Two years anon,' Olins says, 'you'll be on the board when the pfaffing ends and the real work begins!' And so it comes to pass. So does public notoriety of a sort. My opinion is sought by the trade and general press. My mug shot begins to appear in articles on advertising; my byline is all over the place. I begin to be profiled and invitations appear on my desk to all the smarmiest parties in town. I am given a spacious company flat overlooking the sea at Malabar Hill, a car, a chauffeur yet! An expense account and membership to two of Bombay's toniest clubs. I don't have time to enjoy any of this because I am worked like the proverbial dog. There are five directors on the board. I handle seventy-five per cent of the turnover and the Delhi and Calcutta operations; Mani handles Madras and helps out in Calcutta. Between the two of us we handle eighty-five per cent of the company's turnover. Olins departs. (Wiltshire, Bannerman and Brown have long since folded their tents and faded away). The buzzword is Indianization and yet another pukka brown sahib is imported from London. I discover that he knows nothing about advertising just as I learn (salaries are closely guarded secrets) that I earn less than half of what the other directors are making. Mani and I are up in arms. There is a board confrontation. The new CEO incumbent is too confused to know what is happening. My arch enemy, who runs him like a puppet, observes with great delicacy that even directors – no matter how valuable – are dispensable. 'All sorts of people have come and gone, the company carries on.' The agency is riven. Clients, executives, creative high flyers, footsoldiers, even the peons, take sides.

The noise is heard in London. Olins flies down. I make him an offer I hope he can't refuse. A second agency which I shall start, and run, and own fifty percent of equity ('All right then, forty-nine'). The Indian company can own the rest. I report directly to London. 'London will buy it,' Olins says, 'I'm not too sure of the Indian board.' He's right. London says yes, yes and yes again (Maurice Crane now sits on its board) but Bombay threaten to resign en masse.

I put in my papers.

Wadhwani says, 'Dat's great news kid. Now I'll have to pay ya on time.'

'In advance,' I say.

He roars with laughter. 'Have anudder drink!'

I hang out my shingle

It reads, 'Frank Simoes Advertising Private Limited.' A month later I realize that this is misleading. It should have read, 'Piles and Ulcers Incorporated'. Four clients and five executives have moved with me. The plus side. The downside: I haven't a roof over my head, nor a car, a driver, club memberships, expense accounts or credit. I have to pay the media in advance till I accumulate a decent account with them for twelve months. This is the good news. The bad news: All my savings will carry the agency for just three months. Bankers who pursued me relentlessly just a while ago now refuse to answer my calls. Friends who urged me on with glad cries – 'just tell us how we can help' – disappear into the wilderness. And where will I sleep nights? Kersey Katrak, now riding the crest of the omnivorous MCM, offers me room and board free of cost. The guest wing at the far end of his football ground office premises (with a separate entrance yet). I do not say no. It is a large double bedroom with an attached bath, air-conditioned, with an amply stocked bar, a refrigerator and a note pinned on to the pillow, 'Get drunk tonight!' Speechless with gratitude, I do so. The next morning I slink out through a separate entrance and stand in a queue like the rest of the world waiting for a bus to take me to work ...

If I was, twenty years into the future, to write a Before and After advertisement about myself, it would have read something like this:

Before	After
Slim, Athletic	Unable to locate ankles without bending over
Raven-haired	White – not quite – getting there rapidly
Clear-eyed	Fuzzy-eyed more often than not what with two retinal operations
Aggressively single	Permanently married
Church mouse poor	Filthy rich
Hasn't owned a thing in his life	Guards his considerable assets with his life
Hasn't written a non-advertising word in years	Journalist, Columnist, Biographer!
Insufferable	Insufferable

It is the best of times; it is the worst of times. I come to the frightening conclusion that somebody up there actually likes me. In moments of crisis when industry pundits wouldn't have given a snowball's chance in hell for my survival, something or the other happens to pull me out of the bog. One of my largest clients – Murphy – reneges on six months' worth of advertising; I have paid the media (if I don't I will be delicensed) by discounting Murphy's bills with my bank. The bills are now due. Rs. 25 lakhs. I am capitalized at Rs. 2 lakhs, am overdrawn by another fifteen and have to pay the bank back twenty-five in seven days. The credit manager (Sod. I have slaughtered the fatted calf for him every week, on the week, for the past year) says coldly, 'You have all of my sympathy but we are a foreign bank and the people up there' – he waves vaguely towards the ceiling – 'are sticklers for the rules. Sorry Frank but there you are.' There I'm not. I go above his head – despite howls of anguish from my financial director – to his boss, the general manager, a soft-spoken, mild-mannered Sindhi, Gurbaxani, who hears me out patiently for an hour, then says, 'I'll see what I can do.' He keeps the wolf from my door – brave man – for eighteen months, then uses his clout with one of Murphy's bankers to get them to pay up. There are other signs of heavenly intervention. Two years into the agency we lose half our turnover (invested in a single client) through no fault of ours (they all say that!). We are – overnight – in a loss situation I cannot sustain beyond three months. I test my shingle. It removes easily. Then I shop around for business. There isn't any. Now I know how it feels to have the man in the white coat look you in the eye and say, 'Three months I'm afraid.' Then, out of the blue, the phone rings. A spokesman for Reliance. Dhirubhai Ambani is shopping around for an agency. Would I agree to a speculative pitch. Would I! The grapevine sizzles. This is news. Simoes is one of twelve agencies shortlisted. The other eleven are big league players. The minnow – called upon to present first – will die the death. I get phone calls from well-wishers advising me to decline presentation. 'If you lose, Frank, that's it. The agency won't have a shred of credibility.' I pitch. If I don't, I die. At three in the morning, the Fates smile down upon me. I am gifted a line which will make Reliance immortal. 'Only Vimal ...' I present to a dozen of the Reliance board. Ambani is there and not there. He is elsewhere and elsewhen playing poker with the Gods. I conclude my pitch. I am thanked and sent packing without another word. We win the account. I sit across a long table alone with Ambani. He says, 'I liked your line. That's the way I feel about Vimal. I won't change a word of your advertising provided that facts and company policy are respected.' That's it. Not quite. Three years to the day, I sit across the desk again. Ambani says, 'I'm going public, Frank, for the first time. The shares are priced at ten rupees. I've allotted you 2,500.' I've learned to tell Ambani the truth, the whole, nothing but. 'I don't have the money,' I say and that's no lie. Every rupee of profit has been ploughed back into the business. Ambani is unmoved. 'Beg, borrow, steal, pawn Gita's gold. Take up those shares.' But, try as I will, I am unable to. A month later – a week before the issue goes public – the phone rings. A South Indian banker from Manipal. He wants the name of my Bombay bank and personal account number. 'We have been instructed to offer you an interest-free loan payable as and when.' I do not ask the name of my benefactor nor do I look a gift horse.

Again, at the Pushkar fair, on a photographic/writing assignment for an American publication, the retina in my right eye bursts, the left tears one-third across the lower spectrum. Flashes, jagged forks of white-hot light, a celestial fireworks. I am flown back to Bombay. There are seven out of ten chances that I will go blind. I sit in a darkened room in silence and terror while the surgeons argue my case. The universe of my being has been reduced to the torn and shattered blood vessels of my eyes. They talk options and procedures. Should they puncture the eyeballs, use lasers or liquid nitrogen, insert silicon implants. The best scenario: I will have to spend six weeks in hospital, eyes bandaged, flat on my back. Six weeks I can ill afford. The agency has just begun to show some signs of stability after a tottering start. Then a small miracle happens. The next day I have visitors: everyone of my clients, suppliers, staff, my largest media creditors and Wadhwani with a bottle of Bourbon, 'You're gonna be fine, kid.' How could I not?

And yet another intervention by the powers that be. A kind, generous, beautiful, wise and good young woman decides to marry me. No ifs, buts or maybes. Once again, I do not look a gift horse ...

The years pass swiftly. Milestones appear and recede with bewildering speed. Within twelve months I am invited to participate in a five-agency consortium to present India's advertising proposals at the Asian Advertising Congress in Delhi. Nobody has the faintest idea why FSA, the newest plAiyer in the game, wet behind the ears, and with no track record to speak of, should be accorded this honour in the company of such ball-breaking successes as Lintas, Thompsons, MCM etc. Neither have I, I reflect as, facing the most terrifying moment of my life, I launch into our part of the presentation (the very plum, the press campaign) before an audience of five thousand delegates. I do not let the side down. The campaign is a roaring success and, six months down the road as we try to convert myth into reality, a singular failure. No matter. FSA is on its way. There are other milestones. Within five years we are counted among the top fifteen agencies in India and have garnered, in the process, half a century of awards, thirty clients, and the Advertising Campaign of the Year Award twice. I find myself consultant to the National Association for the Blind, the Spastic Society, Beauty. Without Cruelty, the Government of Maharashtra's Anti-Beggary Committee and – hallelujah! – co-chairman with Charles Correa of a committee to advise the Goa cabinet on central town planning (of which I know absolutely nothing). Once I get to know the cabinet, I realize I am eminently qualified. Tourism and economic development. Nemesis again. I am back – with pleasing and welcome frequency – to the green and pleasant land of my ancestors. I meet, and become friends with a truly great man, Vasudev Salgaocar, little realizing that three years on, I would be asked by his family to write his posthumous biography. In the advertising industry I am rapidly, much to my dismay and boredom, assuming the role of an Elder Statesman. I am called upon to address seminars, chair committees, contribute learned articles to supplements on advertising and marketing, guest lecture at various MBA institutions and generally live a life which goes deeply against the grain. The law of diminishing returns begins to apply. I tot up my losses:

1. The more money I make, the less time or inclination I have to use it. (I discover Finance Catch 22: In order to protect agency profits, we go into leasing only to discover that we have to protect leasing profits, so we go into finance and investment, only to ...)
2. The more I discover the joys of Goa, the less time I have to enjoy them.
3. The better I write (the Salgaocar book is published to good reviews and reader reaction) the less writing I do.
4. The bigger the agency grows, the more I have to manage (which I loathe) and the less I create personally (the only aspect of the business left which I still enjoy).
5. The only real assets I have are my family, my talent and the rest of my life. Are these to be sold short in the advertising business?

How do I disengage? If hanging out my own shingle was difficult, disengaging gracefully was near impossible. But I must. I say not a word to a soul; within a week the industry is buzzing with rumours. Strange industrialists with even stranger-sounding companies want to buy me out with an important proviso (I must stay on as consultant for three years, five, ten ...) I fail to understand the logic. If I am to continue to be responsible, why should I sell? The Goa house now rises like some impossibly compelling, impossibly beautiful mirage on God's own acre on a Goan beach. It shall – I vow – be celebrated. I announce the closure of the agency on an auspicious day – 27 February. Radhika's birthday. She is not impressed. To the press hounds who pursue me I have a single-line explanation, otherwise my lips are sealed: 'I want to write.' Nobody believes this. The rumour mill churns. I am debilitated by an incurable disease. I have run into serious financial trouble and it was a choice between closure or bankruptcy. My marriage has broken up. I am a burnt-out advertising case. Threatened client defections – and my inability to secure new business – led to the inevitable. I have siphoned off agency profits to distant Bahamian havens and there is no money to run the factory ....

Unmindful, I arrange a management buy-out for the Delhi executive staff and safe berths for my Bombay executives. How and where will I begin to write? Fate again. Khushwant Singh phones from Delhi. Will I contribute a chapter to Viking-Penguin's sixtieth anniversary volume *Uncertain Liasons* on sex in advertising. I WILL I WILL. The critics are rude about the book, kind about my chapter. David Davidar writes post-haste – he doesn't miss a trick – will I extend the chapter to a book. I cannot, I write back, quick as a flash, but here are a few chapters on a Goan memoir. A lightning swift return. Will I sign a contract for the Goa book with an option on the advertising book. YES. YES. YES.

I spare a smidgen of a thought for thirty years in the advertising business and, with a touch of regret and nostalgia, say firmly, goodbye to all that ....

****

So You Want To Start
An Ad Agency

You have decided to start your own advertising agency. It is the fruit of much thought and deliberation. You have studied case histories and can quote chapter and verse. Consider that young stripling Nanda. Started on a shoestring just a few years ago. Now turning over ten crores. *Ten crores!* Mother of God! Then there's what's his name. A few years at it and eating subsidized foie gras at the Taj. Or take da Cunha. Not so much as a sonnet while gainfully employed at ASP. Now knocking off at five and writing plays, for God's sake. And hardly an ulcer between the three of them.

As a Senior Member of the Club, I have been asked to record my Thoughts and Comments for you, brave spirit, poised on the brink of starting his own – his very own – ad agency. Each thought is followed by an extended comment and in the manner of Swift (who's he?) I may or may not mean what I say. One final caveat before I press on. If the editor disclaims responsibility for the views I express, he's lying. Here goes:

Acquire a good friend, mentor and guide. Never make the mistake of listening to him.

When I decided to start an advertising agency, I went and talked to Kersy Katrak. 'I have the clients,' I said. 'I have the premises. I think I have the money. I know I have fire in my belly and stars in my eyes. I will prevail.' Kersy listened intently, brow quivering in sympathy. After all, had he not once, himself, felt similarly? Then, enthusiasm writ in every golden syllable, he said, 'I shall employ you as a copywriter.' In the event, he gave me a roof over my head for six months. To this day, I consult Kersy Katrak on matters of consequence and, believe me, it takes a lot of willpower not to listen to him.

God bless other agencies. May their days be numbered ...

When eventually I ascend to that corner of Valhalla reserved for valiant advertising men, these words will honour my place of rest. I have not, naturally, revealed my feelings. To the world at large I say that Lintas is a fine and creative agency. I draw attention to the Rediffusion coat of arms and the originality of its inscription, 'We are the Resurrection and the Life.' When I hear somebody say 'Ulka' I say, 'Hot dog!' But I am less than honest. I confess to dark thoughts by the light of the moon. I wish Mani Aiyer would be less happy. I would like Sylvie da Cunha to perpetrate a howler in one of his columns. At this very moment, thousands of people all over the country are tripping and spraining their ankles. Why should Arun Nanda step so blithely? There is no easy way out. This cross you will have to bear. Learn to muffle the gnashing of your teeth when the client says, 'Rediffusion has the best copywriters in the country', or 'R.K. Swamy is a busy man but I've never known him to duck a sales conference.'

The Creative Urge. If it shows signs of life, kill it.

You will, being a man of much experience, realize that the name of the game is Peace of Mind. By dint of wholesome effort you have managed to create advertising that nobody reads, sees, hears or talks about. What's more, you've managed to sustain this invisibility for twelve months. No small achievement. The clients are happy. They read the advertising. The products are nice and big. The logos are large and pretty. Your bills are paid. Life is good. Life is almost lyrical. Watch out. One morning your copy chief, working on an ad for your biggest client, bursts into your room, wild-eyed and feverish, picking at his shirt front. He has an original concept. Horrible, monstrous thought! An original concept running rampant in your nice little agency. Titillating your typists. Nipping at your visualisers. Spreading joy and subversion. It is a serious, nay a grave moment. Do not panic. Make everyone exposed to the concept write one hundred times, 'An original concept is a bad and wicked thing'. Do not relent. Ever. Let your watchword be Eternal Vigilance.

When I say 'Jump!' you shall quiver, do a triple somersault and enquire respectfully, 'How high, sir?' on your way up.

Up to now your ego has been in a perilously fragile state. Your managing director controlled your destiny. Your board of directors controlled his. Your clients controlled theirs. All you could do was hurl moody epithets at your secretary when not looking at her legs. Now all is changed. You control the lives and fortunes of many. Your ego roars like a lion seeking what it may devour. Let it run rampant. It is good for the soul. But do not be foolish. Like most things in life this too requires discipline and organization. Begin by reading the biographies of de Sade, Crowley, Beria. Redesign your desk and chair so that you sit six inches higher than the trembling wretches across from you. Play both ends against the middle before turning the middle inside out. Instill fear and envy. Sack people at a day's notice. Be fatherly to others. Practise wrath before the mirror each morning. Snarl and learn to smoke cigars. Reduce all the confidence you see around you to a small heap of ashes. Exploit your employees. When they get too expensive, sack them and employ others on a pittance. From time to time, rage.

With clients, be nice.

Singh? Oh, you mean Khushwant ...

Forget all you've learned about one-upmanship. Crude. Strictly for the lower orders. You are, remember, the Head of an Agency. Learn instead to be superior in all manner of things. Take the nicety of name-dropping. Never drop names. Drop first names. Better still, initials. Always drop names and initials elliptically. For instance, do not say, 'I met JRD at the races,' but insinuate, 'I put my money on Final Spree. JRD warned me, typical of him. He backed an outsider and it romped home of course.' This refinement of edge is useful in other areas. Never offer your clients caviar. Run a languid eye over the menu and declare nonchalantly that the Beluga in Bombay is never as good as the Malossol. It is passé to be seen with many beautiful women. Ensure that you are always seen tête-à-tête with your wife at the most public of places. If, by some mischance, you encounter someone at dinner who – God forbid – might really know about food and drink, raise an indulgent eyebrow and sop up the gravy with a crust, implying that you are so far beyond it all, that nothing matters.

Who was that Mercedes I saw you with last night?

When you close your books at the end of the first year, and realize that concurrent with an impressive loss, the bank has come through with a fat overdraft, you will begin to be plagued by a strange and inexplicable phenomenon. All over town your Fiat will be overtaken by limousines carrying other Agency Heads. Arun Nanda will swoop by you along Marine Drive in his Chevy Nova. Alyque Padamsee's Dodge will bully you out of the right of way on Apollo Bunder. Bal Mundkur will whiz past you in his Mercedes.

You will begin to feel restless, bothered and distraught. You may be rude to the dog. You will certainly snap at your wife. You will begin to dream of sexy hubcaps and sleek body-lines, or V-8 engines and tachometers. Finally, one morning, you will reach for the door of the Fiat and pause. The scales will fall from your eyes. You will see it for what it truly is. A square, graceless box on four wheels, hopelessly outdated, wholly devoid of character, spirit, élan … You have reached the point of no return. And when, months later, behind the wheel of a silver Peugeot 504, you realize that the distant rattle in the boot is really the wolf scrabbling at the door, take heart. A silver Peugeot is a silver Peugeot while it lasts.

Win the love, respect and trust of your creditors.

By all means be optimistic and cheerful. But you will pile up debts. Because all clients do not pay on time all the time. All agencies pile up debts. With printers, block makers, studio supplies, and (whoa, boy!) even, occasionally, the mass media. Having studied the matter carefully with my group of One Financial Expert, I have come to the conclusion that an agency's debts, outstanding over ninety days, are precisely fifteen times the amount of its paid-up capital. As a result you will have to face creditors. A creditor will rarely ask you for money. He will drop by to wish you well, ask after the state of your garden, talk about the weather, all the while looking at you sorrowfully and accusingly.

Your first reaction is to respond in kind: wish him well, talk at length about the garden, discuss the weather, all the while looking evasive and guilty. Bad strategy. Worse tactics. Look him shiningly in the eye and say, 'I am ashamed of myself and how you can bear to sit and converse with me, I will never understand.' Proceed to tell him how much you owe him (overestimating generously). Praise him for his patience and consideration. Call attention to the supreme quality of his goods and services. Point out that any other man in his place would refuse to have anything further to do with you. Mean every word you say and pay him *something*. If you can't then don't but always tell him why. Truthfully.

How to confound the rumour mill.

Like it or not, you have set yourself apart. Success or failure will make little difference to what people will say about you. The truth, no matter how dramatic, can't hold a candle to the Original Lie. Your agency may be floundering on the rock of insolvency but the word will get around that it's nothing as serious as that: you are merely afflicted with a rare and terminal disease with three months to go. There is only one way to deal with the rumour mill. Gum up the works. Surely you can invent more interesting lies than people who haven't started agencies. Say anything but do not repeat yourself. Some suggestions: You are emigrating to South Africa. Your marriage is hopelessly on the rocks over a nubile young thing: his name is Bert. *India Today* has bought over your agency for a phenomenal price through a secret holding company and Alyque Padamsee is to be chairman. You've pinched the Indian Tobacco account from Thompsons and Clarion. Let your fancy take flight. The only sin is lying small.

If you are 'born with the gift of laughter and a sense that the world is mad', it helps.

You have read these words of cautionary wisdom and are undeterred. Good lad. Let's see now. You take off with a steel account, textiles and cosmetics. Stop grinning. Did you know that:

1. Kersy Katrak and the chairman of the steel account both write poetry. And actually swap poems before publication?
2. R.K. Swamy and the brother of the man who owns the textile business sit together on six committees. Six!
3. Nergis Wadia went to college with the wife of the man who runs the cosmetic company? They live next door and like each other.

Join the Club.

****

A Perfect Pair of Breasts

In the summer of '63, merriment ran high in the creative group in the British advertising agency, S.H. Benson, in Bombay. I had been summoned by the account director, a Brit, who looked after the Maidenform bra account.

'I need a perfect pair of breasts,' he said, 'get a ripple on and don't return without them.'

When I reported back to the creative department, the joy was unconfined. Helpful suggestions regarding colour, weight, shape and size flew about the room. Ribald mirth greeted each sally.

'Do your homework,' the lady copy chief said, 'check out their diet. Does asli ghee help? Will fish make a difference?'

'Resist the urge to handle the merchandise,' the art director chortled.

A female copywriter, who had just recently spurned my offer of coffee and other illicit pleasures at Bombelli, our favourite watering hole, bowdlerized the famous slogan. 'Frank dreamt he had the perfect pair of breasts in a Maidenform bra ... '

The office fell about with merry laughter. The creative director – another expat – had the last word. 'Don't just stand there salivating,' he said, 'get on with it.'

I got on with it.

Bhagwan Wadhwani, the chairman of the company which had the exclusive Indian franchise for Maidenform bras, Jockey underwear, Jantzen swimwear and Liberty shirts, was a boisterous, unrestrained child of nature. A Sindhi with an Italian accent (he had spent fifteen years in the rag trade in Milan), he looked and dressed like the mafia don, Lucky Luciano, in the Thirties. In five short years, all of his brands were market leaders by long margins. His advertising budget was among the top five in our roster of clients.

Dozens of copywriters and directors had come to grief grappling with the metaphysics of the carnal shirt: how did you make a collar sexy: invest bedroom ardour into the cut of a cuff; evoke priapic ebullience out of checks, stripes and textures? A month earlier, he had turned down the latest batch of advertising concepts for Liberty shirts because 'they wouldn't make a rabbit rut!' Management – seeking a breather – decided that a little blood on the floor would distract the beast: I was thrown to the lion.

When I presented myself, Wadhwani looked at me with utter disbelief.

'Who are you?'

I told him.

'What do you know about shirts?' he asked.

That was easy: I went on at length.

'Bullshit!' A deathly silence descended on the room. 'Guys wear fancy shirts because they want to sleep with fancy girls. Jusk like you and me. Now go back and write a campaign.'

Being scared witless helped. I wrote five advertisements in two days. Here, without apology, is the first:

'It was the stuff of dreams. Warm sensuous dreams. Heavenly lemon stripes. Close, intimate ...

'A space the width of her tiniest finger kept them apart. And a single, darling, downy, lilac stripe, yearning to be stroked. She was barely able to contain herself. Oh well, she thought with a happy sigh ... "Tinker," she said, "Tailor." Another button, "Soldier, Sailor". Each syllable soft as a kiss. "Rich man, poor man, beggar man ..." Inspiration failed. Happy chaos took its place. "Oops, darling," she chuckled, "no more buttons." His shirt dropped to the floor. Was that any way to treat a Liberty shirt?'

All of this nonsense was superimposed in coy 12-pt Baskerville Serif on a picture shot in caressing half-light: a woman's slim, elegant hand (no wham-bam-thank-you-ma'am here; this was class!)

unbuttoning a shirt. The man's face is hidden in shadow: the line of cheek and jaw will brook no denial: it is resonant! Eyes downcast (it was, after all the early Sixties) she rests her head lightly on his shoulder, a swathe of thick black hair curves softly down her cheek: an inscrutable Mona Lisa smile plays about her lips. This is one naughty lady …

Without a word, I laid all five advertisements on the table before Wadhwani. A huge feral grin lit his eyes (Luciano: 'Take that you rat!'). He said, 'Great, run them.'

We did so, with some misgivings, but in the event Bhagwan Wadhwani proved right: you could never go broke by overestimating the sexual repression of the Indian male.

That season sales of Liberty shirts doubled and the advertising concept, with variations, was to run for three years. Sex in the Sixties in India was the stuff of dreams for a virtual majority of young Indians. The mandatory condom in wallet (bought surreptitiously, like pornography, in plain wrapper) was pure fudge, regretful nostalgia for an act eagerly read about, lusted over, fantasized in solitary, sweaty guilt, in the wee hours, lied about with lip-licking invention, rarely ever dared. The truth was sadly prosaic: the average Indian male, healthily endowed but woefully unrequited, would never be a conquering hero to his member.

At about the same time in the United States, a great act of cultural insemination was to change sexual, musical and drug mores forever. A flower child placing a lily in the barrel of a national guardsman's rifle – in a classic confrontation between the anarchic, establishmentarian bullet and universal love and peace – became the visual icon of the time. 'Make love not war' was emblazoned on a million T-shirts.

It would take years before this tectonic change would find a full seismic response in India … for the main part. It was an age of touching sexual innocence. I remember vividly the trauma in our very Catholic family when my youngest sister, all of fifteen, went to church on Sunday in a sleeveless, breezy summer dress. It took six severe novenas, and as many weeks of ostracized penitence, to remove the stigma of the Scarlet Woman. She carries the psychic scar to this day. One morning, Kabir (who had begun a highly visible relationship with Protima Gupta, who had yet to streak starkers across the nation's tabloids and into its psyche) asked my secretary for an appointment, a strangely formal request between good friends. He came into my office, hugely embarrassed; it sat awkwardly on a personality which was, even then, larger than life. 'If Protima and I,' he said, carefully, measuring his words, 'live together, will the management object?' Not as paranoid a notion as it might appear today. Normal, heterosexual sex was fettered with medieval chastity belts and locked away in dark, musty closets. As for the love which dare not speak its name, nobody did. Dost thou art, and dost thou will remain, was an idea thirty years short of its time.

But Wadhwani was unfazed. He believed that breasts were big business and after my debut with the Liberty shirt campaign, he chuckled whenever we met. Now he waved bra after bra before my nose, while providing a running commentary. 'This is an illusion. It makes a thirty-two look like a thirty-six, and no one notices the padding. Look at this plunging V-shape. You would never believe she had one on. Now, here's my favourite. Sheer, almost transparent,' and he stretched and held it up to the light – 'the nipple comes into its own.' Not a hint of the prurient: he could have been extolling the merits of haulage trucks. He went into a thoughtful silence, then his eyebrows shot up. ('Dis is one offer, pal, you don't refuse!')

He said, 'Gina!'

I hadn't a clue. I smiled with complete understanding and warm, unqualified approval.

Wadhwani scowled. ('You know from nothin', kid!'), then sighed, produced an American film magazine, and tossed it to me. 'Lollobrigida,' he said, 'that's what I call perfect bosoms.'

Where, I wondered, did she keep the other pair? But he had a point (or two), I had seen pictures of La Lolla before, in careless déshabillé, and had become an instant convert to her cause. No question about it, Bhagwan Wadhwani knew his bosoms. Now all I had to do was find the perfect pair. Word spread like wildfire in the modelling agencies and while we were not permitted to view the goods, *au naturel*, hundreds of pictures of all manner of bosoms (female optimism at its sunniest, more often than not in the face of dire evidence to the contrary) clad in the sheerest of bikini tops, deluged the agency. Never in the annals of the company's history, observed our Welsh managing director, had so many senior executives dropped all to serve one client's (chuckle) pressing needs.

When we found her, the search was well worth the effort: Lise Jones, a lovely Anglo-Indian model, with the face of a Renaissance angel and a body made for sin. Wadhwani grinned. Lit a cigar. ('I gotta hand it to you, kid'). The eyebrows wiggled. 'Wonderful bosoms!'

It would be nice to record an advertising triumph as grand as the Liberty shirt campaign, but while the advertisements looked gorgeous, this was still India mid-Sixties, and I shouldn't have been surprised by the letter which arrived from a leading newspaper group, rejecting the campaign, ' ... the lighting, the camera angles, the poses, indeed the very purpose of the pictures, seem to be to excite the prurient reader. They draw attention to the bosoms (not again!) of the female model and underplay the garment being advertised. In fact, in one of the pictures, she appears to have nothing on at all.' So much for Maidenform's tribute to the nipple. We offered a compromise. The air-brush was ruthlessly employed. Curves, voluptuous in their sweep and promises, shrank visibly overnight; cleavages assumed a chagrined modesty; you could now count the stitches to the inch in a bra which could have been put together from plaster of Paris. The campaign was resubmitted for release, and returned yet again, for the unkindest cut of all. This was performed with due solemnity and India's nippleless pair of bosoms in a Maidenform bra made a somewhat diminished debut in the Indian press.

Lise Jones was not amused.

But the times they were a-changing. Breasts grew nipples again in the Seventies and became a cause célèbre in hearths and homes across the land. A young East Indian, Ross Deas must take responsibility for the renaissance of the Indian bosom. Swift success in making men's muscles bigger and better with a spring contraption encouraged him to seek fresh horizons, and he brought manic energy and evangelical fervour to the uplift of the Indian bosom. He designed an ingenious, pliable, metal-and-spring device (no mincing words, he called it 'the bust developer'; unkind observers called it 'the booby trap') which would have made a Spanish Inquisitor proud. A mechanical engineer and a physiotherapist assisted in its creation. Strenuous effort was required to exercise with the gadget, pulling and releasing it, hither and thither, at various contortionist angles. And while it needed willpower and a high pain threshold to make its wonders work, Ross' trials, conducted in the strictest secrecy, showed that it did.

The campaign broke with the 'before-and-after' theme, flagged with such attention-grabbers as 'Brand New', 'Never Before' 'First Time in India' and suchlike. And if the 'before' picture evoked pity if not downright sorrow, the results of six weeks' early morning work with the bust developer prompted awe, a touch of disbelief, a rush of emotion: Gosh ... would it really? ... could it be true? ... should I? ... no one will ever know. A masterstroke, that last nudge.

Whenever I am asked the asinine question, 'Does advertising work?' I am reminded of the bust developer. Thousands of women – from cities as light years apart as Bombay and Bhusawal – rushed to mail their money orders, a resounding testament to the triumph of hope over reason.

*

If anyone in Indian advertising can lay claim to taking sex by the horn (in a manner of speaking) one need look no further than Kersey Katrak.

To Katrak and a handful of young, anarchic, iconoclastic copywriters (in MCM and a few other agencies), whose motto could well have been 'Who dares, wins!', must go the credit for the coming of age of sex in Indian advertising. They created a seminal shift in the existing paradigm. Ivan Arthur, creative director of Hindustan Thomson Associates (HTA), India's oldest and largest advertising agency, calls the movement, 'the first wave': 'The wave was an exhilarating one. Every day we opened the newspapers to look for breakthroughs, and we found them – in the advertising produced by da Cunha, MCM and Frank Simoes, campaigns which pointed the way to the future.

'This first wave was like an explosion; it shattered old ideas and attitudes ... it introduced style, surprise, aesthetics, stimulation, sophistication and guts into the advertising itself and it revolutionized attitudes, interactions and styles of operation.'

Who would have thought that one of the earliest harbingers of sexual upheaval in advertising would emerge, priapic and triumphant, from a bottle of orange pop? (Katrak and his art director, Panna Jain, natch!) Today, the Gold Spot campaign, conceived by MCM in the Seventies, may seem about as sexually explicit as the Yellow Pages but, for the time, it was revolutionary. Up to that watershed, a soft drink was an ice-cold, flavoured thirst-quencher for a hot day, and promoted exclusively as such. Why then, reasoned Katrak and Jain, in an inspired flight of intuition, was the bottle shaped like a phallus in coital frenzy? And why were young couples sipping from two straws out of a single bottle? Soon, under their wily and subversive ministration, Gold Spot was the only encouragement a couple needed to hop into bed. The slogan did not quibble; 'Live a little hot ... sip a Gold Spot.' But, variety, as we all know, is the spice of sexual life and two years later, Gold Spot urged the young to 'Get a taste of something fresh', leaving no room for confusion: there they are, a young and handsome couple, but all is not well. She is sad and wistful; he is bored and nearly out of it, until he notices – at propositioning distance – the Other Woman: they exchange a glance of shimmering incandescence, reminding us that earlier flames, extinguished, may always be rekindled, 'Livva little hot ... ' RIP.

Ten years on Trikaya Grey, a new hot shop, would have none of this waffling. An Amazonian bondage queen is surrounded by three muscular fawning males. The slogan cracks a whip. 'Don't just think about it, don't just talk about it. Do it!' 'Do it', as you will have guessed, was a low-calorie coke. The campaign was a runaway success.

Will somebody please tell me how sex in advertising works?

The decade was to see the full flowering of sex as a legitimate means of advertising expression, from the first nude in Indian advertising (Nivea cream with – surprise, surprise – Lise Jones) to the rose-tinted romantic ideal (the Charms cigarette campaign). There were more blatant offerings. How Wadhwani would have warmed to the hero of the Frenchie underwear advertisement: hung like a water-buffalo, starkers, except for a pair of Frenchies two sizes too small, delivering a karate strike to an innocent passerby in a suit (suit? Serves the sod right), while a nubile young thing looks on adoringly.

A benchmark of the Eighties was the launch of a new, raunchy magazine, *Debonair*. It was a refreshingly catholic exploration of the life and times of the contemporary Indian male. *Debonair* made no bones about the fact that the affairs of the mind and the liveliness of the prostrate were delightfully compatible.

Fifteen years earlier, an attempt at a similar magazine for men folded up in six months for lack of advertising support. *Debonair* marked a threshold in the sexual emancipation of the Indian advertiser. The future had arrived. The condom manufacturers were ecstatic; here, at last, was the perfectly 'cost-effective' medium. No wastage. Every reader was a potential customer. They leaped – at times with disastrous results – on the *Debonair* bandwagon. One such abortive attempt offered a condom of a different colour, from fire engine red to pulse-racing purple – for every day of the week. There were five advertisements, each in living colour, as the blurbs say, and they were (quite unwittingly) hilarious. The visual of the first advertisement had a young couple on a swing, at its apogee, awkwardly balanced, and in imminent danger of grave injury.

But condoms were no laughing matter, as we were soon to discover: they had the power to move and shake. In October 1991, critical mass reached fusion in the condom business with a plutonium trigger by the inspired brand name, 'Kama Sutra'. This was no quickie piece of plebian latex for brief encounters of the furtive kind. This was the ultimate 'pleasure enhancer'. If no romantic evening was complete without the Jag, the champagne and roses, candlelight and violins, the perfumed suite with velvet drapes, making love would never be the same again once you slipped on a Kama Sutra, or, noblesse oblige, 'let her put it on for you.'

It seems fitting that Katrak – arch instigator of the nascent sex-in-advertising movement of the Sixties – should preside over its apotheosis thirty years into the future. In Gautam Singhania, he found the ideal client.

They did their homework and the results were depressing. Research revealed that, for every hundred men who understood the need to use the product, only seven actually did. It was the classic 'downer': the condom was perceived as a clumsy rubber sheath, used out of necessity or fear, an artificial denial of both spontaneity and pleasure. Katrak and Singhania took a risky and calculated decision: they would go for broke, a total reversal of existing attitudes – from product to communications with no-holds-barred en route. It was all or nothing.

The product was ultra-thin, textured, contoured, dotted on the outside to 'give the woman extra pleasure': India's first truly sexy condom. The pack was slim, flat, modestly rectangular, no hint of the tell-tale bulge in his wallet (or, for that matter, her purse). A white signature on midnight black, with the letters 'K' and 'S' picked out in red. No lavatorial sniggering here; it would do honour to your drawing-room, montaged à la Andy Warhol, opposite the Salvador Dali. The brand name was chosen with care – out of scores – as much for its explicitness as for advertising potential. Indeed, the copy in all three advertisements began with the brand name in the headline: 'The Kama Sutra On Acting Like A Man ... A man should gather from the actions of the woman of what disposition she is and what way she likes to be enjoyed (Book II, Part VIII).' More in the same vein in the body copy, though it's hard to concentrate what with Pooja Bedi (Kabir and Protima's daughter, a neat example of Jungian fulfillment) in orgasmic abandon in the arms of a memorably forgettable stud.

The thirty-second TV commercial was pure sexual whimsy (Katrak snarls!). Through a blue filter. Pooja does a sizzling number with the sexiest showerhead on the idiot box – a glistening silver phallus so mesmerising in her naughty little hands, that when the real thing makes an appearance – attached to a male hunk who leaps out of a rowing-boat, disrobes and joins her – one feels it should be declared instantly redundant, excised, stuffed, mounted and hung up on the wall with her other trophies, leaving Pooja and that gorgeous showerhead to get on with it! The soundtrack (no flies on Katrak) is a single word – Kama Sutra – repeated, huskily, every four seconds.

Nothing succeeds like excess. A 20-page, full colour supplement in *Debonair* engaged the reader's attention with such gems of arcanea as the world's oldest condom (Egyptian linen, 3,000 years ago); Casanova's you-can't-be-too-careful answer to the problem (condoms made from animal intestines); and hats off to the Original Inventor, King Charles II's personal physician Dr Condom, who created a sheath for the Royal Member. All quite incidental to the denouement, unfolding over three pages; Pooja heavy-lidded, post-coital, arms folded modestly over a pair of bosoms (!) which would have won Wadhwani's instant approval and stuck on as a footnote, the real thing: a free sample of the product, with the coy advice, 'Ask for KS'. Stuff and nonsense. The Indian male was ready for sexual nirvana. To a man, they said, KAMA SUTRA!

Three months after the campaign was launched, stocks ran out in the shops and the advertising was called to a halt.

Kama Sutra had made the earth move.

Bhagwan Wadhwani, gone before with honour and distinction, would have raised three cheers.

'You gotta hand it to dem, kid!'

****

I sidled into the advertising business unnoticed and unsung at the age of twenty as a copy trainee in a venerable British advertising agency in Bombay. It was called, if memory serves, BOMAS, an acronym for Bensons Overseas Advertising and Marketing Services, the largest company of its kind in the Commonwealth. The founder-chairman in London was a retired Admiral of the Fleet. His years before the mast had encouraged the more robust kind of Imperial management and he made sure that the far-flung outposts of the BOMAS empire were run by Brits of stern nautical persuasion who believed that bread-water-and-shackles-below-decks was a benevolent form of discipline. My official title was copy trainee, but I was really ship's boy, the lowest form of animal life on board.

As a copy trainee I learned to write advertising campaigns. I was, sad to say, good at it. But there is just so much inspiration one can bring to the greater glory of cooking oil and condoms. Ten years later, called to the board, I was still writing campaigns with no end in sight. With a fiendishly agile leap of lateral thinking, I set up my own advertising agency. As chairman, no one would dare ask me to write a campaign again. They did. I did. But I learned to employ evasive tactics with the enemy. At the slightest excuse (the appearance of a bulky campaign 'brief' for instance), I would plead creative angst, pack toothbrush and portable, and hare off to Goa where, among other delightful pastimes, I would moonlight as journalist manqué, a role I rather fancied. My vice president, client servicing, was not amused:

TO FS CANDOLIM GOA
FROM VP CS BOMBAY
    ITS BEEN A WEEK STOP WE SENT YOU OFF WITH THREE CAMPAIGN BRIEFS AND A FORTNIGHTS DEADLINE STOP YOU HAVE NO EXCUSES STOP WHEN YOU SPENT MONTHS WALLOWING IN GOAN FLESHPOTS IN SEARCH OF QUOTE PERFECT ACRE UNQUOTE NO ONE BELIEVED YOU BUT WE LET IT PASS STOP WHEN YOU SPENT EVERY OTHER WEEK DRINKING AND CAROUSING IN CANDOLIM FOR A YEAR UNDER PRETEXT OF BUILDING HOUSE WE INDULGED YOU BECAUSE YOU PAID OUR BILLS STOP THIS IS THE MOMENT OF TRUTH STOP YOU HAVE SEVEN DAYS TO SALVAGE WHATS LEFT OF YOUR GOOD NAME

TO VP CS BOMBAY
FROM FS CANDOLIM GOA
    RADHIKAS LIFE SAVED JUST BARELY FROM BLACK COBRA ATTACK BY BRAVE DOG JIMI STOP AM IN SWEATY HEART THUMPING MEETINGS ALL DAY WITH SARPANCH FORESTRY OFFICERS LOCAL SNAKE CATCHERS OTHER REPTILE CONSULTANTS WORKING OUT WAYS AND MEANS TO KEEP VENOMOUS COBRAS KRAITS VIPERS AWAY FROM MY DAUGHTER STOP THERE ARE SOME THINGS MORE IMPORTANT THAN ADVERTISING CAMPAIGNS STOP IF YOU WERE EVER BITTEN BY POISONOUS SNAKE YOU WOULD REALIZE IT IS NOT A CALMING EXPERIENCE ADVERTISING CAMPAIGNS FORSOOTH (!)

TO FS CANDOLIM GOA
FROM VP CS BOMBAY
    PLEASE CONVEY DEEPEST SYMPATHY AND FELLOW FEELING TO BLACK COBRA ON NOT SO CLOSE ENCOUNTER (SADLY UNREQUITED) WITH MOST ASTONISHING LIAR IN THE BUSINESS STOP HOW COME 2500 WORD LEAD ARTICLE YOUR BYLINE APPEARED IN SUNDAY

    TO VP CS BOMBAY
    FROM FS CANDOLIM GOA
    ARTICLE WRITTEN MONTH AGO YOU NEVER DO YOUR

HOMEWORK THAT'S ALWAYS BEEN YOUR PROBLEM STOP SNAKES ARE SERIOUS BUSINESS REPEAT DEADLY SERIOUS AND REQUIRE EVERY LAST OUNCE OF STRATEGIC AND TACTICAL PLANNING SKILLS DO YOU KNOW THAT A FIVE FOOT RAT SNAKE CAN SCALE A SIX FOOT WALL STOP ID LIKE TO SEE YOU COPE WITH THAT (!)

TO FS CANDOLIM GOA
FROM VP CS BOMBAY
    LIAR LIAR PANTS ON FIRE STOP ASSTT EDITOR SUNDAY TIMES, CONFIRMS ARTICLE ARRIVED FROM GOA TWO DAYS BEFORE PUBLICATION STOP WHAT HAS BECOME OF TRUTH IN ADVERTISING

TO VP CS BOMBAY
FROM FS CANDOLIM GOA
    PLEASE CONVEY GOOD NEWS TO ALL OF COMPANY 250 EXECS, AND STAFF IN BOMBAY AND DELHI STOP CREEPY CRAWLIES STYMIED WITH SIX FOOT WALL AND FORTY-FIVE DEGREE OVERHANG COATED WITH SPECIAL ANTISNAKE EXTRA SLIPPERY GLAZING WITH CURVED HEMISPHERICAL TRENCH ALL ALONG OUTER BASE OF WALL YOU MAY CONGRATULATE ME NOW I CAN APPLY WHATS LEFT OF MIND TO COSMETICS SCOOTERS AND, READYMADE PANTS

TO FS CANDOLIM GOA
FROM VP CS BOMBAY
    SOMETHING SERIOUSLY AMISS WITH MANAGING COMMITTEE OF ALL INDIA CREATIVE ARTS GUILD STOP SUSPECT THEY HAVE LOST THEIR MARBLES STOP JUST RECEIVED CABLE NOT REPEAT REGRETFULLY NOT LOST IN TRANSIT ELECTING YOU TO HALL OF FAME STOP YOU ARE ONLY SIXTH ELECTEE IN TWENTY YEARS STOP SHOW SIGNS OVERWHELMING GRATITUDE IMMEDIATELY STOP RETURN WITH THREE CAMPAIGNS THATLL KNOCK THEM FLAT

    I did.

****

Twenty years to the day I began, I decided to close down the advertising agency which carried my name, live in Goa for the major part of the year, and – would I never learn? – try to use words to good purpose all over again. It was the hardest decision of my life. I arranged an executive buy-out for some of the senior management and staff. Many of our clients – loyal to the last – agreed to stay on. The new company's name had yet to be decided.

The cable had gone the way of the dinosaur; the telex was as defunct as the dodo; the hour of the fax was at hand. Imagine my surprise when a cable arrived one morning delivered by hand by what was surely the last of a rare species, a postman on a bicycle. It contained two sentences and a hundred and fourteen signatures:

NOW THAT YOU HAVE LEFT US NO CHOICE BUT TO BECOME UNACCUSTOMED TO YOUR FACE WILL YOU LEAVE US YOUR NAME STOP GOOD LUCK AND GODSPEED

I did.

****

The Jaundiced Eye

Those were the days,
my friends. Chords were
struck which made naught
of language, colour and
creed. They would echo
through the Bible,
the Torah and the Gita.

Pythons, Puritans and Perfidy

Shed a tear for Madhu and Milind. There they were, among the bravest of today's brave young people, doing what comes perfectly naturally, only to be flattened by the Chicken Little effect: the sky falls on their heads, presumably the only part of their anatomy the philistines will allow them to expose without fear of arrest and incarceration. Spare a kind thought as well for the hapless python: no reptile has had such a confused press since Eve and the Apple. What was all the fuss about? If I had to spend my life slithering around without legs I'd find a temporary interlude, at such an amorous elevation, a very pleasant way to pass an afternoon provided I could snack on a little chicken now and then. A happier prospect, I would imagine, than having your fangs pulled out and being made to spend the rest of your life in a basket with the blessings of the Tourist Board, entertaining videocam-wielding foreign trippers only to meet with a gory conclusion at the business end of a mongoose. Do I hear a chorus of protest at this beastly behaviour? Not a whimper! Do we cry foul when one of those 'it's-the-Guinness-Book-Of-Records-or-death' maniacs frightens the bejesus out of a few dozen terrified cobras locked in a tiny room with him for a month? We flock in the hundreds to applaud while the media is all pictures and praise at the perfidy.

And how does one cope with the buckets of bile befouling the public print when a lady of the bar bares nearly all (an act of outrageous honesty in a profession notorious for concealing more than it reveals) except to reflect that justice and the law are mutually exclusive and never shall the twain meet. Must all our female barristers wear wigs and bulge in all the wrong places? And must all extracurricular romp and tickle (even the passive, printed kind so many wistful removes from the real thing) be the exclusive prerogative of public figures in high places who are rarely, if ever, brought low? Since when has the liveliness of the libido and the pursuit of the higher values been at odds? Tell that to Wolfgang Mozart and the creators of Khajuraho, to Picasso and Akbar the Great, to Graham Greene and our very own M.F. Husain. It's high time we cast off the blinkers and took a long, hard look at ourselves.

There was a programme on the box the other day where a twittering of Tamilian mums waxed eloquently indignant on the evil influences of Star TV. Never mind that their views were about as relevant as yesterday's masala dosa in today's Kentucky Fried Chicken outlet, what with a satellite dish sprouting over every far-flung hamlet in Tamil Nadu and cable connections writhing in and out of small towns like pythons in sexual frenzy. Had anyone of these abundant matrons paused to consider that well before Star TV brought its blonde, blue-eyed clones and blazing .38s into our hearths and homes, we had preempted all known forms of violence and sexual mischief – and invented a few unknown to the barbaric West – several aeons earlier. Snakes alive! I have yet to find more stomach-churning sexual innuendo than in your friendly neighbourhood Indian feature film blockbuster. The tentacled writhings, the oh-so-close but never penetrative encounters of the contortionist kind, the convoluted sexual desecration of tree trunks, babbling brooks (you'd end up babbling as well if you were treated like that) and the wicked things done to flowers. Flowers! In the land of the ritual marigold? Where are you Maneka when we need you most?

Beating Kentucky Fried Chicken over the head with a monosodium glutamate stick (Ajin-o-Moto if you speak only Chinese). Sinisterly known – shudder! – to cause cancer, warts, hiccups and – newly discovered but kept strictly under wraps – nocturnal bed-wetting. Shame and fie! Never mind that every other Indian Chinese eatery from Kulu to Kanyakumari has used lashings of the stuff from Day One and who cares if the chicken we've been eating for the past twenty-five years are factory-raised in wire mesh cages so tiny they can't move, force-fed by tube with a revolting mush of fish meal, vitamins, hormones and antibiotics to destroy life-sustaining bacteria in the digestive tract and make them fat and bleaching agents to reduce muscle and tissue to the jaundiced off white so popular with the proles. No evil multinationals here. Just good ole Swadeshi git up and go. And not a peep from the fascist police.

But before I am accused of puerility of the most superficial kind, let us return to the concerns of our matrons in Madras. The promotion of gratuitous violence, casual sex, conscienceless greed and the undermining of our high cultural and ethical values. Let's not labour the obvious and suggest that they switch to the news, sports, cartoons or all those excellent and impeccably correct BBC documentaries which put you so easily to sleep. Ninety per cent of time on the box is given over to the relentless mayhem of the Indian feature film: slaughtered bodies by the cartload, hour upon bloody hour of unmitigated violence, acres of arson and dollops of torture, mutilation and rape thrown in when the script begins to sag. With greed, treachery and dishonour very nearly winning the day and the villains and vixens always infinitely more compelling than the blow-dried heros and modestly dimpled heroines. And let us draw a merciful veil over the front pages of our daily newspapers where life outdoes art – the Bhagalpur blindings; the rape, torture and murder of children; the slaughter of hundreds in the name of God and community; the ritual sacrifice of infants; the burning of meagerly dowried brides; the ingenious new employment of the tandoor; the horrible female infanticide on a scale that defies the imagination; the routine gun-toting coercion of the electorate; the gangland executions reported by the media with such lip-smacking salacity; and the new extra-judicial services so thoughtfully provided by the underworld to a grateful citizenry – from the settlement of tenancy and labour disputes to swift termination with extreme prejudice for a price.

We need no foreign lessons in gratuitous violence, thank you very much, nor in sex in its basest form of expression. Bachi Karkaria, just returned from an international AIDS conference in Thailand informs us in a lead article in *The Times of India* that 750,000 adult Indians have the tragic distinction of carrying the HIV virus and 2,000,000 will by the year 2000. Small cause for surprise when you consider that whore-mongering is a major national illicit industry. I know that it is now politically incorrect to use the word 'prostitution'. But 'sex worker' is another one of those weasel Western imports: it implies freedom of movement, freedom of choice, a living wage, medical and social benefits and the right to dignity, no matter how servile the labour. Come to think of it, we don't have prostitution or sex workers in India, we have sex slaves in bondage to criminals, disease, violence, official corruption and premature death. In the hundreds of thousands. In the world's largest, most virulently contaminated, corrupt and criminalized red light areas – Falkand Road in Bombay, Sonagachi in Calcutta and smaller but no less vicious satellites in every major Indian city. Where you can buy a body – male, female, neutered, adult, child – for a fistful of rupees. Nowhere on the planet is child prostitution more rampant, overtly as in the brothels, covertly where children are used illegally as labour by day and sex disposal units by night. Brutalized children grow up to become brutalizing adults and the venom spreads.

Greed? Avarice? Dishonour? *The Bold and The Beautiful* and *Santa Barbara* are Sunday school clases; Machiavelli is a pussy cat, to the back of the class, Richard Nixon. Make way for the big, bad boys of Bofors; multibillion dollar share market scams; the pipeline diversion of aid to the stricken (Latur, Bhopal) observed by unimpeachable witnesses, to the bottomless pits of the black market; godmen who could teach dear old Rasputin a thing or two; the hawala industry cocking a merry snook at COFEPOSA; crime and politics rolling in the hay and producing monstrous offspring; bundles of thousand of rupees stamped Black Is Beautiful; the democratization of higher education at a price; not forgetting the telephone at home which never works until you make the local linesman a permanent, paid consultant. We are a larcenous nation and if we were ever to export our talent in this area our balance of payments would be solidly in the black (pun intended) unto the fifth generation.

In the stormy years ahead (don't look now!) how are our Madhus and Milinds to cope with the furies? Here's a prayer for the future: may they ride a fair wind, with the sun at their backs and in the eyes of the enemy, waving aloft the only motto that matters: when the going gets tough, the Tuff get going!

****

Next Year's Words
Await Another Voice ...

When I began the daunting task of reviewing fifty years of unparalleled change in two thousand words, T.S. Eliot's elegiac epitaph to all our times past returned unbidden: 'Last year's words belong to last year's language. Next year's words await another voice.' Written for a different time, in another place, it remains the perfect swansong to the past and a poignant metaphor for an unknowable future. No more telling definition of burial and renewal comes to mind when looking back at independent India's first half century and the seismic changes that will alter the landscape of the national psyche beyond all recognition in the millennium ahead.

By a quirk of destiny my life has been congruent with the nation's these past fifty years and I – rarely with ascendant hope, more often in the mire of despair – have been witness and participant in the bewilderingly swift transformation of mores, values and expectations which has cast the die in a wholly new direction, pointing the way to a future where the beliefs and aspirations of our founding fathers are finally extinguished in the bonfire of new and alien vanities. Where has change been most potent? When were links severed with a sanctified past? How did the evils of corruption and communalism find genesis and fruition and, finally, a weary indifference? When did illegal wealth and unbridled power become such all-pervasive icons of success? Or were we always this way and the decades of idealism and sacrifice of the generation of Indians which fought for and won independence merely a temporary aberration forged in the white-hot incandescence of revolutionary fervour?

Sadly for all of us the debate is now academic. It has been reduced to the lame-duck rhetoric encountered in Republic Day editorials and public slanging matches between opposing politicians of equally black hue. Today the founding fathers and their days of glory are mere grist to the social historian's mill, and purely incidental to the vastly more intriguing material at hand. The more perceptive purveyors of the past tell us that the seeds of our rancorous and poisonous harvest were sown post-independence when, by one of those ironic contradictions whereby fate thwarts the plans of mice and men, the very act of independence found the forces of liberation making common cause with the dark powers of doctrinaire socialist suppression on the one hand and politically sanctioned and protected capitalist immorality on the other. Hypocrisy became the currency of the body politic. Public breast-beating camouflaged enormous private gain. Black money gained definition, sophistication, status and, before long, primary as the real lifeblood of the nation. Today's public smears, Bofors, Harshad Mehta, the telecom and sugar scandals, the political/industrial/criminal nexus, the hawala shenanigans of cabinet ministers; and the daily hiccups, the policeman's, postman's and telephone linesman's haftas – can trace their beginnings to the early fifties when a cabal of unscrupulous industrialists, the real evil geniuses of our republic, began to suborn the system and turn it to their will.

From scurrilous example set at the very top of the pyramid was born precept. Precept became practice and, with time, practice was incorporated into the fabric of the nation as first principle. The editorialists lamented the loss of innocence. They were wrong. Innocence like birth is, by definition, encrypted with the harbingers of its own doom. In *The Quiet American*, Graham Greene's cynical English protagonist observes of his American antagonist, 'God protect us from the innocent, at least the guilty know what they are about.' True, but to what degree and to what appalling end? Did our freedom fighters, sacrificing all – their liberty, their futures, often their lives – ever expect it would end like this: with a wink, a smirk and a bagful of black money?

In retrospect all of it seems like a game of simple monopoly. Penal rates of income tax at the highest levels – ninety per cent and more – encouraged the creation of a parallel black money economy. This, in turn, fuelled the political process which, in cynical quid pro quo, provided markets protected from overseas competition by swadeshi diktat and politically controlled by the licence raj. The higher you bid in black the more lucrative the licences. They were licences to print money. Black markets flourished and, lubricated by cash of the wrong colour, spread swift and deadly tentacles beyond goods and commodities to real estate, smuggling, flight capital, crime, the political system and, in the process, created huge and impregnable cartels which suborned all to their will – the politicians, the administration, the customs, excise and tax apparatuses, the forces of law and order until, tragically, the common citizen saw the light as well and was embraced into the fold. 'God protect us from the innocent, at least the guilty know what they are about' has become the golden motto for the new millennium.

The generation to which my daughter belongs wonders what the fuss is all about. I was recently and briefly reluctant adviser on publicity to a group of young entrepreneurs, all weightily qualified with MBAs from American universities who, without batting an eyelash, worked into their project report black money cash flows in terms of capital investment, income and outgoings. When I advised caution and restraint I was made to feel about as relevant as the dodo and even less plausible. 'Which planet are you from?' I was asked good-naturedly. Which planet indeed! The received wisdom was clear and unambiguous: corruption, by any other name, makes good business sense.

Kicking over the traces it used to be called in the good old days when we still had access to our rural inhibitions and the equinine metaphor implied violent and heroic exertion to topple existing mores. No longer. Old mores have been interred without trace. The new generation has the freedom to go its own way and does so blithely, without so much as a smidgen of old cobweb to brush aside. Helped no end, it must be said, by the revolution in communications and all that it has wrought. This is increasingly apparent in the microcosm: the ease with which the traditional

Indian nuclear family disintegrates and swans about in bits and pieces all over the globe; the rise and rise of inter-community marriages and more unconventional liaisons; the mega weddings with casts of thousands at a cost of millions, the increasing acceptance of female infidelity as a legitimate response to male oppression; and public acknowledgement, if not outright applause, of homosexuality in both sexes as a matter of individual biological imperative and decision. Not forgetting the nascent movement towards the liberation of women in terms that are specific to our country and culture.

In the macrocosm, changing mores may be encapsulated in the single phrase, 'I want it now!' never more in evidence than in the Gadarene rush for political and administrative appointment as a swift shortcut to the accumulation of illegal assets and a 'Damn the price!' mentality: the mortgaging of future earnings to present gratification in the mindless acquisition of consumer goods on the never-never; the debasement of the rupee at the cost of countless impoverished millions which sees a can of coke at fifteen rupees, a packet of potato chips at twenty-five, imported Parmesan cheese in Bombay in short supply yet at Rs 2500 per kg, a designed salwar kameez at Rs 10,000, a hut in a slum at Nepean Sea Road in Bombay at Rs 20,000 that's right – per square foot and the 'people's car', in its cheapest version at a cool three lakhs plus. While millions of children below the poverty line go blind each year for lack of a few doses of Vitamin A.

There is more than a little nonsense bandied about in the public print regarding the causes of change, furious tilting at the symptomatic windmills of 'sybaritic lifestyle', 'value erosion', 'parental neglect', 'debasement of authority' and all the rest of that woeful litany. True perhaps but where's the reason why? The real truth of the matter is simpler and deadlier by far. The true nature of the beast is brought home to us each day in living colour in a box in our sitting rooms. Apocalypse is here and now: greed, avarice, envy; murder, rape, acreage, genocide: plague and pestilence; the brutal and bloody exploitation of the species by the species in the name of God, flag, race, plunder or just for the sheer sadistic joy of it. No country is spared the disfiguring mark of Cain and the killing grounds which bear gruesome witness to our unholy alliance with the powers of darkness invade our living rooms each day. Small wonder then that we willfully forget the day before and fear the day after.

Our parents and grandparents were spared the horrors of immediacy. They lived relatively cloistered lives sheltered in every particular that mattered. Travel, if at all, was an annual proposition, no further than city to the ancestral village. Families lived together for generations, under a single roof, mutually supportive, in a hierarchy of respect and concern, from grandparent, to parent, to child. The city, the country, the world and their doings were brief intrusions in black and white newsprint, short on pictures, long on words, barely glanced at each morning. The future was known, planned, paced and unfolded with comfortable inevitability. No longer. The future is here and now and too unbearable to contemplate. Grab what you can while you can. Tomorrow may never arrive.

The great current debate on the liberalization process – pro and con – virtually ignored the seminal central issue. This has little to do with Kentucky Fried Chicken or *The Bold and The Beautiful*, with the decadent subversions of Coke or *Playboy's* centerfolds, with the irrelevance of fuzzy logic machines or the obscene cost of Guccis. It has to do with primal exposure. The computer, the internet, cyberspace and the satellite dish have stripped us naked and exposed the species to the species in real time with the unblinking and merciless dissection of an MRI scan. No longer will a child be disemboweled in a Bosnian village: it will be dismembered in our home. Governments will have no choice but to cease and desist from deceit and subterfuge. They will be exposed instantly by a cyberspace nerd in the bowels of Bhopal or CNN's info nerve centre in Atlanta. The world's lunatic fringe – pederasts in Oslo, moonies in Philadelphia, disenfranchised hijras in Varanasi, transvestites in Tokyo, serial killers in Seoul – will be conjured out of airy nothingness by tapping the keyboard on a computer. All of the world's knowledge, for good or evil, will lie at the fingertips of our children and censorship as we know it will die the death. The power of the new electronic technology lies in its inherent ability to transcend all known forms of suppression and to increase this potency exponentially. It will also lead us, instantly and unerringly, to our higher and lower selves. 'Know thyself,' the Bible exhorts. Now we shall be forced to.

The harbingers of this evolutionary change have been with us for quite some time and, in their more mundane manifestations may be observed in such herd phenomena as group travel abroad, the swift osmosis by which fashion, music and mores transcend frontiers, the cross-pollination of art and culture and knowledge (Indian authors invading bestseller lists in the west; Israeli and German teenagers, in their thousands, organizing ecstasy raves on Goan beaches via cyberspace; Indians in far-flung townships trawling the E-mail circuits of the globe; an expert retinal opinion, from one of the world's leading surgeons in Boston which a friend in Baroda obtained in twenty-four hours ...).

There is no end in sight to the boundless fertility of cyberspace. And no fathoming what the future will bring. Only one thing is certain. We stand as a single bonded species, soon to be indivisibly fused, at a new evolutionary frontier. And we shall never be the same again.

****

Those Were the Days, My Friends

The swiftly turning days, the lingering seasons of my youth, golden, ambrosial days, celebrated on Bombay's meaner streets, where secularism had yet to become a dirty word: it awaited an unholy lexicon which the future would compile with shame, blood and tears. To all of us – Jew and Christian, Hindu, Muslim and Parsi, Jain and Jehovah's Witness – it was simply a way of life, a compelling tapestry which offered and fulfilled many-splendoured promises.

We were disenfranchised Goans, lost in the polyglot immensity of Bombay's lower middle classes. Our immediate neighbours were Khoja; above, noisily Iranian; Keralite below; spiritedly Anglo-Indian across the landing; invisibly Gujarati at the rear and, tucked away in a tiny corner flat, crustily British, a retired colonel, who did his bit for the fellowship of nations by introducing me to Chivers Thick-Cut Marmalade.

Those were the days when the unfolding wonder of our diversity was measured by joyful personal discovery. Sandy Solomen, a white Jew, national welter-weight champion, taught me to box at the Nagpada Neighbourhood House. His legendary skills in the ring were held in slightly less awe than his heroic bouts of carousing and, yes, I learned other things with him as well. With Abdul, our Pathan's son, I ate like a prince at the break of the Muhurram fast in the bylanes of Mohamedali Road. Sawant Navlekar, schoolmate and partner in truancy, discovered a kite shop in darkest Madanpura where we bought the world's finest manjar and six lethal fighting kites. For days, risking life and limb, we did honourable battle from neighbouring terraces till sunset and evening star drove us home.

I will never forget the kindness of strangers.

When I look a clock in the face an indelible image returns: a cubicle in a wall three feet above the pavement, an ancient Allahabadi tucked into it, shelves with dozens of watches and clocks in intriguing states of disrepair. Magnifying glass pressed into the folds of his right eye, he worked with unerring dexterity, hour upon hour, bringing dead watches back to life. He spent much time telling me how watches worked, why they fell sick and how they could be made well. He lent me a book, *How The World Marks Time*, and made a friend for life.

Where, I wonder, is the koli fisherwoman whose name I never came to know, who defined compassion for me in terms I shall never forget. I shopped every morning at the local market. Goans lived on fish; there were seven of us, and never enough money. I would enter the fish market with a wistful appreciation of the Miracle of the Loaves and Fishes. She never let me down. From the first day when she reached out, touched the cross at my neck and smiled, the price of fish assumed a miraculous elasticity. We never went without.

Those were the days, my friends. Chords were struck which made naught of language, colour and creed. They would echo through all the Bible, the Torah and the Gita, all the holy books, expressed a universal yearning, the need to reach out and touch, to help, to heal, to give and receive; a yearning to believe that life at its most meaningful was a fertile symbiosis between all things. Or it was nothing.

Those were the days when Aligarh stood for a great seat of Muslim learning, not an obscenity for the slaughter of infants, when the glories of Agra made a united nation proud, the days before the bloody icons of Ayodhya and the cold, calculated homicidal ravings of cynical men.

Those were the days, my friends.

****

The Hour of the Beast

The gardener named him Bacchan and he grew up to be a big, handsome and friendly dog, one of the three we kept in our beach home in Goa. When I heard he had been found with his throat torn open and deep lacerations on his body, I left for Goa at once. There was trouble in the territory. The Konkani/Marathi language agitation had taken on an ugly Catholic/non-Catholic hue. No one could explain Bacchan's death. We buried him and I sat up late on the balcony unable to sleep. At midnight a group of young men in shorts and white vests filed past. They formed a square on the beach in front of the house. A single voice was raised, 'Bacchan is dead.' Another, 'But there are two more dogs alive.' A third, 'And a child.' A fourth, 'Who knows what might happen?' A fifth, 'Anything might happen.' After a while they left, as silently as they came. They never returned.

In *The Second Coming*, the great Irish poet and Nobel Laureate, Y.B. Yeats, wrote, 'Things fall apart; the centre cannot hold/Mere anarchy is loosed upon the world/The blood-dimmed tide is loosed, and everywhere/The ceremony of innocence is drowned/The best lack all conviction, while the worst/Are full of passionate intensity.' He ends the poem, 'And what rough beast, its hour come round at last/Slouches towards Bethlehem to be born?' Prophetic words, composed when the Nazis had taken their first jack-booted strides on the long and bloody road to power in Germany.

Closer to 1939 and the Second World War, Carl Jung, who was

practising psychoanalysis in Vienna, reported a disturbing new phenomenon in his patients, both Jewish and Gentile: the increasing emergence of a terrifying new icon from the unconscious, the Nazi swastika. The symbol recurred in dream after dream and was always associated with terror, overpowering evil, blood and death. The world will never forget the aftermath: carnage and devastation on a scale never before witnessed by the species and the institutionalized murder of six million innocent Jews.

History has taught us that the propensity for slaughter lies skin-deep in the human psyche, ready to uncoil. Once unleashed, it feeds on its own evil raison d'être, turns on provocateur and victim alike and will not be denied. This – and not Ayodhya – is the central issue. The incantations, symbols and rituals which rouse the Beast are myriad. They are drawn from the languages of all races – German, Arabic, Hindi, Yiddish, French, English; they respect neither caste, nor creed, nor colour, only a hideous democracy which does not discriminate between black and white, yellow and brown, Aryan and Jew, Jew and Palestinian, Hindu and Muslim, Iraqi and Kurd, Khmer Rouge and Cambodian, black American and white American, True Believer and Infidel; the cause – real or fictitious – is immaterial: Marxist or religious fundamentalism, racial bigotry, colour prejudice, caste, feudal and tribal hatreds. There are only two constants in this danse macabre: the evil victim and the righteous victor, one in minority, the other in overwhelming majority; and the High Priests of both, calling the faithful to violent arms, oblivious of the dark and evil forces about to be unleashed.

It remains only for good men and true to do nothing.

Ask not, said Donne, for whom the bell tolls.

Today, it tolls for us all.

****

Radhika and The Bomb

When you are fourteen the universe unfolds with an abundance of joy, wonder, revelation and, now and again, a tear. The fledgling years do not prepare you for the corruption in the flesh, the gathering darkness in the butterfly's brief glory, the harbingers of death as the petals on the rose begin to wilt. Until an obscenity beyond all comprehension exposes the betrayal in the illusion. Radhika had been set a school project on The Bomb, its genesis, monstrous denouement and the terrible aftermath of its begetting. The devastation wrought on Hiroshima and Nagasaki was graphically demonstrated: the bodies scorched and mutilated in a manner hitherto unknown; the survivors soon to perish with the radioactive mark of Cain; the unborn doomed to stillbirth, deformity and cancer. As she told me of this her voice tightened with agitation. I remembered Jonathan Schell's funeral elegy, *The Fate of the Earth* and its tragic conclusion: the most evil of The Bomb's legacies was the irreparable psychic trauma it has inflicted on us and our children.

What could I say to Radhika? The consolation of half-truths, no matter how beguilingly constructed, would serve the purpose ill. Children are far more perceptive than adults will ever know. With Radhika I am merely first among equals and even that is often in doubt. The truth then as I saw it, with the caveat that all truths apply first and last to observer and observed, and personal truths travel indifferently rarely arriving at their destinations. So I decided to gather together the little I knew, give it a semblance of order and coherence, and offer Radhika a brief for her project.

Now that the rhetoric of nuclear machismo (Me Tarzan, You Jerk!) has settled into the absurd minuet of wary retreat, snarls, growls and insincere promises of terminal reprisals, it is high time we stepped back and set The Bomb in its true context. Beyond the current imbroglio of nuclear haves and have-nots, real and imagined threats, weaponization, unstoppable escalations to critical-mass thresholds, and all the rest of that ancient garbage, we need to look at The Bomb in the context of our species, all other species and, indeed, evolution in general. It is not an analysis conducive to peace of mind and restful ease. The evidence to date points inexorably to a single conclusion: from black holes consuming entire galaxies, to natural disasters destroying tens of thousands, to a cobra's fangs sinking into living flesh, life as we know it is violent and unforgiving.

I hope, Radhika, that I don't rouse the ire of the World Wildlife Fund with my next observation, but nature is neither benign nor compassionate. We have watched with you with relentless inattention, (I with rueful déjà vu) wildlife programmes on TV, at the end of which one is left with the depressing notion that herbivores (with the exception of those prehistoric dead-ends, the elephant, hippo and rhino) are a luckless lot, created exclusively to provide mobile meals for carnivores. And lunch is always a painful and messy business. Another myth is laid to rest: animals kill only for food or in self-defence. Animals (herbivores included) destroy each other for dominance – sexual, territorial, leadership – and, with some of the big cats, sharks, grizzlies, wolves and the bigger apes, just for the aggressive joy of it, even as we do. And the violence is more than intrinsic to the process, it is vitally essential. Life destroys life to sustain and improve on life. There is method in all of this madness. The weak go to the wall so that the strong may become stronger. The strongest, the quickest to learn, the most ruthless, prevail and their genes make future generations that much more capable of environmental dominance. And the thesis is everywhere in evidence, from the cells in your body and the life of plants to war between nations and the cosmic fireworks of supernova.

What has all this to do with The Bomb, you might well ask? Bear with me Radhika, first things first. All life is violent; we are merely the most violent manifestation of life to date, withal the most compassionate, virile, inventive, collaborative, creative and anguished. It all goes with the territory. Why? Because homo sapiens developed a forebrain and, oh dear, the trouble it's caused. The conflict between the reptilian brain that lies at the base of our skulls, the animal brain that occupies most of it, and the forebrain, is the root cause of the deaths of six million Jews in Nazi gas chambers, twenty million Russians in Stalin's gulags and countless million victims of genocide in Ethiopia, Cambodia and Yugoslavia; but it has also given us the gifts of Albert Schwietzer and Mother Teresa, Jonas Salk who gave us a cure for polio, Lister who gave us pencillin, Mozart, Picasso and Nijinsky who gave us joy, and Christ and Buddha who illuminated the way to the liberation of the human predicament. And, lest we forget, the bhelpuriwallah around the corner who gives a beggar a free plate of ragra. Whales, pandas and cuddly seals don't.

Our future as a species is ambiguous at best, poised on the razor's edge of decision and the decision does not lie in our hands. Did it lie in the hands of a prehistoric hominid who brained a sibling with the shinbone of an animal and discovered a weapon? Before he could say, 'Take that you nerd!' all the other hominids, armed with shinbones, were laying waste with homicidal abandon. Until our alpha hominid, realizing that safety was a prerequisite to slaughter if one was to slaughter again, invented the throwing spear. This was the ultimate horror. There you were one moment, getting merrily high on fermented berries and – thud! crunch! splatter! – oblivion. Still and all, the spear was only as effective as your throwing arm and, after a few skulls-full of roughly brewed mammoth's blood, one's aim tended to go awry. The millennia sped past with not a little degree of frustration. Then some bright spark invented the bow and arrow and there was no looking back. The Chinese got into the act (don't they always) with gunpowder and in the time it took to say Guy Fawkes you could reduce dozens of the enemy into bite-sized pieces. Whoopee! Now things really got going. The cannon made its presence gruesomely felt. The rifle made a striking debut. Gatling invented the machine gun. An evil genius created poison gas; you could now be dispatched in your sleep in a trench as tens of thousands were in the First World War. The dive bomber made an explosive entry; it could reduce a modest township to rubble in minutes. Killer submarines could decimate battleships with the speed of sharks in a school of mackerel. Nothing was sacroscant. The sky, the sea, the land, the very breath you took, was given over to mayhem. Then came The Bomb and a poisoned mushroom took up permanent residence in the human psyche.

What conclusions may we reach from all of this inspired carnage, Radhika? First, we seek always to kill larger numbers, at longer distances, with greater efficiency. (A thousand years hence our descendants, manipulating killer lasers in deep space to annihilate entire planets, will no doubt look back nostalgically on our puny nuclear explosions with the wry amusement we direct at our hominid ancestors and their shinbone clubs.) Second, self-preservation: our own survival takes precedence over the destruction of our enemies. Third, new means of dealing death may never be kept secret; no sooner invented they become the common property of the entire species. Fourth, paradoxical as it may seem, little understood and perhaps most important of all, the other side of the coin of aggression is phenomenal evolutionary progress.

From the club to the Bomb, no weapon has been successfully contained. It has been displaced by a bigger, better bang for the buck. The atom bomb ... the hydrogen bomb ... the neutron bomb. It took fifty years – from the time Einstein, Fermi, Teller, Bohr, Oppenheimer and the rest of Dr Strangelove's merry men began tinkering with the atom with nary a clue as to what they were up to – till The Bomb, encouraged no end by the Second World War, cast its mortuary shadow on the Nevada desert. Ten years later, five countries possessed it. Today, eight countries are in the club and at least five more have the technology to build an arsenal. Lyall Watson, biologist and author, is unsurprised. He once observed and reported how important discoveries take metaphysical leaps across physical barriers. A fishing boat was shipwrecked on one of a group of islands in the North Pacific populated by herbivorous monkeys. The fishermen began catching fish in the shallow for food. The alpha monkeys, observing this, started catching and eating fish. Simultaneously, monkeys on the other uninhabited islands became fish catchers and eaters. He concluded, like many other biologists, that life is a process, whole complete, indivisible and evolutionary. Knowledge for a part is knowledge for the whole. An individual life, or millions of lives, are of utter inconsequence to the leaping, incandescent sweep of life.

Consider this Radhika. Despite the decimation we have wrought on our species, despite nature's periodic culls (tens of millions in the Black Death of the Middle Ages; twenty million in this century's killer 'flu epidemic; countless millions in the coming millennium's AIDS devastation) our species continues to grow exponentially and more of us are, today, healthier, better-fed, longer-lived, more intelligent and inventive than ever before in our calamitous history. Thanks in large measure to the accelerated progress war brings to medicine, science, transport, communications, agriculture, learning and virtually anything you care to name. Nuclear medicine and the nuclear bomb are parts of the same conundrum.

As you are Radhika, and I, and your mother, The Bomb, and Snoopy the Dog Who Knows No Fear, and the rage of the breaking monsoon as it ravishes the land, and the dolphins off Candolim beach who make gentle sport of your awkward way with waves. And all that has gone before, all that is now, and all that lies beyond. Seamless. Indivisible. One. A paradox, enfolded in enigma, shrouded in mystery. Violently antagonistic, purposefully osmotic; awesomely self-destructive, wonderfully nurturing; blissfully amoral but always in triumphant ascendancy. Will we ever understand why we are? Or are we condemned to opening Chinese boxes to infinity? Two thousand years ago the first and last question was asked, quo vadis? Wither goest thou? Will we ever find an answer? I think not Radhika. For us there is only the quest, the rest is not our business.

There is a golden horizon.

Hold your head high.

Do not be afraid.

Remember the words of the poet, 'After the first death, there is no other.'

Take the power and the promise of your life in your hands.

And let it take wing.

****

The Portrait Painter

He fought the good fight till
he drew his last breath.
Our perception of life was
enhanced by the example of
his own; today, in equal
measure, we are diminished
by his death.

Three Thunder-boxes
and a Mandolin

My friend, Remo Fernandes, is a man of many admirable parts. I admire his character, informed as it is with the finest of Goan virtues, held in tempered, understated balance. I am in awe of his success in India and the world at large; it has given fresh meaning to the phrase, 'self-made'. His knowledge of Goan esoterica never ceases to amaze me. His commitment to family, friends and the good Goan earth is as unwavering as my own. I strongly applaud his love of the simpler pleasures: good food and drink, the company of children, dogs and books, a twilight evening alone by the Siolim backwaters with a meditative flute. But there is one thing about him I shall always envy: his childhood; it was the stuff of happy dreams.

We played a game once at Remo's birthday party. Each of us had to recall two of our first memories, the happiest and the funniest. When he was six years old and his musical talent had begun to be seriously noticed, his parents gave him a birthday gift of a mandolin. It was the happiest moment of his life and his joy was unconfined. He and the mandolin were inseparable. He mastered the instrument in months, as well he might, given practice of such dedication that it began early in the morning while he sat on one of three thunder-boxes in a shed above a pigsty out in the yard. Then, as now to a great extent in rural Goa, sanitation was brutally elementary but ecologically sound; loos were located well away from the main house above a trough where the family's pigs fed. One eased oneself, in Remo's words, 'to the soothing rumble of pigs at breakfast'.

The morning's ablutions presented him with his first funniest memory. The commodes were placed on a single platform two feet apart. Remo, his father, perhaps an uncle, shared the loo while engaged in friendly evacuation. Remo strummed on the mandolin; the older men began their day with a companionable chat, a bit of gossip, a quick run through of the headlines in *O Heraldo*, a review of the day's agenda. A felicitous arrangement. It suited the pigs, as well, splendidly: three breakfasts at one serving. Their contented grunts, according to Remo, was a sound as easeful to the spirit as to bowels.

Then, a foreign guest, 'a most proper Austrian gentleman' came to stay. It was his first visit to Goa and his arrival was celebrated in the grand manner — *mea casa, tua casa* — with a feast of truly impressive proportions, a groaning board long on fish, flesh and fowl but, sad to say, short indeed on essential roughage. Spurred on by three large caju fenis, a good half bottle of wine and two coffee liqueurs, the Austrian did himself generously. The next morning, a wee bit the worse for wear, perplexed by Remo's father's invitation, but keen to enter into the spirit of the occasion, off he went, with Remo, his father (the mandolin and *O Heraldo* in tow) to the communal loo. 'It may have been the dinner,' Remo recalls, 'or the unusualness of the surroundings, but the poor man was making rough weather of it.'

Indeed, the Austrian displayed every sign of growing unease. He shifted his weight from buttock to buttock, made small despairing sounds, rocked ever so slightly forward and backward on his heels. It was clear that there was to be little joy this morning. Then the porker below his thunder-box, disappointed at the lack of adequate sustenance, grunted loudly in annoyance, and decided to investigate the cause of this unusual deprivation. It poked a hairy snout up the bottom of the commode, squealed mightily, and snuffled this way and that. The Austrian glanced between his legs, swore an incomprehensible oath in a strange language, leaped off the commode, and rushed across the yard, struggling with his trousers. That morning, claiming urgent and unavoidable business, he departed, bag and baggage, for Panjim and was never heard from again. Had Remo composed a neat little ditty to honour the event, I asked, a musical ode to the Goan commode? Remo smiled. His lips are sealed. We shall never know.

Thirty years on the only porker in sight is on a buffet plate. The venue: the Regal Room at Bombay's Oberoi Inter-Continental, ever-so-correctly sanitized for an exclusive celebration, the star-spangled tenth anniversary of Aroon Purie's elitist *Bombay* magazine. The guest list: Bombay's best and brightest (if you aren't invited, you don't exist). The evening's main attraction: Remo Fernandes, Goa's supremely gifted rock star and, arguably, India's finest entertainer.

Remo is not particularly sanguine about the success of the show. He faces a motley assortment of socialites, high-flying journalists, business tycoons, film stars, celebrity authors, the mandatory flutter of catwalk models and a brace or two from the current crop of artists in vogue. Bombay's *crème de la crème* make an incestuous, blasé gathering. They are the chosen: cheek touches cheek; languid greetings fly about the place; the Scotch and water flows; the canapés are ignored, as is a group of hapless entertainers (Bombay's premier jazz ballet ensemble) which could well be invisible. Generously lubricated, the buzz of chatter rises as the evening wears on. Then, with no warning, the lights soften. There is a thunderous drum-roll and Remo appears centre-stage. He moves on the balls of his feet, with a cat's fluid grace, tracked by a single golden spotlight. His fingers race along the guitar strings in a medley of explosive chords, a superbly controlled riff. His magnificent voice – a voice for all seasons – hurls a challenge that echoes across the Regal Room, 'Are you ready for the magic?' A moment's silence. Then the city's elite, on their feet, cheering, respond with a joyful, 'yeah!' Bombay's movers and shakers will swing into the wee hours of the morning.

Remo Fernandes is India's most charismatic rock star, a rare combination of riveting stage presence and electrifying performance. Precociously talented as a child (he led his own school band), and entirely self-taught, he has pursued his vocation for forty years with the dedication of a Trappist monk and the kaleidoscopic talents of a Renaissance polymath. The press has labelled him, inelegantly, 'a one-man band' and 'a music industry', but there is no question that he is a musical phenomenon. From concept to concert, he does it all: composes the music; writes the lyrics; plays a range of instruments; arranges the score; mixes and records; designs the album cover and the advertising; and celebrates the final creation on stage and film.

It is a singular pleasure to spend an afternoon with Remo, his French wife Michele, their two young sons, Jonah and Noah, and to discover that the family honours are evenly distributed. In fine Gallic style, Michele presides over a memorable lunch: a cheese soufflé that rises triumphantly to the occasion, a roast ox tongue with a clever Provençale sauce, a fragrant prawn pulao (how does Remo keep his figure?), a salad Nicoise with impeccable credentials and as sublime a chocolate mousse as you are likely to meet this side of the Eiffel Tower. Later, over coffee and cognac in the flagstoned garden – a riotous mélange of flowering plants, a gulmohar tree, recent litters of kittens and puppies, canvas recliners to fall asleep in – Remo plays a tape from an album in progress on Mother Teresa.

His studio occupies a separate room in this lovely old Goan house (the ancestral home, sold and bought back within the week by Remo, who has an abiding love for the place and finds ingenious excuses not to move). It was here that he created the albums that were to make his name an inspirational icon to the young of all ages, wherever rock reigns in India. Drawing on the rich motherlodes of his Goan heritage, with roots in the Konkan *mando*, the Portuguese *fado* and the Indian classical tradition, taking his talent farther afield to the fertile pastures of Europe and North Africa, and, finally, fusing all of his experience and musical knowledge into personal art, expressed in original compositions of enduring virtuosity.

He is tall, slim, with the proportions and grace of a ballet dancer, and looks a good ten years younger than his age. Understated and soft-spoken in private, he performs with the kinetic energy of the early Mick Jagger, and an incandescent stage presence that will brook no authority other than its own. His audiences will have it no other way. At his favourite gig, the Haystack in Anjuna village in Goa, where, in season, the faithful gather under the stars every Friday,

Remo comes on close to midnight. This is not polite, creamy Bombay, but local, highly vocal Goa. A roar of joyful expectancy from hundreds of loyal fans greets his arrival. They are never disappointed and, within minutes, have fallen under his spell. The range, power and timbre of his voice are astonishing; more so, when one learns that he perfected the art busking in the great cities of Europe – Paris, London, Venice, Rome, Madrid – where, down and out, he literally sang for his supper. Tonight is not so much performance, as reverential communion. We have heard most of the songs before, but they are, in some wonderful way, fresh and new again. He draws on a repertoire that goes back ten years and a bit, selecting old and new favourites from a half dozen albums that have made Indian recording history.

But no bets were being laid when Remo began his long odyssey; indeed, in 1983, when he made the rounds of the established labels with his first album, *Goan Crazy*, the odds were dismal by any reckoning and he was given short shrift. 'No one,' he was told curtly by a producer who has lived to eat his words, 'wants to hear original songs in English composed by an Indian.' But hope springs eternal in the Goan psyche. Unfazed, Remo decided to go it alone. He set up a production company, Goana, in his house at Siolim. By a charitable suspension of disbelief, the recording equipment could, perhaps, have been described as archaic. The distribution network, as well, was distinctly modest: it consisted of Remo on a yellow scooter, a sight that would soon prompt wry affection the length and breadth of Goa. Goans love happy endings. *Goan Crazy* proved a runaway success. It brought Remo to national attention and, more importantly, to the discerning eye of the country's best film producers. His work for the cinema – entire scores, theme songs, orchestration for dance ensembles – was widely acclaimed.

Remo had arrived. Ten years later, with a shelf-full of national hit albums to his credit and scores of live appearances the world over, he was awarded the Grand Prix at the Dresden Festival, where, the previous year, he had won three major awards competing against the world's best from twenty countries. His latest album, *Politicians Don't Know How To Rock 'n' Roll* sold out in days and augurs well to set yet another national record. Remo would be noticeably embarrassed if I were to refer to him as a musical institution, but his career speaks for itself. He is India's leading performer at home and abroad. The year 1985 saw him at the head of a cultural troupe at the Festival of India in Hong Kong and Macao. Three years later he was invited to sing at the 'Save the Children' extravaganza in London. In Moscow, he performed before the Presidents of the USSR and India and an audience of 120,000 at the closing ceremony of the Festival of India (within the week 3,000 Muscovites bought *Bombay City*). That year, he sang at the grand finale of the Soviet Festival in New Delhi, before Rajiv Gandhi and Mikhael Gorbachov, prompting one press report to describe him as 'the most popular Russian of the evening'. On 31 December, he brought in the New Year on national television.

Yet his career has never been far from controversy. Some of the more savage of his satirical lyrics have struck to the bone: he has exposed cant, corruption and hypocrisy, causing grievous offence in high places, where the accumulated scores of years awaited settling. Opportunity came when Rajiv Gandhi visited the territory. Remo performed for him at a public function. Goa's governor, Cabinet and power elite were in highly visible attendance. Remo sang the cheeky hit, 'Hello Rajiv Gandhi' from his first album, *Goan Crazy*; Goa's top brass – not best pleased – sat in stone-faced silence. The storm broke the next day. Remo was a disgrace; his performance cheap and vulgar; Goa had been shamed. For weeks, Remo was pilloried by a section of the press and public – attacks as ugly as they were unjustified – until a certain person decided that enough was sufficient, and Remo received a crested letterhead in the mail.

It read:

Dear Remo,

We had a pleasant evening and enjoyed both your songs and all the other items in the cultural programme. So long as you are sincere in your art, I do not think you should let a little criticism in the press upset you.

With best wishes.

It was signed by the Prime Minister of India, Rajiv Gandhi.

To this day, no one knows how the letter leaked to the press on the same day Remo received it: newspapers across the country printed Rajiv Gandhi's letter with glowing editorial approval.

For Remo Fernandes, Goa's minstrel with the golden voice, ever 'sincere to his art', there would be no looking back, except, once in a while, to three thunder-boxes and a mandolin ...

****

Why We Do Not Speak
Ill of the Dead

If I grieved at the death of my friend, Rajni Patel, I was immeasurably saddened by Khushwant Singh's degrading epiphany last Sunday. From time to time, one has observed Mr Singh putting the boot into a prostrate foe (distressing but forgivable; it is not a nice world and attack is often the only possible defence). But sticking a knife into a dead body is self-inflicted mutilation, the castration of the psyche, and serves no useful purpose. Sick at heart, I read the piece. Here was a man I respect, talented, capable of true friendship and generosity, brought shamefully low by an act of blind, unthinking folly.

He begins with faint, damning praise, compliments which are not merely left-handed, but terminally palsied. We are quickly told that Rajni Patel's principles were as elastic as his loyalties; that he liked his drink and women in equal and large measure; that his colossal fund-raising efforts (the example in question: Maharashtra's Drought Relief Fund) were conducted in the environment of an exclusive and sybaritic rich men's club – the finest Scotch, Royal Salute no less, French champagne, interruptions by urgent trunk calls from a fawning Centre; that he switched political allegiance with a view to personal power and little else; that his behaviour to his previous wife was cruel to the point of heartlessness. And so, ad nauseam, on.

Mr Singh is entitled to the public expression of his opinions, no matter if these are in dubious taste, but opinions differ and there are people in all walks of life who have good reason to count Rajni Patel a good and faithful friend. Yes, we sat down together, Rajni, Bakul, my wife and I, and drank Black Label as we discussed the Nehru Memorial Centre, a cause dear to his heart. He talked of the project with intense absorption and enthusiasm, leavened by a hard-headed practicality; there was total commitment here limned by a sense of purpose and – yes, I shall use the word – reverence. I will gladly aid and abet, and drink gallons of Scotch with any man (provided he leaves the dead in peace) who can give of himself for a good cause so completely.

None of us are all of one cloth, Mr Singh; angels and demons dance on the crown of each of our countless cells, and it is worth looking carefully at the biological imperative which makes this so. Our brains are part reptile, part animal and only recently human; hence the blind, reptilian strike of the conditioned reflex, the insatiable urge for territory, sex and the other cardinal imperatives of the mammal; all perpetually at odds with the yearnings of the forebrain, true cause for sacred awe, the dimly perceived, yet deeply felt need for love and compassion, peace, harmony and the realization of self. The battle lines are drawn within each of us, while the resolution of the conflict – for a single human being or the entire race – is wholly uncertain.

Even as you or I, Mr Singh, perhaps Rajni Patel had occasion to feel emotional turmoil, shame, bitterness at shabby motives too late revealed, the heart-rending despair of conflicting personal loyalties; perhaps he had to often take the hard decision, leaving blood on the floor; certainly he made enemies, as all men do who lead successful public lives, but he made steadfast friends as well, and left behind a legacy, among others in the field of social work, which is well worth nurturing. I have written elsewhere of my own memories of Rajni Patel: 'A good man died a short while ago after a long and courageous battle with cancer ... A realist, he worked within the frailties of his fellow man, yet he held that the true and the just were inviolate. Scant weeks before his death, he flew back from London for a day (where he had been operated for nodules on the intestine) to fight a case in court, win it, and return the following morning (for further surgery). He fought the good fight till he drew his last breath. Our perception of life was enhanced by the example of his own; today, in equal measure, we are diminished by his death.'

Yet he could be silly like the rest of us.

When he equates whisky with damnation, and condemns the good fellowship and fine intentions it so often encourages, Mr Singh is being less than honest, and we both know it. It is not confusion but a holier-than-thou conceit that clouds his perception of means and ends. An attitude worth examining, rooted, as it so often is, in positions of extreme polarity. One proclaims, 'The end, no matter how noble, never justifies ignoble means.' The other holds that we have no choice but to use whatever means are to hand if the end is worth achieving. Both positions are rigid and absolute, falsely sacramental, dangerous fascist doctrines. The honest truth of the matter is that ends and means are always in delicate and critical balance, and the scales may shift, with complete moral justification, in the hand that holds them. So it is with a single life. The actions of a man's life may only be judged, in the final analysis, by his contribution to the common weal. The greatest good of the greatest number may never be measured by the compromises and venalities of the moment, and, equally, may never be used to justify great crimes. The good one does in a lifetime thus remains a matter of personal belief, judgement and decision till one dies and the carrion – and with luck, the honestly critical – take it from there.

There is a touching innocence in Mr Singh's lament, '… all our wretched politicians and journalists could say about him were cliché-ridden eulogies they spout about every celebrity when he departs …' Any student of thanatology could tell Mr Singh that the rituals for the dead over millennia, across cultures and history, correspond in essentials and are primarily honorific. Egyptian hieroglyphics, in the tombs of pharaoh and farmer alike, speak well of the departed. Cannibal rites in New Guinea praise the courage and strength of the victim even as the heart is consumed. Prehistoric symbols and artefacts discovered in cave burial sites in Northern China reveal that the living, grunt though they might, wished the best for the dead. This too, with excellent reason, is part of the biological imperative.

When Mr Singh passes on, as all of us must, what will he be remembered by? The public accusations of calculated sycophancy (but haven't we all, at some time or other, to greater or lesser degree, made obeisance to that which made us feel ashamed and ever so slightly unclean?); the cynical manipulation of soiled principles (which of us has not bent a belief to the needs of the moment?); the charge of vulgarity in the public print (the best of us have been known to break wind in places of worship); the perpetration of – Lord God forgive me! – bad prose (but then, I, too, have split infinitives with the worst of them).

No, Mr Singh, for my part I shall remember your novel, *Train to Pakistan*, a book I read when I was very young. Seriously flawed, even so it taught me to look with charity and compassion on the least of my brethren. I shall recall the hundreds of young American students to whom you made the gift beyond price, the gift of your knowledge and understanding. And your history of the Sikhs will remain, in my view, a moving, honest and proud account of the lives and times of a great people.

We do not speak ill of the dead, Mr Singh, because singularly and as a species, contrary to all of the evidence, we need passionately to believe that there is hope for the living.

****

Bombay's Busybee Seizes
the Sabbath

If Merchant and Ivory were to make a film about a gentle, sixtyish antiquarian collector of illuminated manuscripts, it would not surprise me if they asked Behram Contractor to play the part; and when, as the plot unfolds, the antiquarian settles into his study with a wicked twinkle in his eye and tosses the dust cover off an ancient Underwood typewriter, I'd know that all was well with Busybee, Contractor's nom de plume. Every day of the week in Bombay, fifty thousand of my fellow citizens and I look forward to the arrival of the *Afternoon Despatch and Courier*. With a frisson of anticipation, rarely disappointed, we turn first to the last page, last column, 'Round and About' by Busybee, and for a few moments, the burden of a life in Bombay is measurably lighter.

When the column completed twenty-five years last April, Bombay's Dynasty Club, the city's cultural heartbeat, honoured Behram Contractor by hosting an evening's celebration of the life and times of Busybee. Scripted by Bachi Karkaria, leading lights of Bombay's stage – enthusiastic volunteers all – performed with flair, ebullience and a sense of high enjoyment noticeably absent from some of their commercial offerings. An inspired collection of musical skits was created around Busybee and his characters – Bolshoi, the Russian Boxer who speaks impeccable English but has, alas, never managed to master Hindi; the preposterous (but ever engaging) multimillionaire on the twenty-first floor; Busybee's fictitious family (where, for once, life did imitate art – read on) and vignettes from a life as colourful as it has been unconventional. The show ran to packed houses for three consecutive evenings. It was a spontaneous and unprecedented tribute from a grateful city to a favourite son.

Bouquets and brickbats (he's had a fair share of both in the past thirty years) are carried lightly in the airy twentieth floor apartment on Bombay's Malabar Hill. Rarely, as his wife Farzana observes, does Behram relax at an interview, but now he takes his ease, with a Scotch to keep imposition at bay, and talks about his childhood. Distinctly unmemorable. While his performance at school did not give the faculty cause for cheer, he does recall making his presence felt by sheer invisibility. Unnoticed, unremarked, he went on to complete his Bachelor of Arts, then, rejected by journalism, he read law and, with two unwanted degrees to his name, he took off for Europe, hitch-hiking, doing odd jobs, making unlikely friends and sowing wild oats with a will – all grist to a later mill. Back home, *The Free Press Journal* gave him a break. He became a cub reporter. It was 1955 and his real education commenced in earnest. He covered crime, sports, politics, social events; he learned to raise a glad glass with the best of them in Bombay's illegal dives (a greasy-palmed prohibition was rampant); he made lifelong friends among the city's lowlife, and its more acceptable residents, and to this day, he never allows prejudice to impair good judgement. Says Shobhaa De, author and columnist, 'In a field where almost everybody's integrity is suspect, Behram commands enormous respect.'

In a few months at the *Journal*, now an established dogsbody of the fourth estate, Behram was a familiar sight – in police stations across the city (he covered the slaying of Suraiya, and the pursuit and capture of the mass murderer Rama Raghavan); in the municipal corporation, where he developed a jaundiced eye for the shenanigans of elected politicians; at football matches, beauty contests, film award nights and other silly season frivolities. His slight figure, amiable manner and a natural self effacement were quite at odds with the quality of his work – crisp, objective and accurate. He developed an uncheatable palate for good food and drink in the city's dhabas and bylanes and today writes regularly – and with scrupulous fairness – about the perils and pleasures of eating out. Reporting became, and remains, his first love, and while he had set his heart on a chief reporter's hat, he was to wait twenty-four years for the privilege.

In 1962, he was poached from the *Free Press* by *The Times of India*. Today he says ruefully of his initiation, 'I have never worked harder in my life.' He reported, edited, rewrote, interviewed and produced six miniprofiles a week, and contributed – as many other reporters did – to a column called 'Round and About' by Busybee. Each reporter was allowed his own byline. Competition for the column was fierce and, political athleticism being notably absent from his talents, Behram was shouldered out. But his column had caught the vigilant eye of Russy Karanjia, ebullient crusader for the Left and founder-editor of *Blitz*. One never says no to Russy. 'I want you to write like Art Buchwald,' Russy declared. Behram found himself bylined in the *Blitz*. The response was instant and enthusiastic if, on occasion, confused. In one of his columns, Behram conducted an imaginary conversation with S.K. Patil, the legendary Congress strongman. Patil's secretary responded with an angry letter denying the interview. Years later, when K.K. Shah, a minister in Indira Gandhi's Cabinet celebrated for his sycophancy, was axed by the lady and demoted to governor of Tamil Nadu, there to await final execution, Behram wrote a satirical column of commiseration. He received a reply which began, 'How can I thank you for your unstinted praise ...' On a happier note, he tells of Busybee's fictitious family (regarded with much affection by the column's fans), particularly the sons, Denzil and Derek – names he had appropriated from a bar owner's children he knew briefly in his early drinking days. Twenty years on, an unannounced visitor arrived at Behram's office – six feet and one hundred and seventy pounds of intimidation – smiled broadly, held out a hand and said, 'We've never met, but I'm your son Derek.'

Ranging far and wide writing for the *Blitz*, Behram perfected his style – gently satirical, deceptively simple and informed – in the lightest of brushstrokes – with 'the gift of laughter'. Says Vinod Mehta, editor of *The Pioneer*, 'There is no finer craftsman in Indian journalism.' A few critics have accused Behram of Buchwaldism, but in my considered opinion, this is untrue. Where Buchwald's prose is muscular and brash, with an eye to the quick effect and an ear cocked for the applause of the gallerier, Contractor is gentle and subtle; the man and the column are seamless; he is the way he writes and this quality more than any other has captured and held the loyalty of thousands of readers. But not, as it turned out, Russy Karanjia's. The Sino-Indian conflict had erupted and Karanjia felt the column was inappropriate for a time of war and high national purpose. The *Times* quickly took it back and, with uncharacteristic generosity, rewarded Behram with exclusivity and an extra Rs.6.80 per column!

For seventeen years the column appeared daily in the *Evening News* and, in the process, achieved that rare distinction in journalism, it became a cherished public emblem, a property so valuable to the paper's prestige and circulation that no price could be put on it. So much so, that when Behram came to leave, with not a little regret ('The *Times* had become home') and decided to take his column with him, the management called in the paper's lawyers. Should they take it to the courts? Obtain a restraining order? Wiser counsel prevailed. Legal action would only confirm publicly what every reader knew: it was Behram's column. 'I had no quarrel with the *Times*,' Behram says. He wanted to be chief reporter; at the *Times*; because of strictly observed promotion by seniority, he never would. Weeks later, over a drink at the Press Club, he said to Khalid Ansari, the publisher, half in jest, 'If you ever start an evening paper let me know.' Three months later, Khalid had worded out a proposal and *Midday* was born.

Thirty thousand Busybee loyalists shifted allegiance overnight. The fledgling paper's stars were good: a lightning strike hit the *Times* group; the *Free Press* offices caught fire. Big stories broke over the next few weeks: the Janata party lost the elections; the Congress was returned in triumph; Sanjay Gandhi died. And *Midday* – with Behram Contractor at long last chief reporter – took off like a rocket. The next few years were among the best in his life. Finally, he was able to mould to his own purpose the many elements which contribute to a good paper – content, style, design, colour and, above all, a spirited and committed young team; it was here that he first met Farzana Khan, whom he was to marry, and it was here that he was to face the first major trauma of his professional career. Irreconcilable differences (which to this day he is loath to talk about) developed between the editorial team and the management. His best efforts to heal the rift proved futile. His team resigned as one, and Behram went with them.

29 January 1985 saw Behram Contractor at fifty-five without a job, a roof over his head or a bank account to his name. Farzana Khan, who has a nice sense of timing about such things, proposed marriage. Behram, a bachelor of awesome conviction, thought it was a good idea. They were married on 31 January. A friend of a friend gave them a tiny room. 'It was a beginning of sorts,' says Behram. Fair-weather friends disappeared. Financiers who had promised all manner of things refused to answer calls. He was offered charge of the *Evening News* and said no. Then Bakul Patel, a friend of many years, introduced him to the industrialist and man-about-politics, Kamal Morarka. They met; Behram outlined his plans for an evening paper. Kamal said, 'How much?' 'Fifteen lakhs,' Behram replied. 'Done,' said Kamal, and they shook hands on it. The *Afternoon Despatch and Courier* hit the stands in March 1985, and publishing history was made.

The formal proprietor/editor relationship changed over the years to friendship and regard. When Behram developed early cataracts in both eyes (and the operations were botched in India) Kamal flew him twice to Johns Hopkins in the USA, underwrote all expenses and was there himself. The cornea transplant and cataract operations were successful. Back in Bombay – in a spanking new computerized office building, Afternoon House, bought from the paper's profits, – Behram bid farewell to his beloved Underwood and made the word processor his own in a day. His friends were unsurprised. 'Behind that sleepy exterior,' says comrade-in-arms Mario Miranda, 'there's a brilliant mind always on the go.'

He will need all the staying power he has. The new *Afternoon On Sunday* joins honourable battle with six of the best and brightest papers in the city. But I believe that Behram Contractor will prevail. Let us wish him well, with the cheering words of Chief Sitting Bull to his warriors on the eve of battle, 'May a swift wind assist your passage, and a valiant sun guide your destiny ...'

He deserves no less.

****

The Satirist

Two cows ravished in
24 hours is no laughing
matter. And a third chased
across a field, now a pale
shadow of her former self.

No Udder Love Have I ... tra-la-la!

Front page headlines in the capital. Delhi is shocked, udderly shocked, as never before. On the cocktail/political/diplomatic circuit the Crime of the Century has displaced scams, celebrity bed-hopping, ISI intrigues and Vajpayee's significant pauses. Only Maneka Gandhi seems unsurprised but, to her credit, she has not gone on record to say, 'I told you so!' Delirious with this unexpected cause macabre Delhi's press has gone bananas. 'Rapist fondled cat at age five' ... 'Capital's French poodles nervous wrecks'... 'Delhi vet invents world's first chastity belt for cows'... 'Black Cats to guard VIP farmhouse buffaloes'. And the police, for once, are preening. 'Caught the badmash with his pants down' – Commissioner Phelwan 'The Scourge' Bhatia – 'about to mount his third operation. The victim was nude. There are no words to describe the scene.'

I interviewed the rapist, under maximum security, in Tihar Jail. Daredevil reporters do not beat about the bush. We do not approach a subject stealthily, from the rear. I took the bull by the horns.

'Why,' I asked, 'did you rape the animal?'

'It wasn't rape. We liked each other. Besides, I had no udder choice. I looked for a sheep first, high and low, no luck. You might say,' – he chuckled – 'that I was on the horns of a dilemma.'

'Two cows ravished in twenty-four hours is no laughing matter. And a third chased across a field, now a pale shadow of her former self.'

'Not cows. Buffaloes. Have you had a good look at a Delhi cow recently? Skin and bones. No oomph. No glad eye. Just a sad, rheumy look. You call that a turn-on?'

'Is that any way to talk about a cow?'

'You press people never get anything right. Not cows. Buffaloes'.

'All right then, buffaloes.'

'Not any old buffaloes. Female buffaloes well into the romp and tickle age. Believe me, they need no urgin'. Wow!'

'This is impossible!'

'Nonsense. That's the problem with you presswallahs. No imagination. No vision. Did Einstein ever use the word impossible?'

I changed tack, determined to get to the bottom – oops – of the matter. 'Aren't you a bit short for a buffalo?'

'I stood on the milking stool.'

'Good God!'

'You should have seen her. Ravishing. Tossing her horns. Curling a lip. At first my intentions were pure. Just a friendly hug or two. She liked that. So did I. Then she swayed those glorious hips, rolled her wicked eyes, batted her beautiful lashes and went moooo. So I got friendlier, wouldn't you? And did she like *that*! Snorted passionately, pawed the ground, bosom heaving all over the place, swished her tail and wiggled her rear at me. That's when I lost all control. Wow!'

'Fifteen years and five off for good behaviour.'

'Worth every minute of it. And who, pray, do I misbehave with in this dump. Not even a cat about.'

The monster! Did he have any idea of the rage and confusion let loose across the land? The feminists are up in arms. A spokesperson called a press conference. 'Female buffaloes – dear, gentle creatures that they are – have been callously abused by brute male buffaloes ever since when. Bruised, battered, gored, beaten black and blue (though you'd never notice it) and forced to have sex when they aren't in the mood. Who gives milk? The female. Who brings up the babies? The female. Who ends up on a plate? The female. And now a man gets into the act! We should (getting her animals a bit confused) hang the swine!' The lady from the SPCA was a trifle more temperate. 'We are for free choice and encourage intimacy between animals and persons. Where there is true love there is no sin. We must not rush to judgement. Has a vet observed Delilah (we understand that's the buffalo's name) after the – ahem – engagement?' A vet had and was alarmed. 'Every time I tried to get close to her, she went moooo, rubbed against me, swished her tail and wiggled her most private parts. And the very sight of a male buffalo sends her into a rage.'

'Do you realize the havoc you've caused?' I said to the rapist. 'You will never be accepted in civilized society again.'

'Who cares.' His smile was beatific; his eyes shone with evangelical fervour. 'I shall retire to a sheep farm in Kulu. Lovely, fluffy sheep. No busybodies about. And baaaa sounds so much nicer than moooo ... '

Good grief. Is nothing sacred?

****

Pages From My Diary

I ask your indulgence for this entry from my diary dated 8 February 1984. It has an ill-tempered air, but there is good reason. I was at the bitter end of a frustrating ten days. Several promising leads had come to naught in my search for an acre by the sea. The season had started and the tourist invasion was on. Hordes of Bavarian butchers, morose Finns, inscrutable Japs and disapproving Brits polluted the beaches, infested the flea markets and drove prices through the roof. Good fresh fish was scarce. Branded feni had begun to appear on the shelves; it stank. Cuts of pork became meaner by the day. So did I. My perfect acre seemed more elusive than ever. In a mood of black misanthropy I made this entry:

Vile Goings-On in Goa

Tanned to a perfect crispness, the tall distinguished stranger with grey hair and an astonishingly young face lay on the sand on his stomach (discreetly on his stomach), chin propped on folded hands and observed, with infinite scorn, the low life on this most perfect of all of Goa's beaches. Caucasians of dubious pedigree, Asians of equally uncertain origin, a furtive hippie or two (this was an *expensive* beach) lay about in various stages of undress while the local beach boys frolicked in the surf and laughed behind their hands.

The stranger came to two jaundiced conclusions. Obesity rode a parabolic curve in direct proportion to affluence and race: the Germans were the largest. And you could never tell about a tan: the

Brits broiled, the Finns peeled; the Americans disappeared under lashings of sunshield and sunglasses; the Italians took off their clothes. Unwieldly Indian ladies, unhinged by hot sun and bare skin, swathed neck to ankle in chiffon sarees, huddled under thatched beach umbrellas and clutched nervously at tender coconuts.

Rage and contempt surged in the handsome stranger's Saraswat Brahmin Roman Catholic Goan heart, as he lay, mute witness to this sacrilege to the sacred soil of his ancestors. Had he not, that very morning at the crack of dawn, in the athletic spirit of his forefathers, jogged five miles down the beach, flying, Hermes-like, past the sinister tents of the Arab sheikh, showing a pair of clean heels to the Nepalese trinket vendors, ignoring the siren calls of the Rajasthani massage ladies; a fleeting, golden figure, lithe as a panther, whom even the hippies rose from their stupor to regard with amazement and awe? Had he not then breakfasted lightly on *poi* and *mangada* and fresh coconut mint chutney (avoiding the massive ingestion of cholesterol, fatty lipids and starch with which the Caucasians so murderously began their day) and then swum a quarter mile out to sea to the place where the dolphins celebrated the music and laughter of the spheres?

Did these goose-pale cretins, these crass despoilers of the holy and the good, these *foreigners* know the sublime and subtle difference between palm and caju feni? Were they aware how, from the ferocious genius of the great Portuguese General Alfonso de Alburquerque, the cavorting centuries had wrought marvellous and merry good? When they offered vacuous applause to the liquid syllables and lilting strains of the mando, did they understand that here were songs of passion and loss, tales of mischief and mortality, all of the yearnings of a people, risen to art, given voice in melodic note and exquisite phrase? And why did they insist, the nerds, on drinking tasteless bottled water, when mineral rich well water lay instantly to hand; water, moreover, which the good earth had purified over countless millennia through layer upon layer of porous volcanic rock? Was nothing sacred?

The stranger had begun his crusade the evening before. The sky glowed a pale, opalescent rose as the sun set vaingloriously behind the palms. He lay in a hammock in the garden of his cottage in the

Taj Holiday Village. Strong caju feni (long and lovingly aged, out of a plain amber bottle roughly corked) stirred the cockles of his immortal soul, while Don Quixote's exalted baritone (from the tape deck in the bedroom) urged him to dream the impossible dream and fight the unbeatable foe. He was ready for anything (that's the way it is with good caju) except, perhaps, the appearance of an ugly, fat little man with an apoplectic complexion and angry porcine blue eyes who stomped out of the neighbouring villa and commanded, 'You vill put off the radio at vunce!'

An unholy glee filled the stranger's heart. 'No spika da Ingleesh,' he said with his very best Sicilian accent. The fat man went purple. 'The radio you vill shut vitout delay,' he screamed. How could one let Quixote down? The stranger shrugged expressively, smiled the gentle, sardonic smile of Marcello Mastrioanni, raised his hands in a gesture of sheer incomprehension. The fat man charged off in the general direction of Authority and tripped over an ornamental bush. 'I vill complain to the direktor,' the words wafted back forlornly on the scented twilight air.

Now the stranger watched with keen loathing as the Nordic Curse, a family of four Scandinavians, descended on the beach. The man carried an inflatable boat in a neat package in one hand; his wife, overflowing out of a bikini two sizes too small, flounced at his side with a furled sail; two small children carried oars and scowled. The Goan lifeguards, wondrously enamoured of anything which floated, rushed as one to admire, aid, abet, assemble, set sail!

The Viking snarled. The lifeguards, perplexed (a snarl on Goan soil? Unthinkable!) backed off. The Nordic Curse went into a huddle, inflated the boat, fixed the oars, unfurled and positioned the sail. The lifeguards, intrigued, approached again and were shooed off like so many flies. The boat was heaved towards the surf. The children tumbled in; the wife, with a wholly unnecessary writhing of buttocks, followed suit. The man began his Sly Stallone act as he did every morning. With a slow, deliberate rippling of shoulders, arms and back, he began to hoist himself aboard. As the drama unfolded, the distinguished stranger's eyes went first brooding and distant, then savagely arctic, then strange and trancelike. A low incantation could be heard from his whispering lips; it sounded oddly like, 'This boat vill capsize at vunce!' And, as if on cue, an empathic wave tipped the boat end over end, depositing the Nordic Curse hurtfully on an unforgiving ocean floor.

That night, after a dinner at St Anthony's Bar which magnificently orchestrated content, texture and taste, replete and in bed, he heard the village band make ancient music by the poolside dance floor. Sedate foxtrots pursued somnolent waltzes. Rarely did a daring tango disturb the rustling palms. Music to be put restfully to sleep by. Then he heard loud Italian voices raised in boisterous protest, challenge, encouragement. Bernado and His Jolly Boys, five ancient parties with a hundred and fifty years between them, began to belt out acid rock with a quavering, geriatric air. Somebody turned the amp up full strength and his villa quivered in protest. Quietly, the stranger rose, opened a drawer, picked up a pair of scissors. Clad in pyjamas, firm resolution in every stride, he walked out of his villa, around the pool, across the dance floor, pulled the amp's plug out of the power socket and snipped the plug off the wire. A quick, disdainful flip of the wrist and the plug sailed out into the night. Turning on his heel, he returned with dignity to his cottage, and slept the sleep of the just and the innocent.

But Goa will not long allow hubris, least of all among Saraswat Brahmin Roman Catholic Goans. The stranger was shortly to have his troubles. Female (!) buffaloes would chase him indecorously across a ploughed field as he attempted a shortcut to the hippie flea market at Anjuna, while the crowds took time off to cheer the buffaloes on. An unfriendly cat with anti-literary tendencies would appear from nowhere, like a disembodied and malicious Cheshire, each time he sat at the portable, and hiss baleful insults, until a nervous muse fluttered off to distant pastures. And – unkindest cut of all – one Black Monday morning the petrol pump attendant at the Calangute service station, addressed him, with the greatest respect, as 'Uncle!' Defeated, the stranger let it pass. The dolt could live to tell the tale ...

****

My Medical Misadventures

A journalist has written a book about the long dying of her husband. But *Heart Sounds* by Martha Weinman Lear, is not really about agony and death, though there is all of that; it is not even about medical ineptitude and callousness; it is, finally, about the courage of a singular man, who celebrates every minute of his life till the last moment of his death. The set-piece opening describes his heart attack in New York. He is a doctor and knows precisely what is happening. His chest is in a tightening vice. He calls an emergency number and is plunged into a black hell worthy of Kafka. 'I am having a heart attack. My doctor's name is ... I am too weak to look up his number. Please call him.' 'Sorry. I can't call your doctor.' 'But I need him.' 'Well, I'm sorry, this is strictly an emergency service.' 'This *is* an emergency. A heart attack.' 'I can't call your doctor' – reproachfully – 'we don't do that.' Later, injected intravenously – and incorrectly – he develops gangrene. During one of several operations, the anesthetist arrives late and fouls up; his brain, deprived of oxygen, is partially damaged. And so on ... a gruesome litany, but in my experience, par for the course.

Flat on the back, gazing up at Klieg lights while men in white masks approach your supine form with sharp knives is not a situation conducive to peace of mind. I have been laid thus, unfortunately horizontal, on four occasions in my life. It is not something one gets used to, but there is a saving grace. Once they put the needle into your arm, all is blessed oblivion till you wake up, like I did one hapless morning after they had opened the jaw and scraped the bone, to find a giggling couple – an intern and a nurse – jabbing a hypodermic into the soft flesh of my inner elbow with much merriment. The nurse simpered. In went the needle, out again, more blood. The intern said laughingly, 'No veins.' Hilarious. 'Try the back of the hand, sir,' and she gave him a Look. Even in my state of terminal fear and loathing, I knew that look for what it was: a stinking invitation to sex. Beasts. 'Use a torniquet,' I snarled, 'or get out of here.' And this is one of our finest hospitals, much touted for the excellence of its equipment and the qualifications of its staff. In the event, when my surgeon made his rounds, and I told him what had happened, all hell broke loose. The blood test wasn't meant for me, but for the pregnant lady with measles next door. Besotted sex fiends, they hadn't even noticed I was the wrong shape.

You might say that earlier events had led up to this day. At the age of twelve, after a party at school where I had pigged excessively, I was laid low with a violent tummy ache. For three days and nights I writhed in bed, while small, malevolent demons laid waste to my insides with red hot pokers. The local quack, Prince of the Instant Diagnosis, said, 'Indigestion,' and plied me with vile purple potions. At midnight on the third day, my appendix ruptured. I vaguely remembered being injected and in a pleasant morphine haze wheeled into an operating theatre. Klieg lights and the next thing I knew, I was awake in bed, my legs wide apart, starkers! A veritable dragon of a nurse ministered to my tenderest parts alternately with ice cold and very hot water. 'You're a good little boy,' she crooned, 'come now, do pee-wee.' Hot. Cold. 'The doctor says you must do pee-wee.' Hot. Cold. Whew! 'DO PEE-WEE!' whereupon she waved a catheter before my nose and threatened instant abominations, unless I did. Did I ever do pee-wee!

Ten years later I was a young adult well on the way to acute hypochondria. When my family physician diagnosed the intermittent pains in my chest in his usual laconic manner, 'Gas,' did I take this fine and intelligent man's word for it? Not on your nelly. Before you could say ischaemia heart disease, there I was in my underwear, wired fore and aft to a machine, my life force reduced to a squiggle on a graph, being keenly observed by a heart specialist while I climbed rapidly up and down a small staircase with three rungs. There is one thing you must clearly understand about a specialist: you exist only as his specialty: I was a Heart. In due course, I was to become a Liver and a pair of Retinas, but that's another story. My heart had an inverted T wave and this was bad news. In fact, said the specialist morosely, it was a symptom of – you've guessed it – ischaemia. Scared witless, my chest pains immediately ceased. I spent a nervous year checking my pulse stealthily a dozen times or so each day until I discovered the Second Opinion. 'Your heart,' he said, 'is as healthy as my own.' So there I was, with two equally eminent men of medicine telling me violently contradictory things. Back I went to the loyal old family retainer who took one look at the cardiogram and snorted. 'Positional', he said. 'Lots of healthy people have that T wave. Go home.'

Now if I'd only consulted him when the Eminent Surgeon said my retinas needed repairing! He spoke casually about laser beams and liquid nitrogen, heat sealing and permanent silicon implants. I am now an Eyeball, I reflected, once more under those awful Klieg lights. The anesthetist was delayed. No one knew why or appeared particularly surprised. The Eminent Surgeon was chatting up my wife over coffee in his office next door. Merry laughter. The laser gun was straight out of *Star Wars* and felt just as lethal as the first of the three hundred laser welds imploded in white hot silence in my head. I survived the experience. Six months later he wanted to do it again but I'd wised up. Off to London where one of the world's leading retinal surgeons said to me, 'Your retinas are as good as mine.' Now where had I heard that before?

Yet, in the dark hour before the dawn, a gloomy scenario persists: I'm under those damn Klieg lights again, laid open from clavicle to gonads. Two gowned and masked figures peer into my innards. First masked figure, irritably, 'Where's that bloody scalpel?' Second masked figure, 'Must you make bad puns at a time like this. Look behind the lower intestine, you twit!'

Where are you, Hippocrates, when we need you most?

****

Super Pseud

'I am plunged in despair,' I say to the Editor, 'lost in the long cafard of doing nothing well. Grappling with the dark night of the soul. My head hurts. It is raining and my feet are wet. The four horsemen prance in the wings, waiting to pounce at the splitting of the smallest of infinitives. Apocalypse when?'

'You'll live, babykins. Pseuds. Monday.'

'Right on, ma'am!'

When did I meet my first, genuine, prime, pseud-on-the-hoof? Memory takes wing. I am eighteen and enthralled by the miracle of words. I have discovered the Holy Trinity. 'I grow old, I grow old, I shall wear the bottoms of my trousers rolled.' Your words honour the firmament Mr Eliot and mermaids shall sing your praises, in wondrous hosannahs forever. 'Lay your sleeping head, my love, human on my faithless arm.' Auden, Auden ... would I remember my first love, Rebecca, without your lullaby to sift the skeins of memory? I swagger drunkenly on dim rooftops, giving praise to Dylan Thomas, preaching valiant mortality to the stars, 'Do not go gentle into that good night ... rage, rage against the dying of the light.'

I tremble at the awesome power of words. 'I am the resurrection and the life.' In wonder I walk the volcanic landscapes of the Old Testament. 'And the word was made flesh and dwelt amongst us.' I live with a single consuming passion: words and their meanings. The joy and terror as they whisper in my mind, informed with a will, a way of their own, impervious to coercion or entreaty, illusive as will-o'-the-wisps, yet, with affection and care and cozening, with patience and purpose, capable of comfort, friendship even, of compassion, tenderness, strength, or rousing symphonies of power and glory.

My soul is captive to their siren call. I will work with words all the days of my years, through the seasons of my life.

But at eighteen, in crisis, they elude me. I cannot find the words which may earn me a living. I labour long and mightily at a copywriter's test and the words flee in pity and shame, immortal words, never to be harnessed to the cause of soap or toilet paper. The pseud runs a languid eye over my pages of typescript and lets them slip through his fingers to settle forlornly on the table top.

'My dear boy,' he says, 'you will never make it in the advertising business.'

I am young, hungry, violent and jobless these three years. I have rampaged out of Byculla with blood in my mouth and fluttering, mindless terror in my heart. 'I want to write more than anything else in the world,' I say, and this man, known and loved in all the land, slams both hands palm down on the table, rises, spins on his heel, strides to the picture window, hands clasped now behind a rigid back, the curls on the nape of his leonine head quivering with barely restrained rage. (Caesar about to pass praetorian judgement!) Is he? – I am ready to die – yes he is. The imperial pronoun is his birthright: he whirls, points a finger at me, says, 'To us, you have a slight talent, nothing more, untidy, indisciplined – where's the word – spotty, yes, spotty.' He seems pleased and I sense reprieve, perhaps a turn of luck. Do I have the good sense to keep a humble silence? Of course not. I am a very young eighteen, awkward as a colt, and I stumble. 'I must work,' I say, 'we need the money at home.'

The furies are let loose. His wrath is biblical. The room is filled with thunder. I am struck dumb by lightning. 'We are not concerned with the coy bud in your bosom striving to burst into literary flower, and if by this remission a great Indian novelist shrivels, so to say, in embryo, we shall doubtless see our way to living with the guilt. And your idiot siblings are of less than burning importance to the industry.

'We are in a tough, brutal, savagely competitive business. The weakest go to the wall. Frail, creative spirits perish by the wayside, as they richly deserve to, in droves!'

Oh, how he r-r-rolled his 'R's'. The vowels slid about his tongue with oiled, orotund ease. The consonants were clipped, edged, attacked! The rhetoric leavened ever so subtly by soft counterpoint, as when, scalpel at my jugular, he sliced down lightly, flirtatiously, 'You juvenile dilettante.'

I did not know it then, being lobotomized for the duration, but I had just lived through an encounter with Super Pseud. He was, and is, essentially a harmless person and meant not a word of what he said. Like all pseuds he could never have enough of the sound of his own voice. And in the event, he gave me wary, guarded introductions which got me into the advertising business, happy hunting ground for pseuds of all persuasion.

How do you know one when you meet one? Watch out for the jargon.

'We create a matrix of polylingual communications beamed strategically at segmented urban demographic groups, mounted in multimedia modalities of mixed verbal, visual and audio characteristics.' This is what he means: he makes ads in English, gets them translated into Indian languages, puts them in newspapers, the cinema and on the radio, and suspects (vaguely) that he knows whom he's talking to. But do they understand what he's trying to say? What's more to the point, does he? One has the sneaky feeling that he does not stay up nights, tossing restlessly about, grappling with the anguish.

The advertising pseud never confuses content with form. 'There you are,' he proceeds, holding up a square of drawing paper on which words are scribbled on, over, or under a picture, 'isn't that a fine tension we've managed between the balance of visual and verbal forces. The weightages are exact, precise, yet dynamic and involving. The eye is drawn immediately to the centre of things, moves in a clockwise direction and lingers finally on the brand name. And between you and me' – the client is beginning to acquire a glazed look in the eye – 'we spent a good three man hours on the typography. What do you think?'

The client wakes up.

'Well,' he says, 'I like the girl, she's nice, but will she sell my boilers?'

Alas, the advertising business produces only common-or-garden type pseuds, woefully bereft of subtlety, the keener forms of intelligence, or the mannered pretensions to be found in the groves of academe, the ripe night soil of contemporary journalism or the dust-and-blood floorboards of the 'professional' theatre.

You ain't seen nuthin' yet, kids.

The academic pseud may, in the sexist fashion of the day, represent the wrong gender, but having said that (Out, damned difference!) all bets are off. She is not merely liberated (a slim volume of published verse or prose may tell of grand passions meanly requited) but looks to blood and war at the drop of the first offensive participle. She seeks out another literary pseud to feud with and they both make the public print with lively exchanges like these:

She: 'I would never ever make invidious comparisons between Virginia Woolf and Sylvia Plath, because I am not that sort of mean-spirited critic. A critic's role is to bring to bear on criticism, a body of compassionate understanding and knowledge which illuminates, informs, enhances, emancipates and makes free. And if he dares put his foul pen to print once more, I'll castrate the bloody sod!'

He: 'And what about Waugh, Auberon I mean, and Greene and that darling man, Forster. Oh dear, I'm getting all my dates confused. And isn't she an awfully violent person wouldn't you say?'

Ho hum.

In the fourth estate pseuds must work their way up, learning to shed in the process of elevation to the think-piece on the edit pages, all originality, keenness, wit, irreverence and style. This takes a quarter of a century and success then is marked by invitations to consular parties, sponsored trips abroad, participation in political symposia and host-playing to visiting firemen of Caucasian and liberal bent who drink Bisleri or nothing, and Decide On India's Future in three clear weeks of five-star insulation.

Small wonder that our pseud tends to write columns which begin, 'We made a moist farewell, Bernard Levin and I, he to fly to London, I to Riyadh. We agreed in a last-minute exchange on the question of Asian immigrants in England, that there were two sides to every problem. I must say that the Saudi Arabian Airline does you proud in the manner of victuals, though I (and the animated German blonde sitting at my side) could have done with a spot of the stuff that cheers. Dashed off two letters on the plane, the first accepting (ghastly chore) the Kingsley Memorial Lecture at Harvard, the second to my old friend Kosygin in Moscow. Yes, I would love to spend two weeks in his Black Sea dacha … Arrived in sweltering 45-degree heat (the Punjab in July!) and was met by my old college chum Ismael (how time flies) now the Saudi Arabian foreign minister, in an air-conditioned Rolls. He said I was to meet the King that evening and the next morning, in the strictest of secrecy of course, Idi Amin's wives …'

This will never do. I must get in on the act. Watch out for further announcements of my next great play, '*Nine Pseuds In Search Of A Character*.' There should be no casting problems.

****

The Reluctant Traveller

Now why can't the English
learn from the French?
This wonderfully tolerant
and laconic race is given to
immediate and justifiable
rage only when confronted
by bad food or bad French.

Destinations

I am off to London on Sunday. The flight attendants will pamper me no end. I shall eat and drink more than is good for me, watch a couple of films I've seen before thanks to our enterprising pirating industry and be bored out of my mind for nine long hours. Who said getting there was more fun than arriving?

Perhaps I shall while away the idle hour remembering livelier journeys and more errant destinations. For starters: getting lost is one of the most intriguing ways of getting there, as I discovered at the tender age of sixteen. Rucksacked, uniformed, tent backpacked and scared witless, I had embarked on the boy scout's equivalent of the rite of passage into manhood – the King's Scout Badge. In order to be awarded this emblem of power and glory on the sleeve of my uniform I was required to camp alone for a fortnight on an island in the middle of a river in the wilderness of the Western Ghats with the bare minimum of survival equipment: a single box of matches, small, measured quantities of dal, rice, tea, sugar, beans and spices, a fishing rod and a series of exercises I had to perform and account for in a diary. A local yokel would spy on me, unseen and unheard, and report flagrant breaches of the code of honour such as stealthy forays into the nearest village market for a chicken or two, fudging on my tests and other transgressions. This Spartan fortnight was kick-started by a fifteen-mile hike from the nearest village to Vasind Island.

Three hours later and the spirit of high derring-do had sunk with the setting sun. Woe was upon me. In near darkness I tramped over hill and dale, along endless ravines, through scrub and thicket and finally, sore at both extremities, laid my rear end on top of a hillock.

I had lost my island!

A village lad appeared like a genie. He was hugely amused at my state of imminent collapse.

'Where,' I asked, murder in my heart, 'is Vasind?'

'You are sitting on it.'

'But Vasind is an island.'

'This is an island.'

'Where is the river?'

'The river,' he said chuckling, 'has dried up. Any fool can see that.' Getting there had been fraught but I had arrived.

Six months on a Japanese freighter and I very nearly didn't. It was Westward Ho at eighteen and I had a small problem. I was, as usual, flat broke. But with the ingenuity for which I am now renowned I beat the odds by signing on as a deckhand on a Mitsui tramp steamer. Two weeks of healthy sea air and high living and I would be in Genoa with a pocketful of loot and all of Europe mine to command. Alas, and for good measure, alack. Six months on board and I understood why the ship was called a tramp and why the Japanese were destined to rule the world.

We darted about all over the southern Mediterranean. A cargo of limes in Limassol? Off we'd go. Olives by the ton in Messina? Here we come. Dried fish in Haifa? What's a little stink among friends. The captain drove us as if there were no tomorrow. I put in a twelve-hour working day washing decks, subsisting on raw fish and trying to avoid grievous injury dodging golf balls attached to long rubber bands which the officers off duty kept whacking all over the deck practising their tee shots. Small wonder then that I squandered my earnings on wassail and revelry at every port of call with not a thought for the future until I found myself in Genoa bleary-eyed but unbowed and – surprise, surprise – stony broke once more.

At least I had arrived in one piece.

Halfway between Tiracol Fort and Arambol beach in Goa no bookie would have given odds on my survival. I discovered Arambol well before the hippies did in the early Sixties when, like the Holy

Grail, it was still part of Goan myth and legend. A magical place far, far to the north, where a crescent of virgin beach was flanked by pristine ocean and sparkling freshwater lake fed by a jungle waterfall. No one bothered to explain that our odyssey would begin at the ruins of Tiracol Fort and a two-hour hike along a 300-foot high cliff on a primitive track known only to mountain goats and an intrepid fisherman or two, one of whom, palm crossed with gold, agreed to be our guide.

I had my jeans rolled up to the knees.

'Put pants down,' he ordered.

I did so.

'Bottoms into your socks.'

'Yes sir.'

I had learned the hard way never to argue with a fisherman. But when he began to cut a three-foot length of bamboo and fashion it with a wicked-looking knife into a club, hefted this in his right hand and made vicious lunges at an imaginary attacker a foot above ground, goosebumps invaded my lower spine but still the penny didn't drop. Half-way up the cliff face with a sheer 100-foot precipice on one side and smooth rock rising as far as I could see on my right, all was made slitheringly clear. A cobra lay coiled before us, head raised, but hood well in, hissing in a friendly sort of way.

'He no bite,' the fisherman said confidently, 'he never seen peoples before.'

'How are you going to get him out of the way?'

'No problem.' And he beat the ground vigorously with the bamboo club. A trifle disappointed at such barbaric behaviour, the cobra slid off leisurely into a bush and we were on our way. Virgin territory indeed! We were forced to give passage to hunting mongooses, leap lithely over scorpions the size of small crabs, risk flailing destruction at every blind turning of the cliff. Mountain goats sneered at us. Fat Russell's vipers, sunning themselves on rock ledges, couldn't be bothered to turn their heads. Nesting hawks screeched indignantly at this violation of their turf. And when at long last the ravishing crescent of Arambol lay at our feet, all joy fled at a new and terrible thought: *we would have to go back the way we came*.

Thank heaven's for later mercies. I would never have to go back again on the *Vietnam*, the cheapest sea passage from Marseilles to Mumbai. Expectation ran high. French food; French wines; French blondes! Oo la la! In the event I found myself incarcerated in the nearest thing to a cattle train on waves. Two hundred and fifty Punjabi and Sikh labourers from the textile bucket-shops of Manchester were my travelling companions. Hammocks were slung along steel pipes in a hold below deck converted to dormitory, dining room and overflowing toilet. Medievally, we were locked and barred in and forbidden to mingle with the aristocracy in cabins. I occupied a space three feet by six, nine feet mid-air accessed by ladder, with Sikh and Punjabi top, bottom, left and right of me. Pungently aromatic sons of the soil. Simmering at such unholy treatment, but rebellion was laid soporifically low by heroic quantities of cheap Algerian red wine. Free. As much as we could drink. A Machiavellian ploy on the part of the ship owners to keep us drunkenly oblivious to the slop we were fed, the dungeon we inhabited and the richly overflowing toilet facilities. I evacuated slushily, hardly ate and bathed not at all. A fortnight later I tumbled on to Princes Dock in Bombay, offloaded like so much cargo and in urgent need of tender, loving care.

Wiser by several decades, I have now devised a foolproof method of travel and arrival. I take a map of the world with India dead centre and draw radiating spokes to all points of the compass. I take a pencil, close my eyes and silently recite, 'Tic, tac, toe, here I go …' And if I end up on the back of a yak in darkest Mongolia, so be it!

****

The World as an Oyster

Well, well, well ... what have we here? Jiggs Kalra yet. Tripping the culinary light fantastic at the World Gourmet Summit in Singapore last summer; dazzling ritzy jet-setters at a gourmet festival in St Moritz this winter, with a brace of Indian whiz-kid chefs in attendance, an overflowing pan-Indian cornucopia of good things, and corporate sponsor Britannia India cheering them on in the wings. What's cooking? Very simply –and delightfully – the globalization of the world's cuisines. Making potential international gourmets of us all.

When I was young, foolish and opinionated above my status about the pleasures of the table, I was invited to a private dinner at the Taj in Mumbai where Paul Bocuse, the legendary creator of the original nouvelle cuisine (as opposed to the bathetic offerings which have since sullied its good name) had been flown in from Paris to celebrate his skills. This was in the mid-eighties, well before the globetrotting Master Chef became a familiar sight at five-star food festivals in India. After a meal of sublimely orchestrated tastes and textures, Bocuse made a modest speech where, among other wise things, he foresaw a not-so-distant future when all of the world's great cuisines, perfectly rendered, would be on offer wherever in the world you happened to be.

Happy prophecy splendidly fulfilled as I discovered last year on a round-the-world trip with a week in Disneyland (we all have our crosses to bear!) specially promised to our daughter Radhika. Loins girth, upper lip stiff as a board I braced myself for horrors beyond the pale, particularly in the matter of food and drink. Unsympathetic friends had, with great good cheer, brought to my attention the perils of an unrelieved diet of Big Macs, hot dogs, fries and Coke. With Kentucky fried chicken nuggets as the peak culinary experience. And then – will wonders ever cease? – at the Portobello Yacht Club on Pleasure Island, after a thirsty wait in a serpentine queue (one and a half hours, mere minutes by Disney time) I sat at a real dining table, with real china, real crystal, real silver, and ate a really magnificent North Italian meal with an Orvieto Classic which lived up to the last drop of its golden promise. From the proscuitto and melon starter, the deep-fried calamari, the knuckle of braised veal in a mushroom and cheese sauce, to the last morsel of tiramisu, I wallowed in the effortless perfection you rarely encounter outside Milan.

And as I travelled west, across the Pacific, through South East Asia, with stopovers in my favourite watering holes in Europe before that, I discovered that Paul Bocuse's gentle prophecy had been realized beyond all my expectations. Good food that not merely made a transcendental leap across national boundaries, but cross-fertilization and fusion – French/Thai, Tex/Mex, Californian nouvelle cuisine – had (with the rare disaster) brought a triumphant new dimension to gastronomy's well-being. I made memorable meals in the unlikeliest of places. A Brazilian fejoada in New York's Union Square as good as anything I have eaten in Rio; Greek – an aubergine tarato and savoury mince dolmas – in San Francisco; elegant, ritualized Japanese at Suntory, Regent Street, London where the sashimi did not quite frolic on the plate but it was a near thing; the perfect Texas panhandle T-bone steak with corn fritters in Hong Kong; in Monmartre olde worlde Louisiana bayou Cajun – chargrilled monkfish, ribs and red-eye beans; and in Cologne of all places, that bastion of the Bavarian sausage sold and consumed by the quarter, half and *full* metre, I ate a magnificent Thai meal where all the other tables were occupied by very large Germans doing what they do best – demolishing very large portions of everything in sight as though there were no tomorrow.

Speciality restaurants, like butterflies, lead brief if colourful lives. Youth in the restaurant business means precisely what it means elsewhere – freshness, surprise, vitality, passion. And brevity. Age withers and stales. And old age (with, it must be said, some grand exceptions) seems to be inversely proportionate to the diminishing quality of the food. Thus the hoariest of Indian restaurants in Paris, London, New York, Tokyo and Hong Kong are, in my seriously considered view, terminally geriatric and best avoided. When abroad if I want to be perfectly certain of a good meal with a decent wine at a reasonable price, I eat where the locals eat, seek true ethnicity above all, and am rarely disappointed. In those cities with large foreign communities, I break the rule, eat en famille so to say, and burp with joy.

At Pacific Heights in Hong Kong, the Swire empire's skyscraper testament to good old Scottish greed and chutzpah, is mightily redeemed by an overwhelming Chinese eatery the size of a small railway station and just a wee bit less noisy. Here the locals (upmarket executives; svelte lady secretaries; prosperous, beady-eyed money-bags; bored, exquisitely slant-eyed wives; dangerous, exquisitely slit-eyed black-belters; and not a tourist in sight) queue hungrily for a table. Five hundred people eat at a time. Two covers at lunch and dinner. Two thousand meals a day. Take your pick from Cantonese, Szechuan, Hunan – all as authentic as they sound. Infinitely more challenging and soul-satisfying than the five-star clip joints where, at a Ming Emperor's banquet you end up hungrier than a slave on the Great Wall of China and poorer by a year's income. The seafood at Pacific Heights is to pray for in future reincarnations and all else is equally distinguished.

Half a planet away on the shores of Zurich's lake, I wandered from Chagall's stained glass windows in an ancient church to a gardened square just behind it. At the far end a Swiss chalet rose, tier upon tier, with window boxes at every level, overflowing with a profusion of spring flowers. An original Swiss guild house. No tourists. No credit cards. Swiss eating Swiss. Fat-to-bursting fresh asparagus steamed, served with a perfect vinaigrette. Sautéed veal in freshly churned butter in a delicately seasoned cheese sauce to which a dash of schnapps had been added at the end of the cooking to bring out the flavours. A salad so fresh it did a little dance on the table. You mix your own dressing if you wish. And Luxemborgis for dessert, those slight, remarkable miracles of meringue, fresh cream and honest-to-goodness strawberry or almond or chocolate or crushed, honeyed, nut fillings. Bliss. Next stop Paris. More bliss!

What can one say about France and food? The ultimate definitive statement? Just this perhaps: that the Creator cast a benevolent eye on the place and the people and bestowed on them an immortal blessing. 'Let there be great nosh in this fair and fruitful land.' And lo and behold! The baguette was born. And ripe Camembert, gold medal foie gras, grand cru Chablis, that rousing fanfare to the fowl, coq-au-vin, bouillabaisse to make strong men weak in the knees, and a patisserie tradition which never ceases to delight in its inventiveness and charm. For my money nowhere are these virtues in such splendid evidence than at Taillevent, the Parisian restaurant where eating well is a fine art. Holy Grail to its patrons these many years. Once you've made a meal of the seafood sausage (lobster, crayfish, pike, truffles) with an authoritative white Burgundy for company, and end your meal with the marquise au chocolate with pistachio cream, you too will join the ranks of the fervently converted.

Ever since I backpacked across Europe in my teens, London has been home away from home. Eighteen, down and out in darkest Clapham, I lived on fish and chips (don't sneer. One could do worse) from a fishmonger's stall. Ploughman's sandwiches. Shepherd's pie. And an infinity of half-pints of bitter. Fortunately for me, better times lay ahead. In no other world capital has the globalization of food made such a salutary impact. My culinary rite of passage in London begins with that most welcome of first rituals, lunch at Senor Sachi at Knightsbridge. Here the best Frascati outside Rome (Colli di Catone '79) offers the perfect foil to the stuffed peppers au gratin, the veal rolls encased with bacon, almonds, suntanas, Parmesan, parsley with a thickly reduced red wine sauce, the mussels baked with herbs, pecorino and crumbs. A festival of fine Italian food. Don't be surprised if, at dinner's end, your waiter bursts into song, an aria perhaps, from *La Bohème*. There will be good reason for celebration.

Unseemly emotional displays are not on offer at those most British of establishments, Alfred at Shaftesbury Avenue and the Tate Gallery restaurant. Just the best of British nosh, with a touch of the modern. I have eaten very well indeed at both, though if asked to make a hard choice, it would have to be Alfred. All the good old stand-bys are at hand – steak-and-kidney pie, roast beef with Yorkshire pudding, toad-in-the-hole – but in lovingly recreated avatars. With imaginative forays into brave new territory: black pudding and bacon, rabbit ragout with caramelized baby carrots, scallops in beer batter. And top marks for the desserts. Full-bodied British and you better believe it! British cuisine no longer hangs its head in apology. The flag flies proud and high over a heady renaissance and if I find the wine lists a bit thin after France, nobody else carps. So there you are.

No such caveats in the home of the brave and the land of the free-range steer. Nothing in New York succeeds like excess. If wine lists weigh you down and menus call for muscle, portions are apparently based on the daunting premise: eat while you may, life is short. Most often quality falls victim to quantity. But diligence and perseverance pay rich dividends here as elsewhere. Five years ago I discovered the Union Square Café, a modest somewhat misleading nom de plume for one of New York's finest and most consistently excellent eateries. Chef Michael Romano's Italian ancestry is conspicuous by its absence from the American-Eclectic menu. New Wave American if you wish. Emphatic flavours which do not overwhelm. The freshest of ingredients (corn-fed, free-range poultry; genuine wild rice and mushrooms; organic salads which you can actually taste; wild salmon, fresh Maine lobster and oysters flown in on the very day) find their place in the culinary sun in Romano's deft, beguiling hands. But you wait and pay for the pleasure. Tables are booked weeks ahead and fifty dollars per person for three courses is the bare minimum.

I save.

Unless I'm being entertained by Nari Hira who treated me, my wife, daughter and a gathering of affectionate colleagues to a real Ming Emperor's banquet in one of those magnificent Chinese restaurants in New York where the sheer brilliance of the pepper and five-spice lobster, the Peking duck, the steamed suimai, the lotus root, black mushroom and crabmeat soup promise a future which all of our fortune cookies confirmed: 'Travel on your stomach. It is good for the soul.'

But my heart still belongs to Paris.

Bon appétit!

****

The Unfair Isles

Be warned. A three-week holiday in the Fair Isles is likely to be a grim and hurtful experience, unless you follow the stern motto of my boy scout days, 'Be Prepared' to the letter. I hadn't travelled to England for a while and was woefully unready.

'I should have gone on a diet,' was the first thought that came alarmingly to mind as I was confronted by the Heathrow Obstacle Course (they never tell you about this in the British Airways advertisements): mile upon mile of freezing co-riders: life and limb threatened at every turn by unstable walkways and vertiginous escalators designed for disaster; dour, cold-eyed Immigration and Customs officials who regard you with expressions that clearly imply it would have been better for everyone if you had stayed at home; free-for-alls over the luggage trolleys (why oh why was the wife allowed to con you into taking five suitcases) from which you emerge bloody, bowed and trolleyless, prove, beyond a shadow of doubt, that you will always remain a mildly developing Asian.

When, eventually, all drooping six feet and one hundred and eighty-three pounds of you – even in the kindest of lights, unevenly distributed – together with one wife, one child in high spirits (adventure!), four handbags and five suitcases, not counting the crate of mangoes, are deposited by a heartless porter who has fled with five pounds (do not, I implore you, convert this into rupees), in sub-zero temperature, in an arctic gale, on a deserted pavement, where nobody has been able to find a taxi in living memory ... take heart, your holiday has begun.

Be Prepared, indeed. With the wisdom of sore experience, I know what I shall do before my next trip. Run a mile every morning, followed by an hour of weight training (all those cases); make my peace with grilled fish and boiled vegetables, turning a stern back on *sorpotel* and *sanas*, roast suckling pig, sausage pulao and all the rest of that lovely grub; practise strict fiscal stringency for the next few years to afford my holiday (thirty rupees buy you a pound; a pound buys you nothing). My survival kit will include a manual on how to cope with racial prejudice (acquire a thick skin or a karate Black Belt); a short aide memoire on food and drink ('Learn to Love Warm Beer' ... 'Hamburgers or Nothing' ... 'London on Fish and Chips'); and, of course, Dale Carnegie's last, unpublished best-seller, *Smile ... What Else Can You Do?*

You arrive accustomed to Goa's calm, unruffled consistency: the unvarying goodness of O Coqueiro's chicken cafreal; the endearing permanence of the collapsed spans of the Mandovi Bridge; the sublime and unchanging quality of Souza Lobo's roast tongue; the decades (so thoughtfully guaranteed by a caring government) of waiting for a water connection. You must now Be Prepared for sudden change and chilling contradiction. When the shop attendant at Marks and Sparks says, 'Thank you very much, sir,' with mechanical courtesy while the hostile contempt in her blue eyes threatens to cause a terminal seizure in one of your major arteries, rest easy. This happens everywhere, with virtually everybody, all the time. If, after saving for your holiday for a couple of years and leaving Goa with moderate riches, you take a look at the prices when you arrive in London and discover that you and your family are as poor as church mice, learn to take the philosophical view: there is always St James' Park and the ducks (if little else) for free; however, if you want to feed the ducks you will have to pay the sort of serious money for peanuts which would keep you in feni for a week back home.

After a couple of days, you may find yourself a trifle bitter while doing the dishes, with one thought uppermost in your mind, 'Is this a holiday?'

Good question. There you were at home in Candolim, happy as a seagull, feet up on the *balcao*, watching the fishing boats, a glass of the very best feni preparing the taste buds so splendidly for the prawn curry your cook Mary was simmering to perfection in the kitchen, while Asha hung the clothes to dry beneath the palms. *Working* on your book. Here you are on *holiday*. Lugging ton-loads of groceries along London's mean streets, not a cab in sight (as if you could afford one!), with the dismal thought of getting back to your service apartment, cooking dinner, laying the table, taking dinner out, eating it, washing the dishes, laying the breakfast table, and missing the only decent programme that the BBC has to offer in the day. (Let us draw a discreet veil over the small garments hanging to dry in the bathroom.) Where are you, Mary and Asha when we need you most?

Try to muffle cries of anguish when you return from an outing with frozen fingertips and no feeling in your toes. You must learn to understand the forecasters' doublespeak. When the weather announcers on television (usually pretty blondes of a dumbness which must be experienced to be believed) gush about clear skies, bright sunshine and luverly warm weather do not believe a word of it; arm yourself with thermal underwear, gloves, muffler, raincoat and keep the brandy handy.

If you find yourself making wistful, nostalgic comparisons, cease and desist at once: brooding unhappiness will be your lot.

Take our newspapers and TV, chock-a-bloc with such stirring events as train crashes killing scores, entire busloads massacred in the Punjab, gang slaughter in Bombay, Kashmir in flames, the burning of brides by the dozen each week, not to mention the grizzly last moments of hundreds laid low by illicit, poisoned hooch – par for the daily course. I shudder to think of the British media and public reaction to such murderous goings-on. Wild hysteria, I would imagine. Questions in Parliament. Royal Commissions. And if these matters were discussed in the Lords (in the sort of excruciating detail the Lords love to indulge in) I can see blue-blooded octogenarians keeling over in the benches every half hour.

The truth of the matter is that nothing much happens in England.

Reams of valuable newsprint, hundreds of man hours of the finest journalistic talent in the world and priceless chunks of the best part of TV each day are devoted to issues of such monumental unimportance as the purchase of estates by pop stars, the presence of salmonella in two eggs in the Hebrides, the appearance of summer's first thrush and Lady Diana's latest show of leg or cleavage; when her husband, Prince Charles, heir to the throne, falls off a polo pony and breaks an arm (his two left feet have, over the years, found boundless sympathy the length and breadth of the land), two-inch, front page banner headlines cause the nation to hold its breath, while the leader writers, without exception, hold forth at voluminous length and in the greatest possible medical detail. Prime-time breakfast TV (Breakfast Trivia?) holds millions in thrall with 'What Your Stars Foretell', 'The Recipe for the Day', 'Letters from the Under Tens' and 'Sally Gets You Into Shape', a severely mauled and censored version of Jane Fonda's body graffiti. Not holiday fare, not by a long shot. How would you feel if three whole columns of *The Herald's* sports page were given over to a breathless examination of Sachin Tendulkar's last tummy upset?

From time to time you will be seized by the desire to be sociable and mingle with the natives. Unwisely, you do not lie down till the feeling goes away, but decide to visit an English person you have never met before – a friend of an acquaintance whose cousin twice-removed once met the man in ... etc. In the finest Goan tradition, you do not phone or otherwise make your presence known, but take an hour's train journey to Blackheath and after tramping around for the better part of the morning, finally locate the Cloisters (which is not a chapel as you had imagined), the abode of your Mr Smith. The door opens. A polite cat regards you with distaste. An astonished Englishman peers at you through horn-rims. 'Hi,' you say, 'I'm D'Souza from Calangute. My cousin Napoleon's brother's wife's sister danced with you last New Year's eve at the Taj Holiday Village. How are you?' 'Do come in,' Mr Smith responds, joylessly; there is frost in his voice and a distinct nip in the air. What he means is, 'Please have the decency to leave at once.' There are other contretemps. When, after knowing an English family for several generations, you are finally invited to share a cold supper, leave all thoughts of groaning Goan boards behind. A sliver or two of ham, a modest piece of a nondescript cheese, a tomato that has seen better days, two slices of the regulatory cottonwool loaf and a glass (no more) of an indifferent white wine ... will leave you weeping for the auld sod and your mother-in-law's Sunday lunch.

If, as with me, you are a Goan who puts his constitutional rights before any other and expects three square meals as a matter of course (the way mother made them), prepare to stiffen the upper lip and tighten the belt a notch or two.

There is good reason why the French (like the Goans, gourmets to the last man, woman and child) refuse to eat in England. I once had occasion to meet two French businessmen who flew to London for the day. Our meeting over, I offered them lunch. 'London,' said Pierre, 'is an uncivilized suburb of Paris. Eat here? Have you ever known an Englishman to smile after a meal? Order me a sandwich. I catch the 5.15 for Orly and have no wish to spoil my dinner.' Too true. Later that day, I phoned room service for a solitary dinner, chicken grilled in a mustard, Parmesan and garlic sauce. It was clear, at first bite, that the unfortunate bird had perished of old age and terminal arthritis aggravated by acute depression. The lashings of Colman's mustard, stale department-store Parmesan and burnt garlic did little to conceal this sad fact. At ten pounds (please do not convert) I felt no sympathy for the hapless fowl.

You will have to learn to grin and bear it.

'Everything,' said my friend and fellow sufferer, Shivanand Salgaocar, who happened to be there with his family, mercifully en route to Scotland, 'tastes synthetic.' There you have it. I could have added: everything seems to taste like everything else. There is reason for this gloomy state of affairs. How do you expect a self-respecting chicken to live up to the glories of a high table, if it is confined from birth to a space slightly larger than itself, fed hormones, antibiotics, dyeing agents and chemicals to get the fat/meal balance and texture/colouring right. Cows are treated no better. There is a strange and lethal illness, raging among English beef herds, called – upon my word – 'Mad Cow's Disease'. The press and public are in a right old tizzy. Taste? Well, the English have no tastebuds anyway, mate.

If I had known, one of my five cases, or a sixth, would have contained nothing but Costa's glorious smoked Goa sausage, their impeccable pork-and-beef croquettes, six jars of Mary's prawn *balchao*, sustaining quantities of the village para, one whole suckling pig baked by Anton and a few kilos of my mother's *sorpotel*. All of which would have made the family very happy and cost me considerably less than a few days' groceries from Sainsburys.

Here we are again, en famille, back in Candolim, giving serious thought to our next holiday. England? France? Italy? Disneyland? Perish the thought. We intend to do ourselves magnificently this year. Expenses be damned! There is a lovely house in Tiracol with not a single tourist for miles around, right up on the beach, with spectacular views and an equally impressive cook. The caju is honestly home-brewed, and the smells from the kitchen will turn the most violently agnostic to profoundly spiritual thoughts.

Tiracol, here we come!

****

The Bottom Line

After two wet and gloomy weeks in London, there I was, in cheerful sunshine at a sidewalk café on the Via Veneto no less, partaking of that most civilized of Roman confections, an espresso with cognac, leafing idly through the many-splendoured offerings of the *Sunday Times*: Kingsley Amis, on a European holiday after five cloistered years in the misty isles, prevails over inferior vintages in forgettable chateaux, and beaches where you can't see the sand for the skin. Clearly, he is disgruntled, but by the time you reach paragraph three, the air of ruffled finer feelings wears thin, and the prose, if not the wine, takes on the mellow flavour of vintage Amis. The novelist gets the better of the traveller, and we are regaled with the telling bon mot, the wry eye for the comic and fallible, and a narrative skill which first engages, then splendidly fulfills its promises to the reader.

I flip a few pages and learn that British Airways lose fifteen million pounds a year on the Concorde. It *is* going to be a good day! The English come miraculously from behind to steal a crucial test from the Australians. 'Coming back from the dead,' says Brearley in screaming headlines. How could one disagree with that? *Cats*, the exuberant musical at the New London Theatre, is a yowling success. Would T.S. Eliot have approved? In a few weeks there will be three million unemployed in Britain. 'Extraordinary,' Mr Matchman, the genial West End theatre agent, had said to me a fortnight earlier, 'here we are, with a frightful recession on, and I'm packing them in at seven quid a go.'

From time to time, I am gently interrupted by affable Romans who offer to sell me things – nubile, virginal, insatiable little things– just round the corner, languishing for lack of loving kindness. The explicitness of their propositions is tempered by a sunny optimism: if only Signore will have a look, all kinds of possibilities will be delightfully clear. Signore's wife will be joining him in a few minutes, Signore says virtuously, but I freely confess that I have been sneaking swift glances of nothing less than the keenest appreciation, at lithe young things, of splendidly enticing gender, passing along.

I make the mistake of turning over to the front page of the *Times*, and the benevolence of a golden Roman afternoon is instantly shattered. Life, the *Times* tells me, is serious and disturbing. Liverpool burns for the third day running. In Southall, the Asians take to the barricades and petrol bomb. Millions of pounds of real estate go up in flames in Manchester to chants of 'Burn, baby, burn!' Where will it all end? 'Anarchy,' screams Enoch Powell, moustache bristling with outrage, 'civil war. Send the blacks back!' The liberals, covered with sackcloth, wheezing through the ashes, wail and lament. The skinheads giggle as they knife yet another dirty brown bugger. And Margaret Thatcher goes on the box to say that she will not allow this nonsense to go on much longer. 'These people loot and steal. Simple greed, that's all it is.' She talks of arming the police with plastic bullets (which have been known to kill, though not so cleanly as the real ones) and water cannons and powers to arrest on suspicion and camps to incarcerate rioters. The iron hand in the iron glove has never been more menacing.

Extreme reactions are to be expected, of course, when the blood is up, and the fire's next door. But now that the politicians have been at it fang and claw, and the editorialists have worried the issue threadbare, it is time to pause, to think deeply and, dare I use the word – profoundly – about what ails the British spirit.

To the bottom of things then, to the toilet, with the shade of Freud cheering by the door. There on the wall, masquerading as a roll of toilet paper, is the source of much that afflicts Queen and country. If an army marches on its stomach, I contend that a nation is only as tolerant as the suppleness of its sphincter muscle, and no sphincter, with the slightest sense of self-preservation, could help but shrink from the harsh reality of English toilet paper. Unforgiving, unyielding (a hard tussle and two mean squares grudgingly come away) it is intended not so much to soothe and cleanse, as to repress with violence. I refer to the most expensive kind, white as the driven snow, with not the suspicion of a hint of the tar brush. There are colours, of course, from a murderous pink to a cringing grey, revealing, in inverse proportions to their distance from the real thing, horrors too awful to write about.

Let us then take the charitable and compassionate view. Can one expect the leader of a nation over which the sun no longer rises, so rudely violated so early in the morning, to spread sweetness, understanding and light? If the sphincter is rigid with fear and loathing, can the iron hand be far behind? The pain runs deep throughout the land. In mean Liverpudlian alleys, stately homes in Somerset, Surrey's stockbroker belt and the hoity-toity boroughs of Mayfair and Knightsbridge, rage and suffering are the order of the day, or to be more precise, the early morning.

Now why can't the English learn from the French? This wonderfully tolerant and laconic race is given to immediate and justifiable rage *only* when confronted by bad food or bad French. The bidet in my bathroom in Paris was serendipitously decorated with mother-of-pearl paisleys and, absorbed by this pleasant little sophistication, I very nearly missed a proper appreciation of the toilet paper. Soft as a butterfly kiss, exquisitely absorbent, lilac fleur de lis on royal blue. No wonder the Foreign Legion was so profoundly inspired. To the distant strains of the *Marseillaise*, I performed serene, lofty, de Gaullian ablutions.

But it was in Venice that I discovered toilet paper's true potential to make the world a better and happier place for us all. A gentle tug and joy was unconfined. Reams of exuberant rainbows whirled rapturously about my ankles, chucked me softly under the chin, and tickled me *there*. Subtle fragrances invited me to linger, take my ease, luxuriate ... Any moment now, Pavarotti would sing an aria from *La Bohème*. Just for me. It was a perfectly irresistible Italian proposition.

One I would dearly love to make to Margaret Thatcher.

****

London: Three Encounters
of the Racist Kind

Take my word for it, Mr Nirad Chaudhuri, never arrange your first racist encounter in England just off a flight at Heathrow, at six of a morning full of wet and dismal prophecy. Jet lag is not conducive to a calm, detached appraisal of what ails blacks and whites in Britain; the intellect will have nothing to do with understanding, balanced perspectives or the importance of history.

I made straight for the open doors halfway down the airport bus and was waved through by a uniformed male attendant. Half in, I noticed that the doors had begun moving towards me, first in slow motion, as the heavy metal responded to the hydraulic drive; then, with a blur and a snarl, they slammed at me from either side. Dignity had no part to play in what happened next, Mr Chaudhuri. I leaped backward, landed on my rump, picked myself up carefully, and checked various portions of the anatomy for signs of damages; only my spirit was bruised.

The male attendant made no attempt to help. He stood five square, good yeoman stock. In another age, he would have hefted a battle axe at Hastings. His eyes were blue and steady and as empty of emotion as the doors of a gas oven. And when he said, 'Isn't that clever!' there was no malice in his voice, or humour. His tone was purely observational: I was a different species, some distance away, and lower down, on a Darwinian scale. This was the face of fascism: absolute belief; a wholly alien order of being. Good and evil were of no consequence; the smoke rising at dusk from the chimneys at Belsen was reason unto itself.

I moved to the front of the bus. The driver, who perched on a high seat, controlled the hydraulic doors from an electronic switchboard. He was giggling behind a hand. I took a seat. The white passengers refused to catch my eye, and their silence was edged with a certain kind of shame.

If Mr Chaudhuri has lived these past eleven years in England, he's led a cloistered life indeed. Colour prejudice is now a fact of everyday life, evident, in greater or lesser degree, at all levels of society. The intensity of the prejudice the average coloured person is likely to encounter is, not to put too fine a point on it, in inverse proportion to his distance from African Equatorial Black. While the media, with rare and inconsequential exceptions, go to town on the stereotype. Thus the West Indian is a spear's throw from the cannibal drumbeats of darkest Africa, answering, with utter violence, the mildest of enquiries from the kindly Bobby on the Liverpudlian beat, while the Indian, if the TV sit-coms are to be believed, are of pathetic, but entertaining, lineage: Peter Sellers out of Kipling's Bengali Baboo, with the occasional dim-witted, but great-hearted Sardar, thrown in to balance things out. And do try to get the accent right, old chap.

There's a weekly TV programme on in London, based on an English language class for foreign adults. The class is run by a Bertie Wooster-type young Englishman perpetually at good-natured odds with the grammar and pronunciation of his foreign students, the funniest of whom are a Pakistani man and an Indian woman. Their inputs are written with a certain degree of depth and sympathy. Here lies the danger; they remain stereotypes, but in the skilled hands of their creators, they are very much more acceptable as the real thing, to very many more people. When I commented that the promotion of coloured stereotypes in the present highly inflammable situation was adding fuel to fire, my companions, Indians of long residence, took quick umbrage. *All* of the students, I was told, German, Dutch, Greek, Italian *et al.*, were equally funny, why was I being so sensitive about Asians? I refrained from pointing out that gangs of skinheads do not knife Germans or Italians in the East

End of London, but did not pursue the point. My friends had assumed the colouration of the environment. Sad. Chameleons only fool themselves.

There is much support, here and in Britain, for Mr Chaudhuri's thesis: there is polarization *only* at the lunatic fringe – the frothing, mad-dog frontiers of the fascist National Front and the Marxist vanguard while the mainstream is free of prejudice. Not true. Today, the attitudes of the bulk of the population are polarized as well, though not so visibly, splintered over a spectrum of positions. Thus the coloured response, aligned more often than not, with length of residence, education, material and/or social success, ranges from the degrading postures of the small, brown Englishman, through retreat and denial, submission, defiance and, currently and most hopefully, organization and militancy.

The white response is infinitely more interesting. Latent racist feelings have seeped to the surface: guilt, indignation, paranoia, shame, outright hostility. The problem can no longer be left to the tidy analyses of the leader writers of the *Guardian* and the *Telegraph*; it refuses to be swept neatly under the carpet: committees are not able to make it sink without trace. *The blacks are putting Brixton to the torch!* This summer in London, there were occasions when my presence, in a shop or pub where I was the only coloured person, prompted a white reaction I had never met with before: a polite, guarded wariness. I embodied the potential of the race for carnage and violent change. I had given the lie to my subservient, immigrant past and could well herald the arrival of a bloody and explosive future.

My second encounter was light-hearted but not without a moral. I was shopping at Selfridges, in the surreptitious manner of a deacon seeking a fetish, a trifle abashed at having to admit at my age that I wanted running shoes. A suave young Indian approached and asked, what it was I wished to buy.

'Running shoes,' I said.

'Would you take a seat for a moment, sir. Won't be a minute.'

He raised a finger at a white colleague who responded with alacrity. 'Dunlops, size nine I should think. Get a ripple on, Bill.' He turned to me then, 'You on holiday here, sir?'

'Sort of,' I said.

'Glad to be getting back, I bet.'

His name was Sharad Patel, and his father had emigrated from India when he was twelve. I encouraged him to talk and he described, without bitterness, the racial prejudice he had to live with: brutal confrontations with skinheads, ' ... the last thing you do is back down'; the trials and tribulations of job-hunting: 'You've got to be twice as good as the white guy, and even then it's a clean toss-up'; subtle condescensions which infuriated him; a few silver linings: 'White girls like brown boys. We're nicer.'

Bill returned with the Dunlops. They fitted like a glove. 'I'll take them,' I said. A look of concern passed fleetingly across Sharad's eyes. 'I see it all the time,' he said regretfully. He ran a hand lightly under the sole of my left foot, 'A couple of years if you aren't careful, sir, and you're in trouble. Bill, a pair of No. 9 insoles and some running socks, there's a good lad.'

'What,' I asked weakly, 'do you do here?'

'Manager of the department,' he smiled, 'you can't keep a good Indian down.'

I left with a shoe horn, a pair of shoe trees, a bottle of superwhite cleansing lotion for my new shoes, insoles, a dozen pairs of socks and, of course, my running shoes. I said good-bye to Sharad. 'Do you ever get to India?' His eyes were troubled, 'My parents won't let me. They know I would never return.'

But I only began to understand the true dimensions of the tragedy the weekend before I left. It was clear to me then that the scars of racial prejudice would forever disfigure; the wounds ran deeper than I would ever know and they would bleed for generations. The girl behind the cash register at the local supermarket was too young to conceal her hatred; perhaps she didn't care. With the whites, she was cheerful and friendly. Her attitude to the coloureds was one of open contempt. 'Don't you know better,' she said to me, 'this is a supermarket not a bank, I don't have change for a twenty.' I let it pass.

She was a third generation Indian emigrant, Mr Chaudhuri, and as black as they come.

****

When the Camels Wept

The lances and swords will never again flash crimson beneath a desert sun. The long silences of the brown and sere plains evoke no memory of thundering cavalry, the clash of arms, the battle cries of chivalrous war. The banners of the warrior kings of Rajasthan have long forsaken the colours of blood and sand. Only memories remain: suits of armour scarred by battle and time; the worn faded colours of the sun and the moon; the weapons of combat – sword, mace, lance, bow and arrow – encased in glass, vaguely menacing, sequestered in the whispering corridors and echoing vaults of Rajasthan's museums.

But the heritage of martial honour was always tempered by the gentle rhythms of a singular culture, born out of a harsh land, given form in an exuberant tapestry of song, art, religion and festival, preceding by millennia the martial heritage it so easily contained and outlived.

If today Rajasthan means the walled turreted fortress cities of Amber, Chittorgarh and Jaisalmer, it means also the marble symphony of Udaipur's Lake Palace; the legend of Mirabai, mystic poetess and lady of a royal line; the exquisite purity of the Jain temple at Ranakpur; the happy defiance of dust and desert in the village wall paintings – gods and goddesses created from a merry and personal mythology, generously interpreted in flowing line and vivid crimsons and turquoises, exuberant counterpoint to the puritan strictures of sun, scrub and sand; the bold colours and extraordinarily fine detail of Rajasthani jewellery, leatherwork and pottery; the flamboyant, cheerful peasantry; the magnificent peacock, royal and honoured bird; the ubiquitous camel; the pink and gilt cities rising like subtle mirages out of the flowing desert ...

It all comes together at Pushkar.

*

The road from Ajmer holds no surprises. It moves direct and swift as the eye to the horizon, flanked by dun hillocks of scrub and sand. Heat waves shimmer in the near distance and cool, delightful mirages appear and vanish even as you look at them. Then the road scythes about a shallow gradient and the desert convulses before you in a wholly unexpected upheaval of dull red and grey rocks, massed in series, rising ever higher in startling arabesques, until you drive along a narrow road high on the side of a mountain which twists and turns and coils into itself while far below a line of pilgrims, tiny points of scarlet on grey, toils among the fallen boulders, following some invisible path, making not the slightest impression on the heights and distances about them.

This is Nag Pahar, the serpent mountain which conceals and protects the sacred lake of Pushkar from the encroaching desert.

A mountain in the heart of a desert. A lake which should never have happened. Oh the unfathomable ways of the gods! It is said that here, when the world was young and the gods playful, the demon Vajranabh made his abode, devouring small children, terrifying the populace and behaving generally as all properly qualified demons do, blissfully unaware that his comeuppance lay just behind the nearest cloud in the form of Brahma the Creator. The Lord of the Universe was casting about for a place to perform a Vedic fire rite or yagna. In his hand Brahma held a lotus flower, symbolic bloom, blossom from out of the heart of water. He slew the demon with the lotus and it floated to earth, lightly touching the desert in three spots. Lakes, fragrant and sweet, came into being and these he called the Elder, the Middle and the Younger Pushkar.

All was made ready for the fire rite. An auspicious hour was appointed. Gods and maharishis descended on Pushkar in large numbers from every far-flung corner of the universe. Even the great Shiva managed to find the time to drop by. When all was finally ready, when the holy moment was a mere breath away, it was discovered, much to everybody's consternation, that Brahma's wife Savitri, was nowhere to be found. This would never do. Man and wife in Hindu mythology are merely two parts of a whole. The fire rite could not begin without Savitri. Yet the very minute was upon them. Brahma, a most resourceful deity, made a quick decision. A wife was the need of the moment. Not *the* wife, merely and happily, *a* wife! His quick and practised gaze settled on the young, comely Gayatri. She was the daughter of a cowherd. What matter? She was both beautiful and modest. And clearly a wife. It was the work of an instant. The two were one. The metaphysical whole was complete. The fire rite could begin.

Savitri turned up of course, as wives do, right at the end of the yagna and nothing would mollify her. Yes, she had been delayed, in a neighbourly chat with a few other gods' wives. But this was neither here nor there. Why had the yagna commenced without her? And who was that woman? Refusing to be appeased she went off in a huff and performed her own yagna, all by herself. Shiva meanwhile, weather eye ever out for a good thing, seized the opportunity to insist, among all the confusion, on his own holy spot. Brahma refused. Shiva promptly introduced a friendly demon, an accomplished poltergeist, into Brahma's fire-rite. Nothing seemed to go right until Brahma, all resistance spent, promised Shiva his very own temple. And, for good measure, Savitri as well.

Whereupon peace and holiness descended on Pushkar.

*

The legends emerge from the mists of antiquity; symbolic representation of the first faint stirrings of man's need for a transcendental reality. Today, the lakes and temples of Pushkar, the holy sanctuaries and sacred, cleansing ghats, are testimony to the truth that out of legend grows belief, precursor to faith. And who is to question that the gods we worship are a lesser reality than the faith which gives them being? It is a living faith and to the hundreds of thousands of pilgrims who make the long odyssey each November from the far corners of India, Pushkar holds equal place with India's other great religious shrines.

*

The light that filtered into my tent was the colour of a pale mulled rose, the light of the desert sun, setting at last, gentled by ancient canvas worn to the colour of old ivory. My cot was rough wood and canvas and rope, but I was grateful for it. I had spent three hours walking the streets of the old city of Pushkar and nothing had prepared me for the experience. I had expected meditative silences and the muted voices of a holy place; revelations of the inner life unfolding in serene bathing ghats, tranquil marble repositories of art and worship, the hushed murmur of pilgrim prayers.

I should have known better for I had read that the religious festival was also the occasion for a cattle fair and other rural fun and games. But to my urban imagination, untouched by the close and beautiful symbiosis between man and animal, a cattle fair conjured up images of herds of polite cows grazing placidly behind stout fences, a horse or two and even, making concession to the desert, the possibility of a camel. I had even decided on the colours and the smells: muted browns and ambers, ancient sere ivories and dull golds; the fragrance of rose petals and incense with just the merest hint of wood smoke

I first realized that my innocence was about to be exuberantly violated when we began the long climb down the snake mountain into the Pushkar valley. We began to overtake pilgrim families, each a sudden and overwhelming community of elders, parents, children, cows, camels, horses, goats, sheep and dogs. One was first aware of a small explosion of violent primary colour in the distance which, as you approached, translated into a magnificent confusion, a riot of exotic hues, sounds and smells; a harlequin medley of man and beast, quite beyond definition.

It was only after several such encounters that I began to detect a pattern: people and animals were happy with each other; little children ran among the gliding legs of camels without mishap. Graceful young men rode beautiful ponies up and down the line while the dogs, sheep and goats politely gave passage. The elders and womenfolk and very junior elements among the children and animals squatted close and companionably in two-wheeled open carts, drawn by camels. It was, I realized happily, a truly rural idea of community, where animals and people mattered to each other and knew it.

The second clear impression concerned colour. Where, at the beginning, its use seemed wild, chaotic and abandoned, now I detected an engaging purpose, a catholic interest in primary colour, in tinsel, mirror and bead work, silver and gold for their own sakes. The bold and imaginative use of these themes, with impartial flair, on camel and chieftain, made for a splendid organic harmony. Brilliantly set off by the dark brooding handsome men, fiercely whiskered, with a single gold piratical earring snuggling beneath an absolute frivolity of a turban, a light, frothy, intricate creation; and the fey gypsy loveliness of the women: golden complexions, deep cozening eyes and a natural pride and challenge in every small movement of hip and hand.

But the detail was lost again as we came nearer Pushkar and the families became whole villages blocking furlongs of road, till our car moved at a crawl, we climbed a crest, and the city lay before us. The road seemed to heave and sway, a living thing of vibrant shimmering hues. Tens of thousands of pilgrim families moved as one great mass, reaching as far as the eye could see, defying credibility, till, in the distance, it merged with the base of a mountain, lilac and rust, shrouded in mist, a pure conical thrusting mass of rock. Right at the summit, catching the sun, passing a glittering benediction on the crowds far below, a white temple with a flag fluttering in the breeze, stood isolated and supreme.

This was clearly no time for the comforts of a car. We were stuck in the crowd like a fly in aspic. Opening the door was a feat of no small proportions. I took a deep breath, exchanged a stern look with a supercilious camel, adjusted the strap of my camera bag, and plunged into Pushkar.

*

Up to that minute I was observer and chronicler, detached, absorbed in the conversion of present experience to future form, but once I became part of the pilgrims of Pushkar, I seemed to lose identity. I was embarked on a rite of passage over which I had little control. Like a twig on a departing tide I was moved hither and yon, with no personal volition, immersed in an ocean of feeling.

Reverence, excitement, joy rippled through the crowds as we passed temples and sanctuaries, the oval white-washed arena which, the next day, would play host to the games, the bazaar and fun fair. Hundreds of colourful stalls crowded shoulder to shoulder, selling everything from life insurance policies to hot grilled partridge. Barkers cajoled, pleaded, bullied through tin megaphones. Tumbling boxes, set up seemingly by whim, anywhere at all, hurled their cargoes of Rajasthani women, shrieking delightedly, into the air, in sudden bursts of soft colour against a blue sky. Every so often a camel and its rider would sway into view, calm and nonchalant, well above the crowd, refusing to be hurried, with all the time in the world at their disposal. I was buffeted and exhilarated, hot and wonderstruck all at once.

I will never understand why I was not instantly trampled underfoot; why I did not once lose patience; why, when an old woman, withered and bright-eyed, touched my face with a gnarled hand and smiled, I felt only awe and a sense of belonging; why the unexpected serenity of a temple in the distance touched a responsive and quiet chord within me; why, three hours later, footsore and weary, flat on my back on my humble wooden cot, an exultant spirit took wing ...

*

Long and long ago, as Kipling would have it, the kings of Rajasthan created a royal drink, gulab, the essence of the rose. Each bottle enshrined the potent and loving distillation of thousands of petals of very young rosebuds. To the Rajput today the gulab of yore is a fragrant memory, now evoked in fiery effect by the commercial product, a squat, brown bottle, splendidly labelled, generously laced with synthetic rose essence. We drank from the bottle, cross-legged on the sand, before a tiny cooking fire.

The dunes merged, receded and overlapped in pensive dialogues of golden light and glowing shadow. The sun was going down and the colours of the desert at dusk were coming into their own. Gone were the brutal contrasts, the harsh primaries, the solid black shadows. On the horizon the low mountain ranges were etched in deep purple against a sky of lilac and rose. The geometric angularities of desert, tent and scrub were now all blurred softnesses, bathed in twilight, lit, wherever the eye turned, by small pools of flickering light from scores of cooking fires.

I had sought food and was reminded gently that I had opted for a tent in the desert and would have to walk three kilometers for a meal. 'It is a two hour walk' – I had gone to the nearest tent to ask – 'because of the crowds.' He then invited me to share his family's supper. We drank gulab and ate grilled mutton and wholewheat chapatis, raw onion and salt, under the stars, while his children giggled behind their mother, a quiet woman, cooking silently, passing us food, her saffron odini covering her head, well over her eyes, but I would catch quick curious glances and once, a smile, barely suppressed, when her husband talked of the strength and speed of his camel which, surely, would win the great race the next morning. I said I hadn't the shadow of a doubt that it would.

I slept like a child that night and remember falling asleep to the voices of camels, calling to each other in the night.

*

Year long they will talk of the last great day of this fair. Of the hours they spent from dawn's early light taking positions of favour on the whitewashed stone benches of the arena. Of the folly of the latecomers, dismissed to hot sun and far corner. Of Ranjit Singh's magnificent bull, a grand black mountain of a beast, worthy of the eminence of the blue riband. In remote desert villages, during the long silences of dusk, they will recall the valour and endurance of Karanjit's camel, swift, graceful, noble dromedary, great-hearted victor of the most exciting camel race in memory. They will tell, in exacting detail, of the merits of the horse riders, of their terrible courage, of the thrust and threats of tent-pegging contests and mock battles. They will recount with a touch of pride the great bargains struck in barter and sale. Laughter and a ribald earthiness will greet memories of heroic drinking bouts and other mild wickednesses. While the women, silent as ever, will turn over, in the mind's eye, memories of a bath by starlight in a holy ghat, the wind sighing among marble columns, the gods evoked in moving shadow and sacred chant.

And they will ask, as they do each year, will there ever be such another Pushkar?

I left the next morning and not an hour's distance from Pushkar we turned along a winding road into a valley where thousands of camels and herders were making ready to depart. There was a murmur in the air which I could not decipher. As we drew nearer it grew into a sad and gentle ululation, rising and falling on a note of lingering anguish. It was then that I understood that the camels were crying.

'They are sad because their young have gone,' a herder told me, 'but they are strong animals , sahib. Soon they will forget and breed again.'

But would I? Would I ever forget that morning in Pushkar when the camels wept?

****

The Gourmand

I was presented with
an apologetic obituary on
an elderly fowl which had
perished from terminal
arthritis.

A Sausage with Soul

In my rare moments of wishful thinking (where would I be without them?), most often after a spectacular Goan meal, I like to pretend that I am a cartographer in an ancient tradition (Here be a Unicorn and a Golden *Bebinca* ... At the Heart of the Magical Forest Lies the Holy Grail of the Revered Goa Sausage') drawing up a map of The Wondrous Ways to The Goan Table. Familiar icons appear on the parchment. That delightful quick-change artiste, the Coconut – tender, ripe, dry; milk, toddy, feni! – making its presence so happily felt in all manner of edibles and potables, from breads and curries to desserts and merry brown bottles, roughly corked. The peerless Malcurada Mango before which all other mangos cringe in shame (to the back of the class Alphonso!) best eaten golden-ripe off the bough or preserved, young and raw, in the irresistible, tongue-tingling pickle, *miscut,* or semi-ripe in an utterly seductive sweet and sour chutney. True-blue sugarcane vinegar, the supreme tempering medium, brewed in-house from fiercely guarded family recipes. A royal bounty of fish and crustacean, straight from boat to kitchen, uncontaminated by such big city abominations as ice and freezer. The lovingly distilled elixir in the voluptuous 12-bottle green glass flagons known as *gararaos*, pure bred caju feni, to a Goan what the sky is to a seagull, a medium of infinite wonder and potential. And, presiding over all, our many-splendoured porker, in its first and last and finest impersonation, the great-hearted Goa Sausage.

Sausage supremacy is a gift from the gods.

If today the Goa sausage hovers over the Goan kitchen like some benign divinity, there is reason. From plump, marbled rump to lean and succulent rib, testimony to a triumphantly imaginative appetite, our noble porker reincarnates into a sausage of exemplary virtue. Hoofing it over such squealing pretenders as the dour, flavourless Cumberland (typical British hogwash), the Spanish chorizo (all chilli and no soul), the overly ballyhooed Italian pepperoni (Mamma mia! just about sums it up), the American frankfurter (now you know where that sad allusion 'a pig in a poke' came from) and the blustering German wiener (which prompts the grim reflection, what good is length without performance?).

The best things in life begin with hearth and home. When I observe the tender loving care bestowed on a pregnant sow in our village by her owner, I am reminded of literature's most famous love affair between peer and pig, Lord Blandings and his Empress, recorded by P.G. Wodehouse with the reverence that grand passion deserves. Small beer, as far as our local porker is concerned. What could be more demeaning than confining a pig to a pen? And mere size is no substitute for chutzpah. In Goa we produce a porker which pays delicious tribute to the good things of life – home-made mash (a rich porridge of rice and leftovers) and inventive snacking at large wherever tantalizing smell calls to investigative snout – under bushes, behind beach shacks, in the mangroves, at friendly kitchen doors. An abundance of fresh air. Lots of happy sex. And regular infusions of high octane adrenalin involving close encounters with bad-tempered goats, feral cats, dogs of mean disposition and gangs of little boys with sticks who seem to have nothing better to do in life than chase piglings up hill and down dale. But the exercise is good for body and soul; it sends the blood coursing to every last extremity and makes for a bigger, fatter, tastier porker. Such is the distinguished pedigree of the Goa sausage. Infused with a dash or two or more of vintage caju feni to provide, shall we say, a certain spiritual elevation.

In Mumbai the Goa sausage has its pretenders. The over-spiced, under-flavoured Bandra sausage, the sad-sack Dhobi Talao sausage, other unsavoury offerings from Marve, Bassein and points north. No contest. They are to the true Goa sausage what Hong Kong Scotch is to a Highland single malt, or the inferior white Italian truffle to the black gold found only in France, or Californian plonk to a white Burgundy Grand Cru. The finest things in life are immutable. Thus, the Goa sausage may only be celebrated in Goa and nowhere else on the planet. Praise the Lord and pass the feni! But in Goa, as in Burgundian vineyards, you will find serious, learned debate over the virtues of the Goa sausage from Saligao and its distant cousin resident in Benaulim. I am on intimate terms with the Saligao sausage as I should be (my maternal village) and can vouch for sterling worth. Full-bodied and of impressive length, it is twice the size of the Benaulim fledgling, and the highest order of care and commitment is lavished on its preparation.

Millimetric attention is paid to the size of the chunks of meat, and the proportion of meat to fat. Meat from rump and undercut is best, finely marbled, with one-third of firm white fat attached to each piece. Given the long hard haul ahead (six months from finished sausage to plated sausage), the quality of meat is of prime importance. Sea salt is rubbed in and the pork is set aside for a day. Then it is washed and dried in the sun. Goa's celebrated red chillies, turmeric, garlic, ginger, peppercorns, cloves and cinnamon are stone-ground to a thick paste in sugarcane vinegar. The finest caju feni is solemnly infused. An enthusiastic blending of pork and paste follows. The sausage meat is carefully spooned into four-inch lengths of tripe casing and knotted. The sausage strings, each two feet long, are laid out in concentric circles on reed mats and dried in the sun for a week. If you think you can now hog, lie down till the feeling goes away. The Goa sausage odyssey has just begun. The sausages are transported to the kitchen and hung from the rafters, a veritable merriment of plump, glistening promise, above the kitchen fires to cure. This takes six long months and tries one's patience to the limit.

In the smoking lies the secret of the Goa sausage's unique flavour and the reason why imitators cower in sackcloth and ashes. The traditional Goan cooking range consists of laterite bricks piled two-high on either side of a wood fire. All cooking is done in earthernware pots. Woodsmoke filtered through unglazed earthernware adds just a hint of smokey flavour to the food and all of that lovely, unforgettable aroma is absorbed by the Goa sausages hanging above for six l-o-n-g months. At the end of it all, cruel and unusual punishment is inflicted on the Goa sausage. It shrinks and shrivels, develops geriatric lumps and creases, becomes dark and mottled as if stricken with a terminal disease hitherto unknown to medical science. At this stage the Goa sausage, now ready to be cooked, prompts grave misgivings in the uninitiated. Will one live to tell the tale?

Ho hum.

For a magnificent resurrection, follow instructions carefully. Cut an appropriate length from the string (three sausages per person, unless you really mean to hog, should do). Arrange in a coil. Place in a pan with Goan well water (gotcha!) to half an inch above sausage level. Peel and pop in a small onion and a generous spoonful of garlic pods. Bring to a brisk boil for a minute or so. Then simmer as gently as possible till the water is reduced to a quarter of an inch. Finish with a splash, no more, of vinegar. Remove sausages. They have now regained their original stature and are plump with the pride of achievement. A renaissance, which never fails to inspire awe and humility. Cease the adoration. Slice lengthwise. Scoop out the meat. Take a deep breath. Plunge in regardless.

Eat as is. In scrambled eggs, in a pulao, in roast chicken bread and giblet stuffing, potato chops, in a toasted Goan bran bun, in a chilli fry with pork crackling and caramelized onion rings, with reachado fried tiger prawns, any which way.

Use your imagination.

And you may, as we all do, make a pig of yourself.

Bon appétit!

****

Hook, Line and Sinker

I am, like all Goans, a fool for fish. Give me a menu and I race past the superfluities till the good word, *poisson* leaps out of the page and I swallow the bait – hook, line and sinker. Blame it on Joaquim Antonio Silveira, catamaran fisherman, who lives in a house by the sea within fly-casting distance of my own in the Goan fishing hamlet of Anna *vaddo*. Joaquim is friend, philosopher and guide. His knowledge of the sea and the life it nurtures is little short of encylopaedic. Ten years earlier, when we first met, he took my education in hand by arranging for a Boys' Own adventure.

Off we went in his catamaran on a full moon night to Grand Island to hunt for the Great Rock Fish. 'He ugly sah,' Joaquim said, 'most ugly fish in whole world. He hide underwater in deep holes in rock.' 'How do you get him to come out?' I asked. 'He no come out,' Joaquim grinned. 'I go down get him.' And he raised his fish spear in one hand and a heavy, marine flashlight in the other. We cast a sea anchor in a rolling swell in the lee of a cliff. Joaquim took a deep breath, crossed himself and plunged in. Just as I was beginning to worry, he broke water and raised the spear triumphantly aloft. Impaled at the end was – without the shadow of a doubt – the Ugliest Fish In The Whole World.

It also proved later in the day to be the most delicious fish I had ever eaten. And I learned an important first lesson in the wily ways of fish. As a general rule, *great flavour and texture in a fish are inversely proportionate to its lack of good looks*. My introduction to the Rock

Fish was followed a couple of weeks later by a close encounter with the elusive Cock Fish, a rarity even among Joaquim and his friends, and perfectly named. If you take a cock in its prime and squash it flat in mid-crow, from beak to tail feather, then inflate it gently three inches around the middle tapering off at the edges, retain the colours but replace the feathers with bony scales, you have the Cock Fish. So amazed was I by this apparition, and so fearful that this bizarre variation on the one that got away would be met with hoots of derision when I later told the tale, that I took the precaution of photographing the fish at once with my Nikon and, for good measure, had Gita paint it in oils for posterity. Contrary to all expectations, it ate like a dream. A week later, grinning from ear to ear, Joaquim brought home a pallo – a fish so ugly, it is hard put to make friends and influence people until it is eaten and you know, with a sigh, that you are at the beginning of a beautiful relationship.

As time went on, I added a few more hard-won principles to the first. *Young fish are tastier by far than grown-up fish.* When I shop for fish at Crawford Market on Saturday morning, I am the despair of the local fisherwomen. Large, fat pomfret are thrust at me. I am urged to stock up on mackerel the size of Arnold Schwarzenegger's forearms. Huge white prawn – with the disappointed look prawns have when they realize they will never grow up to be lobsters – are waved in pairs before my nose. A snip at fifty rupees a brace. It takes fortitude of a high order to keep one's virtue inviolate. Stony-eyed and unbudgeable, I insist on prepubescent pomfret no bigger than the palm of my hand, baby mackerel the size of small sardines and white prawns which – by my own rule of thumb – should be no longer than my index finger. And I do very well indeed. But they are not cost-efficient and you rarely find baby seafood – transcendental as they are – on restaurant menus. Shame on the owners.

Deep sea fish can't hold a candle to freshwater fish and esturians – fish which breed exclusively in the estuaries of rivers where fresh water meets salt. My freshwater fish apprenticeship began in my teens as a boy scout when we fished for our supper with rod and line in a rushing mountain stream in Kulu and Manali, among the clear, rock-strewn upper reaches of streams in Assam and the Nilgiris and along sylvan lakes in the Vale of Kashmir in that happy time when only the rainbow trout were likely to be troublesome. We fished for the lordly mahseer, a majestic fish full of muscle and guile and the small, wiry butchwa ever ready for a brawl; once hooked, you knew you had a fight on your hands. I remember fine moments with the tengara (a rugged and idioscyncratic individualist with impressive whiskers) and the quicksilver murral related to, but vastly more cunning than the pike. Within the hour, the fish were scaled, gutted, filleted or steaked, grilled or fried over woodfires and eaten with a whisk of salt and a generous squeeze of lemon. Magnifique! To the back of the class all you cordon bleu stuffed shirts!

It was here that I learned the last cardinal principle of fine fish cookery. *The very best fish need the very least of culinary artifice.* Cooking should enhance, not suppress, the essential personality of a fish. Thus, while heavy, oily fish such as mackerel and sardines respond gloriously to smoking and grilling, ladyfish, fresh Bombay duck and mullet would die the death if treated so inconsiderately. Mustard oil and green chillies, which sharpen and heighten the flavour of hilsa and roha, would be the ruination of whitebait or baby shark. While baking is an excellent way to prepare large, firm-textured fish for the table (surmai, rawas), you would be courting disaster if you tried this on with lap (Indian cousin to the Dover sole) or, the slim and graceful ladyfish, both best eaten lightly fried.

How do I like my fish? Every which way, as the mood moves me. I am nothing if not eclectic in my pursuit of seafood, though I must admit to a certain ethnic partiality for my neck of the woods. One of my favourites is the Portuguese/Goan fish stew, *caldinho*. Fillets of firm white fish (pomfret, pallo, kingfish) are marinated in salt, pepper and lemon juice and introduced briefly for five minutes or so into a boiling sauce, somewhat reduced, and perfectly wrought with strained coconut milk, salt and sugar, vinegar, tamarind paste, cumin, coriander, turmeric, garlic, sliced onion and crushed green ginger. Unbelievable. And very nearly as good as reachado black pomfret. Sliced above and below the central bone, stuffed with tiny pickled prawns, layered over with tongue-tingling reachado masala, quickly seared on both sides in very hot oil, over a very high flame, so that the skin is crisp and the juices are sealed in. I eat it with an aromatic pulao made with the prawn stock. When I wish merely to snack, there's a gourmet's choice: mackerel smoked in hay with a vinegar sauce, sardines grilled in rock salt, clams, mussels and crabs in dozens of delicious avatars and a positive embarrassment of prawns in all shapes, sizes and inclinations.

But liberated Goan that I am, I must doff a nostalgic cap to Indian seafood at large: the unique distinction which Maharashtra has bestowed so generously on Koliwada pomfret, mackerel and rock crab; that perennial favourite, Parsi patra Ni Machi, where banana leaf and mint chutney celebrate the steamy virtues of fat white pomfret (but why, frustratingly, only met with at Parsi homes and Parsi weddings?); those two exquisite Bengali dishes, Narkol Chingri and Maach Tel Jhaal, respectively, prawns baked in a coconut crust, and that prince of fish, the hilsa, magically stewed in mustard oil, white and black cumin, fenugreek and saunf, with onions, ginger and red chillies for good measure; Sind's flavourful contribution to my Good Fish Guide, that utterly seductive river fish, the palu, filigreed with a latticework of fine bones which melt miraculously when covered with spiced country liquour and baked in a slow oven; and, finally, Michele Fernandes's winning French way with red snapper (no wonder Remo is such a happy rock star!), stuffed with herbed butter and spring onions, flavoured with anise liqueur and baked to perfection.

But, the lady only cooks for close friends. So for all of you out there this, sadly, will be the one that got away ...

****

Will I never learn to face the truth?

'Gas,' I said to my wife defensively, and she smiled, letting my shirts out at the pleats. 'Acid indigestion then,' I suggested moodily, 'brought on by the relentless tensions of a madly successful career.' 'Sure you want hash brown potatoes with your roast chicken for dinner?' this said, naturally, in her most innocent, wide-eyed voice. But I was not to be undone. '*And* the sage and sausage stuffing,' I replied coldly, 'it is a touch of flatulence, nothing more.' The last word is hers. 'It does seem to go on and on though. Strange.'

Blame it all on a Goan childhood. Next to God and the hereafter, there is no more absorbing preoccupation in a Goan household than food. Recipes are a sacred trust, family heirlooms of priceless worth, fiercely protected from the neighbour next door. Vast banquets, meticulously created, are essential accompaniments to all of life's major events. Groaning boards welcome the newborn, encourage the nuptials of the just married and consolingly remind the company at the wake that all is not lost. While I ploughed through my first primer ('The Fish is in the Frying Pan') I was being coached in vastly more important matters: how to test the freshness of a pomfret, for instance, or the tenderness of young bhindis (you press the gills of the one and crisply snap the ends off the other.)

Oh the innocence of the very young. Nobody bothered to tell me that all the nicer things in life are either sinful or fattening.

I put on and lose weight with manic-depressive regularity. The way up is ever so gratifying. The artful Julia Child aids and abets, suggesting a spiced pot roast here, a cunning little Roquefort soufflé there; anon, her very own, wickedly seductive, chocolate-and-cognac mousse. Craig Clairborne rallies around in moments of crisis. Leading knight of the New York Times Round Table, celebrated author of great cookbooks, he is a source of inspiration and solace. For the troubled mind, and the sore at heart, I recommend Clairborne over calmpose any day. Here he is, immortalizing the humble egg, ' ... Saute the onions in the butter until tender. Add the flour, salt, pepper and blend. Stir in the cream until thickened. Fold in the Gruyere cheese until melted. Add the eggs ... ' Sheer poetry and it eats even better than it reads.

My mother completes this happy triumvirate. Her Goan ways with food are informed with delicacy, guile and a splendid disregard for the perils of over-indulgence. One of her creations, the sublime Goan dessert, *bebinca*, begins, 'Take the yolks of forty eggs ... ' I can get rich and retire on her recipes but she refuses to write a cookbook. She will not permit me to eat her *sorpotel* until it has seasoned for three days. All is forgiven though when I lur h on her pork vindaloo and prawn pulao. Calories? Cholesterol? Perish the thought.

Hints, signs and portents darken the way down. Buttons pop. The bathroom scales are terribly wrong. Shirts shrink. I am one short, bitter step from remorse and the diet books. 'Lose up to 20 pounds in 14 days!' promises the Complete Scarsdale Medical Dict. *Vogue's* Dr Atkins tells me grimly that carbohydrates kill. Craig Clairborne's ambrosial prose fades to a poignant, wistful memory before Dr Morton B. Glenn's mean-spirited injunctions, '... if your diet allows you 1 cup (2 portions) of cooked vegetables at a meal, you are to have ½ cup of two different vegetables, *not* (emphasis his) one full cup of one vegetable.' I am not convinced.

It takes a horrifying encounter with Dr Reuben's 'Save Your Life Diet' to bring me back to the straight and narrow. Unless, Dr Reuben informs me sepulchrally, I follow his high-roughage, minimal-protein, low-calorie diet right away, I am a hair's breadth from a mean and untimely end. I will be laid low, in early middle age, by varicose veins, kidney stones, liver dysfunction and terminal constipation. So much for the good news. If I persist in my degenerate ways, why then ... Overwrought, I seek instant comfort in a double-decker cream cheese, ham and water pickle sandwich.

One morning I find I have to lean forward to see my ankles. It is the moment of reckoning. There is nothing for it but professional help, permanent change, a brand new me.

Dr X is slim and dauntingly supple. 'Why,' he asks keenly, 'do you wish to lose weight?' It is no light query. Dark undercurrents are at work here. Why, indeed? Do I wish to stay healthy? But I am. I only feel sick when I diet. For my wife's sake? She knows I always put it on again. Out with it! I want to look slim and sexy, that's why. 'I do not feel fit when I'm fat, doctor,' I say. There's a twinkle in his eye. He's heard that one before.

First, a photograph. 'Turn sideways please. Breathe out. Smile. Good. We'll take another after three months. Before and after. Ha, ha.' He takes my pressure, blood and other unmentionable samples, makes me stick my tongue out (not my most impressive organ at the best of times) and goes, 'Tut, tut.'

'My dear chap,' he says, 'we must take you in hand at once.'

My worst fears are realized: a liquid diet for five days, daily injections of Vitamin B, an appetite depressant, a tranquillizer, minerals, violent exercise and Lasik thrice daily. 'Lasik?' 'Best diuretic there is. Gets all that liquid out. We don't want you to bloat now, do we?'

'And the tranquillizer?'

'So that you don't brood about food.'

'When do I eat again?'

'Come now, is that the right attitude?'

Three days later, I sit at a bone-bare breakfast table, balefully regarding a glass of orange juice. I think bitter thoughts: the man who invented Vitamin B injections is a sadist. Even now, my grand-aunt, eighty-seven years if a day, is settling down to a leisurely Goan breakfast in her cottage in Asagao: a thick, nourishing soojee porridge, sprinkled over with raisins and molasses, hot brown bread baked with toddy, lashings of freshly churned butter, mango preserves, a Goa sausage or two … Eighty-seven! With a bloodline like that I have nothing to fear. A decision is taken. The spirit soars. Join the party Clairborne. I shall never forsake you Julia Child. 'Breakfast,' I roar at the cook and in minutes eggs sizzle, crisp golden toast pops, bacon fries fragrantly and a gentle peace descends, once more, on the old homestead.

****

Well Done, Wagner

At dinner at a five-star French restaurant the other night, I was reminded of the innocence of callow times past. You are young and in Paris. The language adds to your confusion: one man's meat is another man's *pousain*. You run a nervous eye down columns of exquisitely incomprehensible copper-plate. The maître de's lack of expression is carved out of granite. But all is not lost. A single word leaps out and greets you with happy familiarity, *filet*, as in pomfret, of course. Your voice rings with confidence as you declare your intentions, 'I'll have the *Medallion de filet fignon a la Fleuriste.*' A bread of sorts seems indicated and another word, *roti*, warms and comforts. You order the *Roti de Cailles* as well, and what sounds like a jolly good dessert, *Pommes Gaufrettes en Paniers*. Champagne, naturally, for such magnificent nosh, 'a bottle of the *Granite au Champagne*, well chilled.'

The maître de is unperturbed.

'Does Monsieur wish to begin with the roasted quail, the beef or the potatoes? And the management's apologies but we do not serve our champagne sorbet by the bottle.'

Much champagne has splashed on spotless linen since the faux pas of my youth. Paris in the Sixties was wonderfully forgiving of a young man with pretensions; language was the only impediment which stood in the way of a good meal and other moveable feasts. And there was a saving grace: nothing was allowed to intrude on the serious business of eating excellently well. You were given a table, a menu, a wine list, and were expected to get on with it. Minor skirmishes with the language aside, truth was never a casualty to promise. Thus the *Guinea Fowl al la Normande* was a genuine celebration of a free-range bird, poached to perfection in cider, dressed in sour cream and Calvados, garnished with bacon and fried apple slices, served with a fresh green salad picked on the very day. A dessert as simple as a baked custard was a minor triumph, the fresh bread and rolls a tribute to the baker's art. And if the service was brusque, the napery barely adequate, and the bill proportioned as generously as the meal, this was right and just.

Will our home-grown French restaurants, severely retarded clones of the real thing, take note. We were ushered in by a young person whose Carter Road haute out of Ravissant's couture made no bones of the fact that she considered us small potatoes. The manager, in funeral black, led us in the manner of an archdeacon, in worshipful silence, across inlaid marble floors, to a table which dazzled with silver, cut glass and bone china. Six-foot, white-gloved waiters, recently employed no doubt as bouncers in Amritsari video parlours, glided menacingly about on little cat feet. Acrobatic black-belts to the man, every now and again, they leapt at unsuspecting tables brandishing enormous silver tureens which they flung open with a flourish before cringing diners.

I was shoe-horned into a chair; a gloved hand groped for my lap; alarm gave way to mere discomfort as a napkin was arranged so as to hide my lower parts. A heavy, leather-bound, coffee table book was thrust into my hands. The hotel's history? No, the menu. I ordered the *poulet pot-au-feu*, a dish so simple it may only be ruined by a truly inspired order of genius. I had underestimated the chef. I was presented with an apologetic obituary on an elderly fowl which had perished from terminal arthritis, then been hastily interred in a bouillon made from stale chicken cubes and a handful of tired vegetables. Canned button mushrooms, long dead, added insult to terminal injury.

Conspiracy theorists have it that this theatre of the absurd is carefully designed to distract from the appalling absence of good things to eat and nice things to drink, and to prepare one for the moment of reckoning when the waiter, shuffling up to your table and refusing to catch your eye, socks it to you in a discreet brown folder. Be that as it may, much is left to be desired in the way of drama and entertainment. And here I would like to offer our five-star hostelries, a Thought for the Year: why not say it with music? All that's required is imagination and the sort of thingummyjig the Japanese are so good at, stuck under the table, into which a cassette may be slipped surreptitiously with each course.

How nice to be able to say, 'A large Scotch, please, with Handel's *Water Music* on the side, the steak *con brio* if I may, and a large helping of Wagner with that. Well done, the last time I was here it limped along a bit.' Or: '*Pomp and Circumstance*, I think, with the *Chicken a la Kiev*, a cymbalic mushroom or two would help, and could you play the theme from *2001 AD* when your waiters do their thing with the silver tureens.' Or, witheringly, as you return the *Coq au Vin* uneaten: 'The *Unfinished Symphony* would have been appropriate ...' Nor need we neglect our ethnic roots, *Oye Oye* with the kathi kabab, for instance, and to add to the homespun pleasures of our latest village eatery in the capital, the real thing: cries of terminal anguish as all manner of fish, flesh and fowl are done in with blunt sickles to the merry laughter of the local yokels.

And, when courtesy the management, lighter by a month's honest wages, the *Pathetique Symphony* ushers you on your way, thank heaven for small mercies. Given the quality of your meal, it could well have been *The Last Post*.

****

The Drinking Man

In a tiny room
a boot-legging 'Auntie'
of formidable girth and
crucifying eye flanked by
as menacing a brace of
villains as you were likely
to meet in those benighted
parts, stood behind a table.

Blithe Spirit

In the August issue of an English monthly in Goa, the editor vented his spleen at the demeaning of serious Goan values in the national press by – traitorous heresy! – Goan columnists and cartoonists (read, inter alia, Frank Simoes and Mario Miranda). Are Punjabis, he asks (having just returned, no doubt, from a jolly night out with the boys in the Terai) any less fun-loving than Goan? Never before, I suspect, has this invidious comparison been made in the public print. But I was not surprised.

Par for a rancorous course, the editorial was the latest in a vanguard of angry Goan reaction, thankfully in small if highly vocal minority, to any portrayal of the brighter side of life in the green and pleasant land of my ancestors. Let us be charitable. Perhaps the editor in question had neglected to attend a village feast, a christening, a club ball, a wedding, or drop in at his convivial local taverna in the previous month (tut, tut; abstinence so unGoan as to be utterly disgraceful).

Given the blight that afflicts the human spirit wherever one turns in this country, one would imagine that the ability to celebrate the lighter side of life against grim odds would be cause for congratulation. I am glad to report that the naysayers have no future: there is boundless resilience to Goa's blithe spirit; down the applauding centuries it has cocked a snook at the philistines, in rousing voice, with a guitar in one hand and a glass of vintage feni in the other, knowing full well that high spirits and high seriousness (will our dour Goan editor please take note) far from being mutually exclusive are happily and irrevocably symbiotic.

Brewed from two of the least promising candidates in the botanical world – the coconut palm and the cashew fruit – feni is to the Goan psyche what the sky is to a bird, a medium of joyful and kaleidoscopic potential. Clear as vodka, with a slight bouquet in the case of cashew, feni may be drunk neat or mixed, as with its Russian cousin, with almost anything that takes your fancy. Goans drink a great deal of feni: joyfully at births; solemnly at deaths; awesomely at Christmas and other festivals. They drink it before, with and (in the form of a wicked coffee liquer) after meals. They drink it in all ages and conditions: babies are fed a few drops with sugar to ward off a cold; it is rubbed in the joints for rheumatism and generously imbibed by the patient immediately thereafter; come to think of it, Goans drink feni whenever and wherever they please.

Nowhere are they to be seen better pleased than in the local taverna. Here, in a land blessed with many gifts, nature's most thoughtful bounty is enjoyed in full and free measure, by the *copito*. The equivalent of a generous double (the measure is always poured to overflowing and not, as in Bombay, well below the lip), the *copito* is never interpreted literally, for it is less the measure of a drink than a state of mind, a warm invitation to camaraderie, to easy conversation and good fellowship and, as the evening star rises in the night sky, perhaps to a little wassail, laughter and song.

You will be glad to discover that Goa's tavernas are ubiquitous – in town, village and remote hamlet – and always ready to serve. But you would do well to avoid the three- and four-star attempts at meretricious imitation in some of the larger urban centres. Here, dud coinage is offered in lieu of old, minted worth. A swift glance at the racks behind the bar reveals all: a riotous, unsightly display of bottled goods, cock-eyed flights of fancy in shape and ornamentation: a carnival of brands, bewildering to the untutored eye, labelled with a wanton confusion of colour, type and illustration, and a fine disregard for the ethics of design. You may, if your luck holds, find some slight merit in names such as Old Barrel, Red Star, El Nectarino, O Fidalgo, Alegria, Golden Barrell, Black Tiger, Donna Lisa *et al*. But you are more likely to be inflicted with a chemically brutalized, additive-laden apology for the real thing and pay thrice as much. You may, if adventurously inclined, work your way through, with strong heart and stout liver, finding joy where you can. Not that I would recommend it.

Seek out the small taverna instead, where locals gather around rough wooden tables, where a family has, for generations, dispensed good cheer and good nosh to an appreciative and close-knit circle of neighbourhood afficionados, where the feni comes in merry brown bottles, unlabelled, roughly corked. Approach its contents with care and respect, for this is likely to be genuine, pure and wholesome, distilled and nurtured by the family in traditional, inviolate mode, happiest and most true when drunk under its own roof.

The taverna is at its welcoming best at sunset. Visit. Select a seat by a window with a view of village and fields. Get to know the magnificent brew. Its liquid alchemy revives tired cells with the gentlest of encouragement. Time is paced by the tolling of Angelus bells, a black dog trotting across an emerald paddy field at twilight, going home for his dinner, two farmers at the next table enquiring about the health and well-being of each other's pigs. Allow the *copitos* to come as they will. The tavern keeper *knows*. His disposition, god-given, poured from the happy brown bottle, will lead you gently past sunset and evening star, the flicker of oil lamps in village windows, a girl's voice raised in a *fado* cozened by a lone guitar; to quiet introductions and good fellowship as the amber bottle moves once more and you are made welcome as guest, friend, brother; to laughter and song as the witching hour approaches; perhaps a plate of crab or sausage with a loaf or two of the crusty village bread; then the last amber bottle makes the rounds to good-natured if feeble protest, and home across fields fragrant with the scent of dew of paddy and the musky essence of *raat ki rani*. All about you the palms sway beneath the shifting moon as they have before time began, as they will when a new dawn breaks.

Fare forward, blithe spirit!

****

Yo Ho Ho and a Bottle of Rum

Bluebeard … Captain Blood … Long John Silver. Buccaneering scourges of the Caribbean. Armed with unflinching ruthlessness, a cutlass in one hand and a bottle of rum in the other, they sank legions of ponderous Spanish galleons laden with the golden loot of the New World. Do we remember them for the measure of treasure they accumulated over the years? Or the hapless hundreds made to walk the plank? Or their gory gallows end? Perish the thought. All that remains of their claim to fame is Robert Louis Stevenson's rousing ditty:

> Fifteen men on the dead man's chest
> Yo Ho Ho, and a bottle of rum!
> Drink and the devil had done for the rest
> Yo Ho Ho, and a bottle of rum!

Down the intemperate centuries the dramatis personae may have undergone a sea-change and the circumstances gentled somewhat, but who among us can gainsay the stirring virtues of a bottle of fine rum? Or the inspired triumph of mind over matter that it never fails to bring about so swiftly? Man and boy I have pursued twin vocations, the Word and the Water of Life. Both are irresistible, intoxicating and, when celebrated with the spirit of the acolyte, may reward one with small mercies. And while I have found them sorely troublesome on more than one occasion, at the end of the day I have been a better and happier person for the pursuit. Despite the odd fraught memory recalled with rue.

The earliest a rough and ready teenage initiation urged on by gleeful peers in the days when prohibition sat dankly on the land and the only way a Byculla Boy could cut his drinking teeth was at the end of a motley queue in an alleyway off Sankli Street. In a tiny room a bootlegging 'Auntie' of formidable girth and crucifying eye, flanked by as menacing a brace of villains as you were likely to meet in those benighted parts, stood behind a wooden table. On it was a glass. The First Villain snarled. The Second Villain held out an open palm into which you slipped, with trembling fingers, a five-rupee note. 'Auntie' squirted the glass brimful with a noxious brew from a football bladder. Close the eyes. Say a prayer. Down the hatch. A roiling glow in the tummy, a delightful friskiness to the step. To the back of the queue again. Once more with feeling. Then, to my utter astonishment I began to levitate, bobbing up and down, this way and that, like a small inebriated cloud. I remained atmospherically unstable till the next morning when I came to, just, convinced I was dying. My unfeeling friends disabused me – no such luck! But if I wished to avoid a hangover in the future I must learn my limit. Indeed.

Scene II. Two years later. Your hero has earned his sea legs and is now an intrepid sailor on a Japanese freighter. He speaks no Japanese; the thirty-man crew speak no English. They get along famously until the last night on board when the Captain lays on a ceremonial farewell dinner. A teapot steams gently at the side of each place setting, a tiny ceramic bowl beside it. Warm sake. The Captain points cheerfully, pot to bowl, in sign language's most welcome hieroglyphic, 'Drink up.' The fearless deckhand does so in a swift gulp or two. Ha! Mother's milk. When will these inscrutable Orientals learn about the hard stuff? Beer with everything and now … this! Well after the witching hour and the umpteenth toast is done, your man-at-the-mast discovers with alarm that he has no legs below the knees. He does not rise so much as unfold, joint by joint, like an ancient carpenter's rule. The teapot bows to him gravely and takes a short hop backwards; he returns the traditional farewell and they recede, bowing and hopping, into infinity. Not quite. He

backs out of the stateroom and tumbles down the stairs. Gales of
Japanese laughter encourage his downfall ....

Wiser by several decades I now approach avante garde versions
of the Water of Life with circumspection and a couple of hard-won
ground rules. Rule No I: there exists an inversely proportionate
relationship between the innocuous appearance of a spirit and its
lethality. Thus ouzo and aquavit and Pernod are devilish plots in a
bottle created by the Greeks, Scandinavians and French to undermine
the future of your liver (it is easy, on your fourth ouzo, to forget
that you have one). Colourless, smooth as milk, stratospherically
proofed, they plead beguilingly for indiscretion. Resist the
temptation repeating, without moving your lips, 'Whoa boy, you
must live to drink another day.' Even F. Scott Fitzgerald, that sad
and irrepressible tippler, sounded a warning, 'First you take a drink,
then the drink takes a drink, then the drink takes you.' But beware
as well of the lunatic fringe howling at the far end, the philistines,
sprouting like poisonous weeds all over the land even as I write,
who would have us wholly bereft of good cheer. There is only one
riposte to lay them low: quote the American humorist Robert
Benchley's exquisite squasher when told that drinking was a slow
death, 'So who's in a hurry?' I'll drink to that!

Choose your tipple as you would your friends, by inclination,
proximity and congeniality. But keep an open mind and an
investigative outlook or you may miss out on the King's ransom
that India now has on offer. We have, as all know, been keen
purveyors of intoxication for centuries, Rajasthan's gulab and Goa's
feni being just two of dozens of sterling ethnic efforts to keep the
spirits up. But keen research into that ungainly collection of
bureaucratic syllables, Indian Made Foreign Liquor, will reveal that
Lucknow now offers as many ways to get sloshed as London. Our
whiskies have come of age. Pleasant surprises await the dedicated
tippler right across the range, from the modestly-priced, quietly
self-assertive Directors Special to the snootily-christened Antiquarian
(a fine, well-bred whisky nonetheless); from McDowell's doughty
bottlings for malt enthusiasts to the ultra-smooth, high-powered
and accordingly priced Oaken Glow that Seagram's have thoughtfully
brought to market for the well-heeled aficionado; while in all fairness

one must allow, no matter how reluctantly a nod of recognition to the handful of over-priced, country-cousin Scotch whiskies which gather dust where they lie.

The other spirits have kept their end up. Indian rum, gin and vodka are well up to reasonable world standards (will I be forgiven for confessing to a partiality for Alcazar over Smirnoff?) while our beers, particularly the lagers, could grace an English country pub or a Bavarian biergarten with honour and distinction. And I am happy to report that our wine snobs have now got their comeuppance. (The next time a twittering host uncorks a bottle of cheap French plonk and says, 'It has to breathe a bit' I shall say, 'Do the decent thing. Let it die!') European reds travel woefully to the tropics; the finer, drier whites not at all. More times than I care to recall I have been inflicted with terminally ill red Burgundies (more likely their stricken cousins) at Indian summer room temperatures when they should have been chilled to sixty-five degrees thus preserving what little life remained till the roast was done with. But salvation is, at long last, at hand. Indian wines surprise and refresh. While the offerings of our handful of vintners tend to be erratic, hats off to Grover. Pricey, true, but with utter fidelity to quality, character and consistency. Their dry white, rose and red do honour to palate and plate as Grover and the Oberoi, in brilliant alliance masterminded by Jiggs Kalra, Karen Anand and a galaxy of specialist chefs, proved with resounding success at a recent banquet of Indian foods and wine at the Regal Room. I have laid down crates of Grover's wines and must now explain this disgracefully expensive behaviour to the wife.

Perhaps I shall divert her attention with my file of memorabilia concerning the stuff that cheers. Utterly delightful and awesomely useless bits and pieces which I now propose to share with you. Did you know that the Chinese invented beer five thousand years ago, that a bottle of 1805 Chateau Lafite sold at Christies for £8,300, and that – from 'well oiled' to 'one over the eight' – there are 101 ways your friends can accuse you of being sloshed. And if you want to find out if you really are – God forbid! – try saying this, 'Beautiful Betty bought some butter/But, said she, the butter's bitter/So she bought some better butter/And put the better butter in the bitter butter/to make the bitter butter better.' If you can't, take heart. You can always say 'Cheers' in nineteen different languages but would be well advised to avoid the Russian, 'Na Sdorovic.' If you are in Italy you may find saying cheers a trifle exhausting. The average Italian drinks 110 bottles of wine a year, proving that Henry Aldrich was right after all: 'If all be true that I do think/There are five reasons we should drink/Good wine, a friend, or being dry/Or lest we should be by and by/Or any other reason why.'

Bottoms up!

****

Praise the Lord and Pass the Feni

Heaven and hell lay about me in my childhood.

I was born a Saraswat Brahmin Roman Catholic Goan (sort that one out if you can) and when the church bells of my youth tolled the Angelus at dusk, they carried the faintest echoes of the temple bells of my ancestors. Yet Satan sprung real and virulent straight from the pages of the Old Testament, lurked behind the tiniest of sins.

Better to be on the side of the angels and here a Roman Catholic childhood offered magnificent protection: the solace of commandment, precept and ritual demanding nothing less than unconditional acceptance, tempered by the flickering illumination of sacred candlelight, the hypnotic repetition of plainsong and chant, the muted responses of the family rosary at dusk, the bells of the Angelus echoing over twilight spires, the measured revelation of a miracle each Sunday at Mass, the shrouded lamentations of Lent and the joyful, resurrectional hallelujahs of Easter and Christmas.

Small wonder then that I said goodnight to God before I slept and offered grateful prayer to him in the morning for the blessings of a newly minted day. Before lunch and dinner we gave thanks for that which we were about to receive, Amen. I confessed my sins in the shadows of the Stations of the Cross, guilt and retribution sullen on my young soul, as I whispered the words of acknowledgement, 'Father forgive me, for I have sinned ... ' And when I received

Communion the following day, taking the living host on my tongue, the fluted columns and Gothic arches of St Anne's Church shone with the radiance of redemption; the stained glass triptych bewitched the eye, making many-splendid glories of the flooding light; there was a triumphant resonance to the very air; salvation was, by the grace of God, mine again.

But if guilt and redemption were sombre chords (struck still in a somewhat wayward life), the great feast days of the church offered high-spirited crescendos — Easter and Christmas and, more particularly if you were Goan, the exuberant village celebrations on the feasts of Patron Saints. Since the Litany of Saints is nothing if not generously endowed, rarely did a fortnight go by in Goa without some village or the other making excessively merry.

I always found Christmas overwhelming. There was so much to do and so little time to do it in. Now Easter came along in a gentler fashion, a promising glow at the end of the long, dark tunnel of Lent. If I gave up chocolates, fasted on Fridays, attended a three-day religious 'Retreat' barred from all speech, and generally put a brave face on those endless, daunting weeks, the thought of Easter made it all bearable, for the waiting was agreeably leavened by the *preparations* for Easter Sunday, and here the honours were strictly apportioned. My mother and sisters made the kitchen their inviolate territory. The men of the family — my father and his two sons — were to provide the wherewithal for what would, without question, be a memorable feast.

A lifetime's application had prepared my father for this kind of work. Cheerful hewer of song and drawer of laughter, he was born the heir-apparent to a Goan clan. Colvale, our village, or as my grandfather would have it, the ancestral seat, nestles in a fold of the river Snapora and here, in privileged isolation, my father grew to young manhood accepting, with good grace but never entirely seriously, the convictions of the gentry. The family despaired of my father for he seemed too casual to care. If he was ever stern, uncompromising, relentlessly committed, it was, perhaps, when addressing himself to a perfectly done roast suckling pig; when he gave forceful voice, it was to the accompaniment of a guitar; and his guardianship of the family's cherished traditions was never more evident than when concerned with the care and replenishment of the ancestral cellars.

Yet he enjoyed his birthright hugely, without guilt or doubt. Life for him was a celebration of the natural order of things: the miracle of young paddy fields after the first rains, the fellowship of his friends, his sailing boat and the sea, the gifts of laughter, song, a bottle, children, the pleasures of the table ....

Now, the finest hour of the year upon him, ably aided and abetted by his sons, he made his presence tellingly felt in the local markets. The crabs, destined for immortality, baked in the shell, took three trips in the getting, for he had decided firmly on plump, black rock crabs, no other. Gills of innumerable pomfrets were pried open, the interiors closely examined, before six were selected for the fish curry. A foray was made at the crack of dawn into darkest Sonapur, where a villain of a butcher dispensed the only free range pork in the city; one never, but never, compromised on a *sorpotel*. Only chicken which had the run of the countryside were considered eligible for the *cafreal*, and the prawns for the *apa de camaroo* had to be the huge, white prawns which bred, scarcely and expensively, in river estuaries, yearning to be lobsters. Anything less, sacrilege!

One would have thought that high seriousness of this order, sustained over days, would, eventually, allow us to put our feet up. Perish the thought, for this was only food – glorious food to be sure – still ... victuals. Yet to be addressed was the near sacramental question of booze. And here my father was sole and final arbiter. A lifetime's critical experience, a spirit of indefatigable enquiry, a curiousity to rival Einstein's, had brought him in the autumn of his life to the happiest of conclusions. Not for him the noxious effusions sealed with *tin caps (!)*, variously described as vodka, whisky and gin – inferior alcohols chemicalised, tinted, flavoured, caramelized beyond all hope of salvation. It was feni or nothing.

The family appreciated this fine distinction, for feni is, in its more authentic rendering, nectar for the Gods. Palm feni, my tipple of choice today, is as clear and odourless – but far more refreshing – as spring water. Cashew however, is a clear favourite among knowledgeable Goans for it gets you to your destination with a pleasing swiftness. Bottles of the ancestral feni, carefully transported from Colvale where it had matured in the family cellars for five years or more, were now brought forth! Amber bottles, roughly corked, lightly cobwebbed, reverentially dusted off, were laid in a cheerful array on the sideboard. The heady white wine of the Monks of Honte de Guirem was put down to cool. A brace of bottles of an exquisite feni-based coffee liqueur were thoughtfully added to the sideboard display. All was now ready.

To the uninitiated observer, the first question that sprang to mind was, 'Is this a family lunch? Or a banquet?' Well, yes and yes. Every Easter my parents, as the eldest siblings in awesomely extended families, played host to the clan. An assortment of aunts, uncles, cousins, nieces and nephews – some three- or four-dozen strong – would somehow manage to fit into our modest home, resplendent in brand new Easter finery, all blessed with growling Goan appetites and, more to the point, with never-say-die Goan livers! (*On the eighth day, God said, 'Let there be a Liver!' and lo and behold in faraway Goa, there ploppingly appeared* ...)

For the women of the house, it was a time of high drama and low farce. Would the *bebinca* – the most triumphant of Goan desserts, baked layer upon interminable layer, emerge from the open oven with delicacy and restraint? At the last minute, the butcher had failed to deliver the lambs' kidneys. A generational pox on the man! Would the *sorpotel*, lovingly prepared three days earlier, now maturing in a huge earthenware pot, live up to its fragrant reputation? And if the *sanas* that went with it did not turn out to be the fluffiest, lightest, tastiest ever bestowed on an undeserving family, my mother swore she would die the death. Fears happily without foundation, for I *knew* my mother's cooking and in all of these many Easters, I had never been cross with one of her buns.

And on the Day, begun with High Mass, sung by choir and congregation, if there was a distinct lack of penitence in the '*Agnus Deis*', and if the '*Kyrie Eleisons*' were a trifle hurried and informed with a lilt more joyful than usual, all was forgiven as the priest ascended the pulpit, turned towards the faithful, and repeated the words of redemption, 'I am the resurrection and the life ...'

Where shall I be this Easter? Why, in Goa, of course. I shall be going home again, to my village, in the true and holy spirit of the words, where the values of kinship and community are held sacred still, where in every Catholic home at the end of the Rosary at dusk, the ancient blessings are given, parent to child, grandparent to parent, until the very old bless the very young by the charismatic laying on of hands, where it is impossible to tell when the village ends and the fields begin because the symbiosis between man and environment is whole and complete.

Where I shall praise the Lord, pass the feni, and raise a silent toast, 'Happy Easter to one and all!'

****

The Bombaywallah

Rose Cherian's Dobermann
makes an indecent
suggestion to
Lalubhai Desai's irresistibly
alluring Dalmation who is
not disinclined.
Consumation, alas, must
await another sunrise.

When the social historians of the twenty-first century chronicle the self-destruction of a great city, they will point to a micro-map of Bombay in the early Sixties. 'This,' they will say, 'is when the folly began.' Black dots in the urban topography, few, far between, tucked away in the odd, obscure corner, seeking to go unremarked and unobserved. 1981: it is apocalypse now. Like blind, malignant growths, the stains have spread, invading the open spaces violating the green belts, creeping up hillsides, choking the arteries, threatening the vital signs, spawning with a bewildering fecundity, until the very air we breathe is infected by the spores of the slums.

For years we have said to ourselves, if we ignore them they will go away. We look and refuse to see; we cauterize our sensitivity to suffering, and as we pursue our favourite pleasure – the acquisition of power and money, the satiation of greed – our very lifestyles are imperilled by the inexorable tide of the dispossessed and the unwanted. There is one of 'them' now for each one of 'us' and they are beginning to come into their own, to impose organization on chaos, to refuse to remain ciphers in a planner's file. They will no longer allow their lives to be reduced to the cynicism of a voters' list.

In the rabbit warrens in which they exist – where huts are separated by inches and the approach road is a gutter which serves as latrine and passage both, and where you can take your pick between stamping on shit or on a child – in these abominable violations of the human spirit, there is a new and determined gestalt: a brave, affectionate sense of community, of comradeship and strength in numbers; they have nothing to lose and thus must prevail; they will find a place in the sun. A terrible resolve is taking hold. In a single, powerful voice – mercifully not yet informed with violence – they demand to be heard.

We hear the sound, a distant and disturbing turbulence, but cannot, or refuse to understand the words. We have always regarded the slums – on those occasions when we were forced to – as a surgical problem, and excercised one or the other of two options: containment and excision. We have taken what is essentially a human and moral issue – can one fortunate human being allow, within arm's reach, the brutalization of another? – and reduced it to figures; the figures to plans; the plans to money; whereupon, heaving a collective sigh, we spoke wearily of corruption, venality, exploitation and the other unredeemable sins of the victims. *When will we act?* When will we realize that if the slum dweller does not find his rightful place in our city we shall soon, willy-nilly, have to vacate ours?

True, they stand accused on various counts: there are slum landlords, slum capitalists, slum pimps: they exploit each other brutally just as we do in our ivory towers of affluence, but there the similarity ends. They also aid each other in need – quick to comfort, help, defend – because they know that nobody else will. The community, in the final equations of survival or defeat, comes first. If we, the affluent, have begun the process of polarization which, in its first and most damning manifestation says, 'Them and Us', the slum community, united, organized, purposeful as never before, will take it to a violent and tragic conclusion.

Four million people, half the city's population, live in the slums. Human beings, people like you or I, old folks and wage earners, housewives and children. Cut them and they bleed. Tickle the funny bone and they laugh. When a house collapses on them, skulls implode, eyeballs crush and liquefy, bones shatter to splinters, vital organs rupture; they die exactly as we would if the roof had to fall in. 200,000 of them are in imminent danger of just such a death this monsoon: eight and ten to a room, they live in 5,000 ramshackle buildings, ceiling propped up with wooden poles; dwelling places which have long been condemned by the authorities. They have nowhere to go. The slums they inhabit, which may deal death at any moment, are refuge and citadel.

Let us take a quick Cook's tour of a horizontal slum, choosing, for this exercise, Dharavi, the largest slum in Asia. It is a small city within a city, a self-contained sub-culture. A first view of Dharavi approached along the glittering new Ring Road which skirts the slum, is daunting: one gets the impression of a stronghold of a wholly alien kind: the huts facing the road are packed solidly together, phalanx upon phalanx of impenetrable, stoic brick: tiled roofs stretch as far as the eye reaches, an undulation of sepia tones with no open spaces visible; sudden, narrow alleys lead into darkness. A medieval enclave, sullen, barricaded, access by permission or right of residence only; a stranger enters at the risk of violent confrontation, and that is no exaggeration.

I am told that the police make strong bandobast when they have to enter Dharavi, and if they step warily it is with good reason. Violence is endemic; a certain kind of rough justice is rule of law in Dharavi's mean streets; an element of freewheeling, buccaneering enterprise makes itself felt at once. The criminal minority live by smuggling, hard drug peddling, prostitution and bootlegging; a complex social structure is hierarchically inclined. Lawless gangs have established fiefdoms, internecine bonds and territorial imperatives as tenuously and finely spun as a web; there is a working symbiosis – 'Sink or swim together' – with the relatively law-abiding majority.

A good 80 to 85 per cent of the residents of Dharavi attempt to get by as all of us do – by battening on Bombay's enormous generation of wealth in one way or another: the men work as labourers, hawkers, hand cart pushers, low-level office workers; many of the women are employed as daytime servants in middle-class homes; whole families work at cottage industries, making cheap goods and artefacts and, in the process, exploiting child labour in appalling conditions. All of them make do: like lichen in a desert they are conditioned to absolute survival, extracting the last drop of sustenance from a cruel environment. In microcosm, the Dharavi slum holds up a cracked mirror to Bombay's high life. The price of a one-room hut runs to about Rs.15,000, brisk trading sends property values soaring each year; hut owners apply their own leverage by selling 'sleeping' space in shifts for up to one hundred rupees per person per month. It is a seller's market. Even so, the signs of a humble affluence – transistor radio, the Jawa motorcycle, the TV aerial – occur as infrequently as a generous gleam in a miser's eye.

The harsh reality is the hut, the filth, the excrement on the doorstep; the naked children defecating in the mud in which they and their dogs play and eat and often sleep; the tap which serves hundreds and more often than not runs dry; the maggot-infested latrine at the end of the road; the epidemics which scythe through whole communities; the lack or total absence of medical help; the anger and futility at the deaths in the night which need never have happened. 'No one listens, no one cares. We get promises at election time and they are never kept.' He worked as a porter at Dadar railway station. He spoke the truth and I had no answers.

There are answers, of course, there have to be, and as the debate gathers force, the options are dusted off, refurbished and weighed. Should we build bridges across the harbour to the hinterland, opening it up, with a bunch of carrots, to industry to decentralize? Should we use the stick and force industry to decentralize? Should we deed the slums to its inhabitants and provide the basic amenities – water, power, paved streets, medical and social inputs?

Should we bulldoze the horizontal slums, relax the FSI, hand the whole sorry mess over to commercial builders, accommodate the slum dwellers in high rises, and offer the constructors a quid pro quo in the form of additional properties they could then develop and sell for a profit on the open market? Should we go, cap in hand, to the centre to whom we contribute an enormous amount of revenue, asking for some back to ensure that the goose which lays the golden eggs stays healthy and fertile? Or should we begin by containing the issue, legislating against the 300 new immigrant families that come into the city each day? Should we do this, or that, or the other? The questions fly thick and fast, and I have yet to hear the right one: *should we ask the four million slum dwellers what their thoughts are on the subject?* Perhaps they felt that *we* – consuming as rabidly and conspicuously as we do – are the problem.

There are many concerned people in our city, people of probity, influence and honest purpose, who have matured beyond the shackles of cast and the restrictions of community, people for whom the greatest good of the greatest number is more than a homily. They see this city as an inheritance bequeathed to them which, in turn, they must pass on with honour to their children. We must mobilize not just money and resources; we must mobilize the will of such people. We must work with whatever tools are to hand, creating those we need, applying the pressures we must, legislating for the hard disciplines called for, working towards a common end so that, if not in ours, at least in the lifetimes of our children, the cruel distinctions between 'them' and 'us' will blur and merge into the triumphant, affirmative, 'We'.

****

Dear Traffic Commissioner

This letter begins with a caveat. Please understand that I am not merely on your side: I am an admirer, albeit, at times, a confused one. When I encounter, as I do with distressing frequency these days, irate Letters to the Editor, worse still, articles blazing with indignant rhetoric, not to mention the wails of anguish from limping pedestrians deprived of their rightful place in the city's natural order of abuse, I am saddened at the lack of understanding, the shameful absence of any semblance of sympathy with the heroic – nay, athletic – manner in which you have addressed an immensely difficult task.

When, with exemplary chutzpah, you took apart and reassembled the traffic mess at Flora Fountain and Kalaghoda, I had occasion to rap across the knuckles an unkind critic (it takes all sorts, Commissioner) who mentioned that it reminded him of nothing so much as the gay abandon with which his infant daughter rearranged spaghetti on a plate. Radical problems call for revolutionary solutions, I pointed out, you can't make an omelette without breaking eggs etc. One dismisses, as of little consequence, the psychotic episodes involving homicidal BEST buses, pedestrians with acute anxiety attacks and the inexplicable absence of traffic crossings. It is a small price to pay for progress.

The greatest good of the greatest number, that's the ticket. Never mind that I set off at ten-thirty one morning from Nariman Point en route to VT, drove round and round in ever widening circles, only to end up dizzy and cross-eyed at the Bombay Gymkhana at noon. My fault entirely. Now if I had had the foresight to draw a detailed traffic map of South Bombay from your very comprehensive press release (five half columns, no less; naming all the roads with their newest names was a nice touch) would I have been found at lunchtime at the Gym's bar, clutching a glass and quivering like a casuarina in a high wind?

Not, mind you, that there are no compensations. May I recount a cheering incident, when courtesy did not go unrewarded. If you've heard this one before Commissioner, well, chuckle again.

There I was, parked politely behind a bus at the traffic junction between the Oval and Cross Maidan, waiting for the lights to change. Green, and I nipped across smartly, only to have a traffic cop (crisply starched, I was proud to note) wave me to the far side kerb, well away from the rude and scoffing multitude so quick to gather at the scene of a traffic crime. He removed a little black book from his shirt pocket and pointed down the road to a tiny sign thoughtfully hidden behind a bush. THIS LANE FOR BUSES ONLY, it said. Then a strange thing happened. Pen poised above page, my friendly policeman was seized by a *petit* attack of St Vitus' Dance. He shuffled from foot to foot, cast quick glances over both shoulders, while his left eyebrow twitched in urgent solicitation. The penny dropped. I handed over a crisp, large note. He had the good grace to feign reluctance. 'For the Police Widows and Orphans Fund,' I murmured reassuringly, 'and may the Force be with you.'

Warmed the cockles of my heart that did. Do your critics appreciate, Commissioner, that your efforts have brought back to our roads the possibility of happy and unexpected surprise? Take your ingenious device for the alleviation of boredom and the conservation of gas – the car pool. If it weren't for the pool, would I have known that Neighbour C had an embarrassing medical problem, that the tax authorities had raided and uncovered a monumental foreign exchange scam in Neighbour M's offices, while impeccable authority had it that Neighbour D's wife had developed more than a passing affection for Neighbour F's husband? Stirring stuff, it brightens up my day no end. The car pool spurred me on to higher endeavour: I would, henceforth, give rides to despairing fellow citizens trying to hail short haul cabs, an initiative which,

I must confess, met with mixed results. I decided to call it a day when a venerable old party I picked up at Kemp's Corner, chuckled pruriently, said, 'Pssst,' and flashed a life insurance agent's card at me.

In retrospect, a prescient offer, for shortly after that, in a bold, brilliantly innovative masterstroke, you banned the use of horns under pain of fine or worse. The moment of truth came sooner than I would have wished. The dear old Parsi lady who darted across the road at K.C. College presented me with Hobson's choice – manslaughter or misdemeanour. I slammed on brake and horn. He was at my side like a genie, book open, pen poised and the PW & O Fund was richer by twenty rupees. What a way to start a day! The next week I allowed a Great Dane to live with a Rambo-like application of brakes and nary a honk, only to be side-swiped by a soundless ratamobile equally determind to abide by the law. I must admit, Commissioner, to liking you a little less.

I now tool about noiselessly in a heavy-duty Army surplus jeep with reinforced steel bumpers fore and aft and a song in my heart. The other day a street urchin, trying conclusions with my left headlamp, bit the dust. No real damage done. A bruised ego, a bent clavicle, that sort of thing. I could say I was really unhappy about the cyclist I sent into a double flying somersault at Carmichael Road. Careless sod. And last evening, I smashed up a Maruti at Worli Naka. Now that felt terrific!

Thank you, Commissioner. You have brought dancing beams of sweetness and sunshine to our dour lives.

Gratefully yours,

PS. Talk of coincidences. Jung would be chortling in his grave. The mail has arrived with an offer I cannot refuse – your very first book. I always knew you had it in you, Commissioner. Let your detractors bite their tongues!

****

Carmichael Road Dog Lovers
Brace for Battle

Carmichael Road dogs, like Carmichael Road dog owners, like Cumballa Hill along which the road winds, constitute one of the last, inviolate bastions of Mumbai's privileged elite. Here, in the cool of the morning, dogs of distinguished pedigree may be seen taking their owners out for a constitutional. Observe how, at the gate of the Japanese embassy, Colonel Mukherjee's Alsation exchanges notes with Bapsy Crorewallah's Apso. Don't look now but a most uncivic encounter begins outside the Municipal Commissioner's bungalow. Rose Cherian's Dobermann makes an indecent suggestion to Lalubhai Desai's irresistibly alluring Dalmation who is not disinclined ('Is she ever?' Colonel Mukherjee may be heard muttering in his moustache). Consummation, alas, must await another sunrise.

It is interrupted by an unholy commotion down the road, just by the police chowki as Pinkie Durrani's Great Dane contests right of way with a mere ... a mere ... dudhwallah! Pinkie is not amused. 'Carmichael Road,' she announces to anyone who cares to listen, 'is going to the dogs.' Will the police bring the full majesty of authority to bear on this noisy transgression? They do. With quite unexpected speed and efficiency. The dudhwallah is hustled to the side of the pavement and warned NEVER TO LET THIS HAPPEN AGAIN! The Great Dane is unruffled. He cocks a defiant leg at a lamppost to make the point that he is above the law.

But today all is not well. A sense of impending doom, or sizzling outrage, envelops owners and dogs alike. The 'Good-mornings' carry no conviction; the 'Hi Scotties, Rovers, Bonzos,' clearly lack sincerity; there is scant interest in bowel movements, usually the object of keen, if discreet, scrutiny, pet paranoia being an occupational hazard. When, for three days running, young Lalitha Deshmukh ignored her terrier's evacuations for flirtatious banter with the silver-tongued Shanker (Moneybags) Swamy, who literally *dragged* his poor little Dachschund around, veiled threats of anonymous calls to the SPCA caused the azaleas to wilt. But today even Lalitha and the whiz kid are noticeably subdued. Snoopy, the Cocker Who Knows No Fear, urges me on to enquiry. I do so. Colonel Mukherjee, flinty-eyed (he has the enemy in his sights) hands me a printed notice. Its tombstone calligraphy reads, ISSUED BY BRIHANMUMBAI MUNICIPAL CORPORATION ... FOR DOG OWNERS ... A FINE OF RS. 1,000/- FOR DOG OWNERS IF DOGS MAKE A MESS (DOG SHIT) ON THE ROADS/FOOTPATHS.

Dear me, now the fecal matter has really hit the fan.

The gloom is not misplaced; nor is the sense of fear and injustice. Carmichael Road dogs, like their owners, and their homes, and their cars and clubs, are expensive propositions. And while feeble attempts at the tightening of domestic purse strings may occur from time to time, a dog's welfare is not negotiable. Bowel samples (at Rs. 500 a peek) are sent off to the pathologist at the slightest evidence of inconsistency; X-rays, frontier-edge antibiotics, rare vitamins and Harvard-trained vets are par for a cheque-strewn course. And let us draw a discreet veil over valeting, entertainment, monsoon protection, vacations and ... and ... (How could you forget, you brute!) *cordon bleu cuisine*. Bapsy spoke for us all one morning when she declared, with quiet pride, 'How can I deny my Cuddles her Chicken Galantine?' Colonel Mukherjee, as usual, had the last word, 'It's quite impossible to provide a dog with a decent life for less than five thousand a month.' Well said. But a thousand rupees for a morning's heave-ho was surely taking matters a bit too far.

And the sheer unfairness of it all.

Thus far a fine sense of democracy has prevailed in allowing no let or hindrance to nature's calls on Carmichael Road. Crows and pigeons let fly with deadly accuracy. Stray dogs and cats evacuate where they will. On Sunday mornings, performing monkeys and an elephant, so help me God, get into the act. The elephant to a thunderous breaking of wind which creates instant alarm among the barred and shuttered Americans in Washington House. And I am ashamed to report that even some of our more ethnic domestics, accustomed to the great outdoors for the morning ritual, slink like wraiths by dawn's first light into nooks and crannies, there to drop trousers with a casual insouciance. Does the law intervene with a heavy hand? No sir. 'Why then,' Pinkie points out with indisputable logic, 'should our dogs be fined for doing what comes naturally?' It was left, as always, for Colonel Mukherjee to sound the last word of warning. The military has a wonderful way of developing strategy. 'If one of the blighters,' he announced, 'so much as approaches Rover while he's at his business, I shall order him to attack!'

But Bapsy is stricken by a terrifying thought.

'Then they may,' her voice trembles, 'insist on muzzles.'

The dastardly custards! Is nothing sacred? Will they leave no turd unstoned?

Carmichael Road's dog owners brace for battle.

Watch this space.

****

My Dog Days Take
a Turn for the Worse

How the outrage began: In an act of the vilest treachery, the BMC announces that it will exact a spot fine of Rs. 1,000 for every uncleared piece of 'dog shit' (ugh!) on Carmichael Road. Raw courage confronts unbridled tyranny as owners vow to fight to the last turd. Who will win the day? Read on.

Colonel Mukherjee and Rover, his Alsation assassin, chaired the war council. Rover kept uncurling his upper lip and pointing his canines (a fearsome collection) in the direction of the municipal commissioner's bungalow. He was not to be trifled with; neither was the colonel. 'The letter of the law,' he announced cryptically, 'cannot be questioned, but the spirit of the law' – there was an ominous glint in his eye – 'is quite another matter.' 'The law is an ass.' Rose Cherian, who showed signs of wear and tear each morning from the gin and lime excesses of the night before, yanked at her Dobe who was sniffing amorously at Lady, Lallubhai's Dalmation. 'Not first thing in the morning, Clinton.' Was there a hint of regret in her voice? Clinton began licking himself moodily, then, struck by a happy thought, evacuated with great authority. The council cast uneasy glances about them. The Law was nowhere to be seen. 'Biding their time,' Pinkie Durrani observed grimly.

'Well,' Bapsy offered, 'if you want a legal opinion ...' Her nose began a grant elevation; the council braced itself for the

Dropping of a Name. Ratan? Vakil? Lentin? 'I could have a word with Nani. He's a dear, never says no, at least not to me ... Cuddles, you naughty girl, that's not breakfast!' And poor Cuddles' investigation into Clinton's heroic exertions was brought to an abrupt conclusion. The council pretended it hadn't noticed. 'Nani's intervention at this point,' Colonel Mukherjee suggested mildly, 'might be a bit excessive. Anyway, you can't have punishment without proof. They must catch us in the act.' Nobody would look Clinton in the eye; his act was mountainous.

'How will they establish identity?' Colonel Mukherjee was now absorbed by jurisprudence, 'in the face of that lot.' And he pointed up the road, whimsically adorned with a profusion of bowel movements from the lightest of patchwork to robust sand castles, to the devil-may-care, I-don't-give-a-shit depredations of the street's mongrel community. Lallubhai, syntax somewhat dislocated by a sudden flash of enlightenment, spoke for us all. 'They will not know who did what!' 'Precisely,' the colonel issued his first Order of Action. 'We shall have to exercise subterfuge and discretion.'

Creativity took wing. 'Do it behind a car,' Bapsy said triumphantly. 'The blind side of the police chowki,' the colonel offered. 'Nonsense,' Pinkie's indignation seared the laburnums. 'When Clinton has to do it, he does it.' 'No one can see you behind the bushes opposite Carmichael House,' Moneybags Swamy, who else? Lalitha, the brazen hussy, giggled. Colonel Mukherjee brought the meeting to order. 'We shall have to clean up.' 'Not doggie bags,' Bapsy protested. 'Afraid so,' said the colonel, 'take heart, my friends.'

Easier said than done. The minions of the law are not without a certain native cunning. A brace of villains, with mean and hungry looks, pounced mid-turd on a hapless domestic with a Retriever. The First Villain whipped out a pad. The Second Villain gave him a pencil stub. The First Villain scribbled furiously. Pandu, the dogsbody, launched into an impassioned plea: 'I don't *have* a thousand rupees.' The Villains consulted keenly. Dreadful sentence was passed. Take us to your sahib. And they frog-marched Pandu, a shattered man, to Usha Kiran. Only the manacles and shackles were missing.

Good grief! What next? Thumbscrews? The Lash? A firing squad?

Worse, dear reader, much worse.

Order your copy of next Sunday's *Blitz* now.

****

Dark Dog Days at Dawn

The Outrage III: You'd think the BMC's fine of Rs. 1000 for a stray turd was bad enough, and blueblooded Carmichael Roaders clearing up the mess humiliation beyond belief. Now crime rears its ugly head.

It would have been sad if it weren't so brave. Here were Carmichael Road's finest engaged in subterfuge and unwitting farce, albeit with a certain defiance. (The Upper Crust, after all, never lets the Upper Crust down) But down they were, scraping, patting, scooping and putting away. Rear elevations aloft as they did so, offering the keen anthropolgist much cause for delightful speculation. But the creaking of recalcitrant joints, the twinge here and there at unaccustomed contortions, the agitated quickstep as the evidence spread hither and thither, could not repress a saucy try-us-on-for-size panache. The dogs, however, looked on in utter disbelief, with the quizzical expression dogs have when they're thinking, 'Doggone, I don't believe this!'

Improvisation was the order of the day. From Bapsy Crorewallah's Mickey Mouse mug and spoon (where on earth did she get them from?) for Cuddles' frugal offerings, to Pinkie Durrani's seaside spade and bucket (when Great Danes do it, THEY DO IT!), to the enviable invention of Colonel Mukherjee's scooper and container, to Rose Cherian's Cartier paper bag and ivory shoe horn the ingenuity of the Upper Classes was everywhere on display. So was the ability to deceive.

There was Colonel Mukherjee, whistling nonchalantly, guiding
Rover in an evasive military manoeuvre to the space between the
police chowki and the Wadia Mansion, there, out of sight of the
enemy, to ease himself without fear or favour. Freny Tipsywallah
and her irascible Peke sought peace and stealth behind a Sumo
when, much to our disgust, the Peke gave all away while giving
away all by yelping hysterically at a passing tomcat who stopped to
sneer at him. No harm done. The Law had other things on its
mind. It observed, with savage intensity, Moneybags Swamy and
the outrageously glandular Lalitha as, with giggles and guffaws,
they hustled the long-suffering Daisy the Dachshund into the
Carmichael House bushes. The Law slouched behind them.

It was then that Colonel Mukherjee drew our attention to an
inexplicable phenomenon. Down the road ambled Pandu, the
domestic (Carmichael Roaders do not employ servants) with the
Golden Retriever, last seen caught in the act by two minions of the
Law and frogmarched in fear and trembling to his Master in Usha
Kiran. Now here he was, blithe as a lark, a spring in his step, pausing
now and again while the Retriever cocked a leg at every other
lamppost and laid waste, without a care, in the middle of the road.
Where was the Law? Looking the other way! Suspicion reared its
ugly head. And when, a moment or two later, Moneybags and Lalitha
came running up to us, their breathlessness and agitation, alas,
owing nothing to interrupted amour, our darkest fears were
confirmed. 'They ... wanted ... a bribe!' 'And did you give it?'
Moneybags avoided our eyes; Lalitha gave a little sob.

'Extortion,' Colonel Mukherjee muttered through clenched
teeth, 'the dirty dogs.' Nervous speculation flew in all directions.
Would they demand hafta by weight? By consistency? By the day,
week, month? By breed? And how much? 'We gave them a hundred,'
Moneybags admitted, 'and when I said never again, they grinned.'
'An evil grin,' Lalitha added. 'Chota kutta, ek sou. Barra kutta
pakrenga, bap re bap!' Pinkie Durrani gave her Great Dane a hug.
'Just let them try, puppykins.' But it was Colonel Mukherjee who
led us to the light. 'Extortion never stops. Are we to become victims
for life? Threat must be met by threat. We shall marshall our forces
and counter-attack. We are not without resources.' 'Nani!' Bapsy

exclaimed, 'Mendonca. Lentin.' 'No, Frank. He shall write the Commissioner a letter.'

'Who me?' 'Who better?' And they beamed as one. Lalitha threw a swift and tender look at my creative parts. 'Let me help,' she offered, winningly, 'I can type.' Snoopy, the Dog Who Knows No Fear, urged me on to great endeavour. So did my creative parts. Forsooth! To the breach, Frank, to the breach.

Next week: VICTORY!

****

*T*he *Outrage IV*. Hafta for dog turds! How low will the BMC's minions sink? Carmichael Road braces for the final battle. I, for my writing sins, have been appointed Defender of the Faithful. Burning the midnight oil, I hurl a challenge to mortal combat at the enemy. If this column appears no more, you will know why …

Dear Municipal Commissioner,

You can push a person so far, but if that person happens to be a Carmichael Road dog lover, you push at your peril. How dare I address you in this fashion? I am authorized to do so as Honorary Communicator-in-Chief or, if you prefer, Journalist Laureate-in-Residence to DEE-BEE-DI-DO. Before you consign this letter to the shredder (aha! We know your little secrets) you would do well to take pause. We may, at first blush, appear to be a frivolous, even whimsical body (such as the Sales Tax Department, the Sewage Collection Authority or – dare I say it? – the BMC) but nothing could be further from the truth. DEE-BEE-DI-DO is an acronym for Death Before Dishonour To Our Dogs. A certain alliterative licence may be forgiven (Carmichael Road ladies have a weakness for flourish and curlicue) but we are organized, awesomely influential (more anon) and determined to fight to the last turd (don't feign ignorance; *you* authorized the Rs.1000 dog shit fine and fat lot of good that did you. If you haven't collected a paise so far THERE ARE REASONS).

When, five years ago, our telephones began to go dead on us in an utterly mystifying fashion, to be lethargically revived after a couple of weeks only to give up the ghost again, our consternation gave way to enlightenment in the persons of two linesmen. They were polite, efficient and apologetic. Given the elephantine responses of the corporation, they said, the problem – tut, tut – would recur. Now, for a small consideration, a mere bagatelle of Rs. 200 a month, personal inspection would ensure flourishing phones forever and aye. And thus it came to pass. Ten of us, at Rs. 200 a month works out to Rs.20,000 a year. Tax-free and no small potatoes. When six postmen turned up at Diwali for baksheesh of Rs. 100 each (tut-tutting at the growing incidence of dividend warrant pilferage) they were overwhelmed by our generosity; when the same six postmen turned up at Christmas and wished us, as only good Christians can, we bit the bullet and paid up. If our 'Merry Christmas' was a trifle strained, could we really be blamed? And let us draw a discreet veil over the traffic cops, the metre inspectors, *et al.*, who, in the best socialist tradition, encourage the re-distribution of hard-earned wealth.

But a time comes when one must stand fast. Dog shit is not negotiable.

We are not, as indicated earlier, without influence. Colonel Mukherjee, our distinguished chairman, is a personal friend of the G.O.C. Western Command. How would it look if a crack Gurkha platoon, in full battle gear, was to flag march down Carmichael Road? Think of the international repercussions if the Japanese consul's wife were disturbed at her sashimi. Or the dyspeptic fallout if Kali Mody was interrupted mid-Dhansak? Then again, if Bapsy Crorewalla (she's the blue-rinsed lady Cuddles takes for a walk) were to have a quiet word with Nani or Vakil or Lentin, the situation, dear Commissioner, would best be described as dire!

Worse may follow. You may have come across the term 'event management' (and I don't mean ministerial forays into Chowpatty hanky-panky at dead of night). There are lady friends of mine – Dolly, Pali and Neerja – who manage such things with devastating results. Imagine if you will a stage at the Taj Ballroom, a script by none other than Bachi, barking mad at the sheer infamy of it all. The crème de la crème of the press in rapt attention. Alyque's direction has the audience riveted to their seats. Gerson's peerless

254 / The Bombaywallah

diction mesmerizes. Colonel Mukherjee, head bowed, brings in a dejected Rover, a pale shadow of his former self. Bapsy follows with Cuddles, in tears, in her arms. Pinkie's Great Danes' tragic 'Woof' reduces strong men to tears. Lalitha's Dachshund attempts to raise a leg mid-stage (Alyque's genius knows no bounds) when two villains rush on and demand, 'HAFTA!'

The headlines! The editorials! The *pictures*! And if we can persuade Vir Sanghvi to host a programme, 'Going to the Dogs' there's no telling where it will all end. And if all else fails, Commissioner, there's always Busybee's Bolshoi the Boxer. A few well-chosen words from him in the direction of the SPCA and thousands of dog lovers will be baying for blood along Carmichael Road.

Cease and desist, we say.

Remember, every dog has his day!

****

The Best of Times

At nine-thirty this morning the editor of the Bombay edition of *The Times of India*, called for his senior editorial staff. They were grouchy, with reason: they usually began their day at eleven. 'Girls and boys,' he declared, 'this is the first hour of the first day of our next one hundred and fifty-three years. Let's celebrate.' A bottle of Indian champagne was opened. The fizz was flat. They drank glumly out of teacups. At ten the publisher burst into the room. 'This is the second hour of the first day ...' 'Get on with it,' said an assistant editor, stifling a yawn. 'I shall read from my latest collection of poesy,' the publisher announced, 'while slides of my art nouveau renditions will be projected on all four walls, and' – he added thoughtfully – 'the ceiling.' The editorial staff fell asleep. At eleven, the owner, in stonewashed denims and a Pierre Cardin T-shirt, sauntered in and snarled, 'This is the third hour of the first day of our next one hundred and fifty-three years. Wake up and get to work!'

Congratulations are in order. I have shared forty of those one hundred and fifty-three years with the *Times* – as young reader, unsolicited and much-rejected teenage contributor and, latterly, fledgling columnist – and I am glad to note that the Old Lady of Bori Bunder is alive, well and giving the rest of the pack a lively run for its money. But first things first ....

My mother believes to this day that impoverishment is no reason for ignorance, and while I remember as a child that dal and rice was

our lot (with a piece of fish thrown in on a good day), we feasted at
the world's table each morning when the *Times* was slipped under
the front door. It was the only newspaper we received and my real
education began when I returned from St Mary's High School in
the afternoon. My grandfather, bifocals in place, *Times* at the ready,
conducted me on a guided tour of the alarums and excursions of a
wonderfully wayward world.

In my late teens and now a fervent convert to the Word, I felt I
should do my bit to improve the standards of the daily journalism
in the *Times*, wholly ignorant of the fact that I had begun an
impossible odyssey, a lifetime's vocation to give meaning to words,
a conflict without end where honourable defeat would offer rare
consolation to a general condition of abject misery. I dashed off a
3000-word middle, took a tramcar to Bori Bunder and deposited it
with care at the delivery desk. Editorial response was swift, terminal
and arrived in the form of a rejection slip. Those were Spartan times:
the slip was brief and brutal in its denunciation: 'The editor regrets
that he is unable to accept your contribution.' And – unkind cut –
'Unsolicited material is not returned.'

A year and forty rejection slips later, with my journalistic
future now in major jeopardy, I took gloomy stock. Would I ever
learn to craft a sentence with the fine rhetoric of Mr Frank Moraes,
the pointillistic wit of Mr Shawn Mandy, the effortless poise of
Mr N.J. Nanporia, the artful guile of Mr Nihal Singh, the punch
and panache of Mr Girilal Jain (to a man, once and future stars
in the *Times* firmament), to say nothing of the lofty and
unattainable cerebrations of Mr Sham Lal? Clearly, the time for
serious reflection was at hand.

In my final school year at St Mary's, Dom Moraes was the
star distraction. I was part of the large majority of boys who
regarded Dom wistfully and from a respectful distance, lacking
the courage to strike up a friendship. He had written a book on
cricket; it had, alas, been published. As if this was insufficient
cause for injury, it was surreptiously put about that he was a *poet*!
And the most crushing blow of all: his father, Frank Moraes, was
the distinguished editor of the *Times of India*. How did one even
begin to speak to such a person? In the event, I found myself

unable to do so, but now, several years later, shamelessly and with no guilt whatsoever, I wrote to Mr Moraes, claiming bonds of unbreakable fealty with his son, and demanding, as rightful consequence, that he publish the 3000-word middle he would find enclosed with my letter. Changes were not to be made without my permission. Editorial reaction was immediate. Mr Moraes sent me a letter which ran to two pages of typescript, and was as fine an exposition of the art and craft of the middle as will ever be put to paper. I returned to my typewriter, composed five hundred disciplined words of wry self-effacement, 'On Rejection Slips': the *Times* published it: I was paid Rs 25. No cheque has given me greater joy.

Both the *Times* and I have come a long way over a quarter century, and while I admit to no flaws, I do wish the Sunday Review would stop slicing editorial matter down to anorexic fillets interleaved between sunburst celebrations of condoms and after-shave lotions. And it would do no harm to put some of the junior subs out of their misery. But I carp. Where else does one observe secular democracy practised to such rousing effect, not merely in content and expression and the encouragement of opposing points of view, but in the roster of senior editorial talent. Here, Parsi rubs companionable shoulder with Punjabi, Goan crosses swords with Tamilian, iconoclastic Bengali writes, shoulder to shoulder, with prudent Gujarati; the life of the *Times* is, indeed, living testament to the life and times of the highest order of secular Indian journalism. Here, Khushwant Singh, M.V. Kamath, Mario Miranda, Behram Contractor, Minhaz Merchant and a galaxy of distinguished journalists first honed their considerable skills. Here, today, more often than not, the third leader brightens my day; Shalini Devi Holkar and Sangita Advani sparkle; Khalid Mohamed takes my film education engagingly in hand; Swaminathan S. Ankelsaria Aiyar makes me believe that, other than the Hand of God, there may be something to economics after all, while Jug Suraiya and Bachi Karkaria continue to lay waste among holy cows as they have, in their merry and prolific way, these many years. But why is Dina Vakil bylined so thriftily?

Thirty years ago I began writing for the *Times* because I needed to write as much as I needed the money. My work for the *Times* opened the lucrative doors of mainstream advertising; in turn, advertising has given me the financial freedom to write and live as I will. I do so with a sense of joyful déjà vu, while raising the only toast that does justice to the occasion: forever and aye, let the good *Times* roll!

****

The Saraswat Brahmin
Roman Catholic Goan

Swallows swooped and
soared among the wild
bougainvillea. Formations
of gulls explored the skies.
God's chosen acre. Here,
the troubled heart could
learn to be still.

Goa has a winning way with siren calls.

Just when I begin to feel a wee bit jaded with my house on the beach in Candolim, I am nudged gently in a new and serendipitous direction. With a felicity that never ceases to engage and surprise, the green and pleasant land of my ancestors offers yet another revelation: a gem of a hidden cove perhaps, unsullied by hippie or tout, where sandpiper, seagull and sentinel palm hold sway and yours are likely to be the only footprints on the sand; or a serene odyssey by cataraman with my fisherman friend Joaquim Pereira along the tranquil backwaters of the Mandovi and Zuari where the villages emerge like mirages from a world of shimmering emerald, aquamarine and burnt sienna and only the long-legged herons proclaim the virtues of virginal white; or a gift, one beneficient morning, from my good friend Steve Miranda, a *garafao* of the noblest caju feni, brewed on his ancestral estates south of Pernem, golden, ambrosial nectar, worlds removed from the noxious brews inflicted on hapless tourists.

It has always been this way.

For ten years we lived on and off at the Taj Holiday Village while I searched for a perfect acre by the sea. Cottage No. 17 became a home away from home. The view was perfect: pool and palm, emerald lawns, iridescent banks of hyacinth and bougainvillea; beyond, the lambent benediction of sunlight on sand and surf. And sunny Goan smiles all over the place. We ate magnificently under thatch at the Beach Hut, good Goan food cooked with more than a little hint of celebration, and slept to the sound of moonspun surf with a million stars within arm's reach. I rediscovered Goa during those years. My quest for the perfect acre had taken me beachcombing, from the lonely, windswept seascapes of Arambol and Tiracol in the far north, to the mesmerizing backwaters of Betul and Sal in the south; to Baga, Calangute and Sinquerim, where the villages cluster thickly, one to the other; and run down to the sea's edge. I had explored cliff, cove and headland, clambering over broken rock and down craggy hillside, as often as not beating a path through thick brush and scrub. At day's end I was tired to the point of exhaustion, but exhilarated, as I have never been before or since. I was discovering the landscapes of my ancestors and I now knew why the Portuguese and the conquerors before them had been held spellbound by the bewitching loveliness of the land.

The day we broke ground for Rockheart, I stood on the sand and looked out over the dunes as the surf came roaring in on a moon-tossed tide. I gave silent thanks to the powers that guide our destiny. My grandfather, who loved Goa more than any person I know, had once said that no one owns the good Goan earth. I was a guest, no more. As a bee is given a flower and the nightingale its song, I had been granted happy residence for the rest of my mortal time on one of God's chosen acres. I would have it no other way; indeed, if I were sentenced to life on a hammock under a palm tree in our garden at Rockheart, I would rest content. But Goa was not done with her surprises.

The American who turned up at the beach gate one morning did little to promote a feeling of confidence. Six feet and a bit, with golden locks down to his shoulders, bare-bodied, barefooted, a beard well on its way to making a significant statement, a rainbow lungi draped two sexy inches below his belly button, but – thank heaven for small mercies – as sober as a bishop at his brievary.

'Frank Simoysh?' he said.

I was impressed. My surname in Portuguese is pronounced that way. Here was a firangi who knew his polysyllables. And when he presented his card and a letter of introduction from a mutual friend, an American publisher, the penny dropped with a resounding tinkle. This was no itinerant hippie but the bureau chief of the Asian edition

of the *International Herald Tribune*. Patrick Smith was in Goa to do
a major story for his paper and he was not impressed. People, he
said, were wary of his business card; the moment he produced it,
they either clammed up or spouted the received wisdom which was
about as enlightening as a government tourist brochure. So he had
slipped into hippie camouflage, hired an Enfield, and sought the
true Goan experience, without, he added wryly, much joy and more
than a little grief in the persons of the local cops who stopped the
bike, demanded bribes on the threat of drug charges, and turned a
pale green when he presented his credentials. The beaches had left
him cold; he had seen better in Malaysia, Thailand and Bali. 'Where,'
he asked a little plaintively, would he 'discover the real Goa?'

So I decided to do my bit for flag and country and took him off
in the Gypsy to the south. Goa did the rest. My understanding of
southern Goa was at best superficial and for me, as much as for
Patrick, it was a voyage of splendid discovery into uncharted territory.
We abandoned the beaches for the hills and the river valleys; we
lived in guest houses, ate and drank as the locals did and took our
pleasures where we found them. The images return: Lotuleim at
dusk, groves of trees aflame with fireflies; the exquisite baroque
chapel in Mario Miranda's ancestral home, murals from floor to
high ceiling, an altar all of eighteen feet carved from Burma teak;
the fishermen at Betul working canoes out of tree trunks, harvesting
clam mussel in one of the loveliest estuaries in Goa; a wedding
party proceeding down a rustic cart track, with pomp and ceremony,
in the sweltering heat of midsummer, the men in dark suits, the
bride and her entourage, were it not for their complexions, could
well have stepped out of a church in Lisbon; villagers dressed in the
aquamarines, lilacs and ambers of their land, walking a path between
fields of emerald paddy towards a whitewashed church to celebrate
the feast of Our Lady of Immaculate Conception ...

Goa had, once again, taken my higher education in hand.
Patrick Smith returned to Tokyo, a convert to the cause, and wrote
in the *Herald Tribune*:

' ... few visitors ever see much of Goa besides the sand, the tide
and the beachside bars. This is unfortunate, for it is the up-river
interiors that distinguish Goa as more than just another strip of sand.

'Here the rice fields are planted and palms cultivated as they have been for centuries, and the old whitewashed quintas and the people who inhabit them stand as super testimonials to a rather special way of life. To explore this Goa is to take a deep draught of history and to begin to understand that Goan character you will hear, if you listen carefully, in the very cadence of Goan English. Like the Tuscan countryside, Goa yields itself after extended stays, not a week's barnstorming holiday.'

I was soon to realize that this revelatory sojourn was, yet again, merely another prologue to my unfolding discovery of Goa. I had signed a contract with Viking/Penguin for a Goan memoir. I had given it a working title, *Glad Seasons in Goa,* which seemed to me to best express the way I felt about the land and the people. In the year in which it took for the book to gain substance and form, I came to a rueful conclusion: no matter how well I thought I knew Goa, I would never know Goa as well as I should; one lifetime was several lifetimes too few.

My research began with the villages of my mother and father, Saligao and Colvale in Bardez. I returned with a Proustian inclination, with sharp eye and ascendant hope, and I was not disappointed. Saligao lies exactly minutes in the Gypsy from our beach house in Candolim. Once you turn off the Chogam road and take the wayward lane beneath crimson gulmohar into the village, time pauses, turns, drifts, gently retreats, and you could well be a century into the past. The environmental doomsayers are, mercifully, wrong; apocalypse is not around the corner, not, at any rate, in Goa's interior. Saligao remains as sharply etched a reality today as I remember it as a child, an ordered, mannerly, gracious and exquisitely beautiful Goan village. The hand of progress lies lightly, when it rarely does, on the place and the people and in Colvale, my father's village, is markedly conspicuous by its absence. My mother tells me that when she married and moved to Colvale, she remembers a sense of alienness, of being in a time and place frozen in a distant past, far removed from the gentle bustle of Saligao. I recall being puzzled by this; how could one Goan village be so different from another?

When I returned to Colvale to research *Glad Seasons in Goa* I began to understand. Goa shifts focus as if at the turning of a glittering prism. There is a real apartness about Colvale; a sense when you get there of arriving at a last destination with little prospect of return; of doors closing behind you; of a way of life sequestered and exclusive to itself. Yet, paradoxically, it was here that I reclaimed my father's legacy. He left no will – there was nothing to leave – but he gave me a gift of four words in the language. A moveable legacy which I have bequeathed, in turn, to my daughter Radhika.

The first is *phale* from the Konkani and means, literally, tomorrow. This is subterfuge. *Phale*, much to the despair of the visitor, is an unabashed invitation to the pleasures of procrastination. It may really mean the day after, the next month, the following year, or never. When, in the Bombay manner, I seek instant gratification only to encounter '*Phale*', I take immediate refuge in *phale's* crafty sibling, *susegade*, an old, wise Portuguese word which means they also serve who lie and laze: take your restful ease while you may, swing in a hammock, observe the playful fronds of the palm trees. Let your thoughts wander as they will. It is a benign, a bountiful universe. Take counsel with the butterflies. Look to the kingfisher. Observe the brilliance of the gulmohar. See how the eagle makes sport with the wind. Regard again, with grateful thanks, this noble and beneficent palm. Without the fruit, where would one find the true essence of a prawn curry? The fronds offer a fluttering shade and the sap, distilled, gives forth that peerless spirit, feni, a glass of which you now raise to your lips in a silent toast to abandoned resolutions, '*Phale!*'

The other words are Portuguese with no English equivalents. *Alegria* is a way of being; the lilting syllables evoke all of Goa's love and laughter, song and happy fellowship. It is the way we are when we are there. *Saudade* is the way we feel when we are away. It means remembering with melancholy and hope. Melancholy at the passing of a small miracle; hope because we know it will, some day, return ...

****

God's Chosen Acre

Carl Jung, the great Austrian psychoanalyst and Freud's contemporary, did not believe in coincidence, only in metaphysical congruence: happenstance was merely a perceived instance of a wholly alien and profoundly important dimension of existence: a web of complex and life-determining effects, the reasons for which would forever be beyond our understanding. What would he have made of the cosmic arabesque which brought together a working colleague, Rukmini D'Abreu, a lame mongrel puppy, an inspired architect, Sanju Walawalkar, the Goddess Shanta Durga, a distant cousin, thrice-removed, whom I had never met, a seventy-year-old water diviner, convalescing from a bypass, and a sublime acre of Goan beach?

My maternal grandfather would not have been surprised. His house still stands in the village of Saligao in Goa, a magnificent Iberian home of many rooms, with its own chapel and a cottage for the priest who ministered to the household's spiritual needs. The priest is long dead, and the family, flung far and wide by the vagaries of history and circumstance, took the name of da Gama Rose to Brazil and Canada, Great Britain, Portugal and Australia. Yet, home was forever where the heart claimed first residence and this, without question, was the *vaddo* in Saligao where the ancestral house embodied the very best of the Goan sense of *saudade* and *alegria*, nostalgia and joy. 'A strong house,' my grandfather had once said, 'and a good family are greater than the sum of their parts.'

For ten years I had been on a personal odyssey along Goa's beaches searching for the perfect acre by the sea. I discovered it quite by chance, on a tempestuous September afternoon, while exploring a part of the village of Candolim called Scrivado, the place of the scribes (Jung again?). Two dunes, covered by thick, green, man-high scrub and mangrove, dipped to clear white sand, ancient, weathered stone cross and a thatched fisherman's hut, at the very centre of an acre of beguiling serendipity: an azure sea set off a profusion of coconut palms, a drumstick tree weighed down with autumnal abundance, a flowering cashew at the far end. Swallows swooped and soared among the wild bougainvillea. Formations of gulls explored the skies. God's own acre. Here, the troubled heart could learn to be still.

But not, as it soon transpired, without some heartburn. None of the villagers in the fishing hamlet had a clue about the owners. I checked with the sarpanch, the parish priest, old landed gentry, to no avail, and time running out, returned, disheartened to Bombay. Then the kindly hand of congruence dealt me an ace. An office colleague, Rukmini D'Abreau, was leaving for Goa. Hefting a bit of rank I made her promise to visit the land survey office in Panaji. 'Don't come back without a name,' I said. She returned a fortnight later, burst into my office with a beatific smile and announced, 'My uncle owns your piece of beach.'

Gita and I took the next flight to Goa. We acquired a solicitor, bought the land at a price which made me smile, only to discover that we had acquired a tenant as well, a lame female mongrel pup which we came upon abandoned and left to die on the main village road. She would never win a beauty contest, but she had a mind of her own. Yelping with joy (she had discovered affection), she followed us to the property, marked the boundaries in the only way dogs know, and made it clear she had arrived to stay. In deference to her total lack of any kind of canine presence, we named her Aunt Jane.

At Bobb's Inn and Bar that evening, we discussed 'plans and architects' and came to a rueful conclusion. Given our firm – and often wildly divergent – views on what a beach house in Goa should be like, and the monolithic obduracy of the prima donna architects we knew in Bombay and Delhi, it seemed like a lost cause.

Brooding over our fenis, we heard a chuckle. A young slip of a girl with a winning smile and pigtails stood at our table. 'Sorry to interrupt,' she said, 'but I couldn't help eavesdropping. I'm Sanju Walawalkar and I designed the Taj Holiday Village.'

Not only did the chemistry between us prove an alchemist's dream, Sanju was the perfect catalyst. Gita wanted a beautiful house; I wanted a Goan house; both of us wanted a house for our collection of my family's heirloom furniture and Gita's paintings and antiques, and my venerable red Underwood typewriter, and Gita's Portuguese lithographs, and my books; above all, we wanted a house which would make happy and timeless conversation with us and the elements. We wanted everything. Sanju would have none of this. Never did an architect go about designing a house more obliquely. She disappeared with Gita for hours on end on mysterious forays – on catamarans to distant islands, to the university archives, to waterfalls and rain forests, to crumbling monasteries and new plant nurseries, to old, distinguished Goan homes and the huts of fisherfolk with hard cowdung floors. They returned with stars in their eyes and samples of stone and tile, flowering plant and old wood, pottery and stained glass and exotic fish recipes. As for me, Sanju was clearly unimpressed by my architectural opinions, but she insisted on reading every word I had ever written about Goa and my family. She spent evenings plying me with large fenis, while I told her how I *felt* about Goa and why. Once, in a moment of rare introspection, she said, 'A house should be the way you are and the way you feel about life, and each other.'

One morning she announced briskly that she was off to Bombay and would see us in a month with drawings and a plan. Thirty days later we had both, a house and a friend, for life. But finding a contractor proved a strangely difficult proposition. They came; they saw; they quoted and then, mysteriously, at the eleventh hour, they would say no, apologise and flee, never to be heard from again. There was nothing for it but to call in Gopal Kakulo. Very pricey (he had built the Taj Holiday Village) but honest, quick and good at his work. We agreed terms and timescales; a contract was drawn up; then it happened again. Kakulo, immensely unhappy at having to let us down, did so. But he had the good grace to tell us why:

'Shanta Durga will not allow me to build your house unless I shed the blood of a cock on the land.'

At the far north of Candolim, where the village gives over to emerald paddy, in a glade shaded and scented by mango and *raat ki rani*, stands a temple many hundreds of years old, dedicated to the Goddess Shanta Durga. No contractor will build so much as a buffalo shed in the village without performing a special puja seeking the blessings of the Goddess. Exquisitely wrought in brass, four feet and a bit, she has behind her a penumbra of brass leaves, ten at each side, set in a perfect circle, like a peacock's fan. The pundit performs the puja, then soaks a bunch of tulsi leaves in a vessel of holy water and, very carefully, places a green leaf on each of the brass ones; they adhere. When a question is put to the Goddess, she responds: a leaf falls to the ground. If the leaf falls from the left, the answer is yes; from the right, no; the leaves do not fall in sequence, from top to bottom, but at random. All of our earlier contractors, to a man, had asked a single question.

'May I build a house for Gita and Frank Simoes at Scrivado?'
'No.'
Gopal Kakulo, with much trepidation, had gone further.
'Will you let me build the house if I give you an offering?'
'Yes.'
'Flowers and fruit?'
'No.'
'Rice, coconut and mithai?'
'No.'
Dread shaking his heart, 'Blood?'
'Yes.'

A young cock would do nicely, the pundit said, and helpfully offered to perform the maha-puja at a price.

Gita was appalled. Not only is she staunchly vegetarian, but sensitive about animals to a fault. Had we discovered the perfect acre only to find that we could never have a roof over our heads? The next morning, Sanju and Gita went to the temple to plead with the Goddess in person. Subdued, they sat in silence while the pundit went about the ritual. The tulsi leaves were put in place and Gita said, 'I am a Hindu and have a deep reverence for living things.

I believe that all life is sacred and that the spilling of blood will bring abiding unhappiness and ill-luck to the house, the land and my family. Won't you please accept another offering?' For long moments, not a leaf stirred, then three leaves on the left of the circle detached together and floated to the floor. The pundit was amazed. 'Three leaves at once,' he said, well pleased, 'we must give thanks.' That evening, in the centre of the property, just before sunset, the pundit performed a puja that lasted for an hour, with a havan and five kinds of fruit – bananas, apples, mangoes, chickoos and oranges. These, together with agarbatti set alight, kum-kum, a small mirror, holy oil and a ribbon were placed at the foot of the cashew tree. 'It will appease the female spirit who lives in this place,' the pundit said. The next morning they were gone.

The long arm of coincidence had not done with us yet. Nothing – not Shanta Durga's blessings, not the promise of a fat advance, not all of Sanju's powers of persuasion – could make Kakulo change his mind. He would not build our house. As a last resort, a friend in Mapusa suggested we try Carminho da Costa, adding unhelpfully, 'Slim chance. He's a very big government contractor. But you lose nothing by trying.' Carminho da Costa gave Gita polite but short shrift. 'I'll think about it,' he said, 'but its very unlikely. If I'm not at your site tomorrow morning, take it that I'm not interested.' Gita left her visiting card and returned, near tears. The next morning, a jeep bounced across the dunes; a tall, lean figure leaped out, embraced me warmly and exclaimed, 'Francisco!' I hadn't been called Francisco since I was a child. Carminho da Costa turned to Gita and said, 'Why didn't you tell me that you were married to Frank Simoes? He doesn't know it, but I'm his cousin, thrice-removed, from my mother's side.'

But no contractor, no matter how distantly related, can work without water and the PWD engineer was not encouraging. 'The watershed has been mapped along this entire beach,' he said. 'Dig if you like, but you won't get a drop of fresh water.' Was Jung chortling in the wings? I had made a beachcombing friend, an ancient party who shuffled at the water's edge with a cane every evening, startling the sandpipers. He lived in Bombay and was convalescing from a bypass. When I told him of our water problem, he chuckled and said, 'I'll have a go.' He was a water diviner, among other things, and the next morning, there he was, ambling all over our property, with a crescent of thick copper wire held before him, twitching merrily as he went along. 'Dig here,' he said. We did, and lo and behold, an abundance of clear, fresh water burst forth from a perennial spring.

Everything went swimmingly after that. In a matter of days, the foundation had been dug, and our obliging pundit performed a puja on the site, while the parish priest, not to be outdone, prayed over the stones. Two laterite bricks took centre stage in the ceremony. A cross had been carved on one and a small gold cross laid within it. A swastika was inscribed on the other brick and inlaid with the five precious jewels of the zodiac – pearl, coral, sapphire, emerald and ruby. Evil spirits would do well to stay away. And when I climbed down into the foundation, sprinkled holy water on the bricks, and broke a coconut, a collective, 'Ah ... ' went up, for the coconut had split cleanly, at the exact centre, into two perfectly symmetrical halves.

At dusk, a loving congruence gave us one last, immortal blessing. Radhika, two and toddling, was playing in sand. I heard the carpenter's boy take a sharp breath and drop his chisel. Not six feet away from her a black cobra lay coiled, head raised, hood spread, absolutely still. Aunt Jane, taut as a bow string, stood between my daughter and death. Her hackles were up, the upper lip drawn back over her fangs. She growled deep in her throat. For an unbearable moment, the dreadful tableau was frozen in time and space, then the cobra retracted its hood and glided swiftly across the sand and into the mangroves.

That night, I stood on the land and looked out over the dunes as the surf came roaring in on a moonspun tide. I reflected on happenstance, pride and possession, and gave silent thanks to the powers that guide our destiny. No one owns the good earth. I was a guest, no more. As a bee is given a flower and the nightingale its song, I had been allowed happy residence for the rest of my mortal time on one of God's chosen acres.

****

A Wedding in the Family

When I was a child growing up in Goa, Armando Menezes was a name to conjure with. Poet, teacher, defender of the faith, distinguished flag bearer of all things good and Goan, and patriarch of a clan which had made its mark wherever Goa's far-flung émigrés had laid down roots. Now, a generation later, on a golden February evening at the Church of St Laurence on the crest of Sinquerim Hill, Armando Menezes, long gone and lovingly remembered, presided in spirit and verse over the marriage of his grandson Vivek to Noreen Carneiro, worthy daughter of my very own village, Saligao.

There were deeper connections. Armando and my mother were first cousins; Leonard, Vivek's father and I, second cousins, and the clan's fertile restlessness which had seen Lenny make a brilliant career in the United States and Europe, had taken me as well to distant points of the compass; odysseys which had brought us back at last to soil, root and first and best reasons: Lenny and Naomi to five acres of exquisite headland high above the Mandovi river; Gita and I to God's chosen acre on the beach at Candolim.

Now, touched by a wistful déjà vu, I rose with the congregation of family and close friends as the majestic trumpet calls of *The Bridal March* led Noreen on her father's arm and her entourage of flowergirls, pageboys and bridesmaids under the flowing arches of the church porch to a simple, chaste altar made for this day alone, overlooking plunging cliff, sparkling ocean and the crumbling ramparts of the old Portuguese Fort of Aguada. No better metaphor,

I reflected for time and occasion: inexorable termination and life rampant, one indivisible from the other, made more poignant yet by the concluding verse of Armando Menezes' poem, *The Emigrant* with which the marriage ceremony began:

Upon a low grey hill there stands a church
They say it was there they christened me
There, too, my mother sleeps; there I alone
Would pray – pray and forget this fruitless search
Land of my fathers! May'st thou also be
The land my children shall be proud to own

We responded, to a person, with silent hosannahs. The Goan expatriate never leaves home. Bombay, London, Nairobi, Toronto, Sao Paulo ... these are occupations by necessity. Goa is the place in the heart of permanent and loving residence, and our joyful returning is at its most exuberant when the clan gathers for a wedding in the family.

I must confess to a flutter of nervous butterflies when we arrived at the church. The young angel in gossamer who approached with a tray of favours drew back nonplussed. Her coaching had not included so confusing a conundrum. How was she to pin a favour to the lapel of a jacket when there was no lapel? Neither, for that matter, was there a jacket. I wore a silk kurta when all about me were imposing men in dark suits, compellingly lapelled and thus easily favoured. An uneasy moment or two there but, as time went on, I was glad to observe that mine was not the only idiosyncrasy.

Vivek and Noreen, on this the first evening of their lives together, had decided to seize the initiative. They had made the ceremony their very own, planning every last detail, taking wing from venerable tradition, yet with all the essentials in reverential place. Celebratory chords were struck: loving goodness towards each other and the world about them; a tribute to generations gone before and a dedication to a green and golden future. Actively encouraged, it must be approvingly noted, by the wedding's main celebrant, the Reverend Mulchand Bulchand Chablani, Society of Jesus, who aided and abetted with unqualified enthusiasm.

'A Roman Catholic Sindhi Jesuit priest,' whispered my Hindu Sindhi wife in happy awe to her Roman Catholic husband, who added quite unnecessarily and with gloomy pride, 'It takes sixteen years to become a Jesuit.' Sixteen years well spent for, with a twinkle in his eye, Father Chablani applauded the young couple's 'post-Vatican' celebration of the sacrament of marriage while asking us elderly veterans of yesteryear's Vatican rites to brace ourselves for a brave new rendition of the plighting of the troth. Brave indeed! With poetry and song and tomorrow's rituals; and inexpressibly moving when, after the exchange of vows and rings, Vivek Menezes took courage and a guitar in both hands and serenaded his bride with an eloquence that made the very cherubim smile ...

Later that night, five hundred of Goa's finest gathered at a reception on the lawns of the Taj Holiday Village. Wine and cake and a toast; a magnificent dinner created to put good resolutions to chaotic flight; a band inspired to heights of effervescent invention. Goa's movers and shakers made common cause, deploying their considerable energies on the starlit dance floor, in fox-trot and waltz, quickstep and the rousing Bunny Hop, with all of the sleight-of-foot (and, thankfully, none of the tripping up!) that had done them proud on the Assembly floor and other public fora these many years. The spirit urged me to shake a glad leg. My back would have none of it, sprained neck to hip by an unwise gazelle-like foray over soft sand on a dark night. I had stepped on a small boulder half-buried in the sand, lost my balance and pivoted on the ball of my foot to avoid serious damage. With a loud crack, my back seized up. All was not lost however. I sought consolation in the healing prospect of glorious Goan grub!

A small confession here is in order. When the invitations arrived at our flat in Bombay, an unworthy thought – irrepressible, no matter how hard I tried – made its presence delightfully felt over the next couple of weeks. Not one, but two Goan wedding banquets! Praise the Lord and pass the pork please. I would, of course, bear witness to the nuptials and wish the young couple the best of all possible futures; off – as far as I, in happy anticipation, was concerned – to a winning start with the magnificent dinners even now being planned to the last delectable morsel by Vivek's mother Naomi, a relentlessly perfectionist mater de (no more deserving pun has been put to paper!). I was not to be disappointed. Under her inspired guidance, the Taj Holiday Village kitchens excelled beyond their usual excellence (Goan cooks on a grand Goan occasion – girth your loins!) but I supped modestly, as I would the whole of tomorrow as well in order to do great justice to the intimate family dinner at the Colaco mansion on the Mandovi river the next evening.

A boat trip by sunset and evening star down the fragrant lower reaches of the Mandovi and as the benediction of twilight caressed the far bank, a low white jetty, fairy lights among the bougainvillea and along the gracious silhouette of a grand old Goan house, and Emiliano's mandolin beckoned from a lamplit balcony. Nothing rejuvenates the spirit like a Goan wedding en famille. Cheek nuzzles cheek; rib-cracking embraces are in order; formalities are thrown to the winds; the wine flows as generously as the high spirits. Emiliano and his trio serenade where they will, as the mood moves them. Glad laughter and good fellowship greet one at every other turn of emerald lawn and candlelit alcove, chandeliered hall and starlit corridor. The night remains forever young. A new moon rises and the river responds with brushstrokes of shimmering, molten silver. Emiliano's trio are now up in the ballroom and the haunting opening bars of the *Blue Danube* insist that we join them at once. There's nothing like a good Goan wedding to unlimber a bad Goan back. I danced with a suppleness and brio that had even young Vivek throw me a glance of the purest awe. Or was it concern? No matter. Here came the Bunny Hop. I plunged into it with masterful unrestraint. 'What on earth do you think you're doing?' said Gita, a trifle breathlessly. 'Working up an appetite,' I said, with the wonderful sangfroid that knows no tomorrow.

It was well that I did. The groaning board extended from one end of the thirty-foot dining room to the other and on it, splendidly arranged, without an inch to spare, was the most glorious exuberance of great Goan nosh I was ever likely to encounter in several reincarnations. How life's decisions wear one down! Where would I begin? And would it be considered impolite if I took all week? Perhaps if I started at the head of the table and worked my way down … Starters by the dozen, entrees by the score: lobster and crayfish, mussel and clam; smoked sardines, plump *reacheado* mackerel, enormous kingfish glittering in aspic; chicken in a bewildering array of avatars including my favourite, *cafreal verde*; fragrant pulaos, sublime tiger prawn and crab curries, huge, bubbling tureens of *caldinho*; utterly ravishing suckling pig, *feijoada* and *sorpotel, apa da camaro; xacuti de cogumelos, ervilha, tambdi bhaji* (the vegetarians amongst us – where would we find one? – would not go hungry this day!); a salad bar which appeared to have denuded a kitchen garden to its last leaf, and a veritable merriment of desserts showing off on a table all to themselves.

Small talk ceased. A reverential hush descended as we went about the serious business of eating our dinner. But the evening was yet to reach a conclusion. Gerson da Cunha, magical Master of Ceremonies, was called upon to say a few words. He said them in English, in Portuguese and, triumphantly trilingual (to the partisan cheers of one and all), in lusty Konkani. On infrequent occasions, my English has been known to make friends and influence people; my Portuguese, alas, is rusty beyond repair; and when I attempt a few words in Konkani, my Goan friends smile. But by some blessed alchemy of meaning and moment come brilliantly together, Gerson's words transcended the unforgiving strictures of Anglo-Saxon correctness, celebrated every last lilting, liquid syllable of evocative Portuguese and gave Konkani its robust, jocular due.

They struck a wonderfully responsive chord and, as one, we joined him in a rousing toast to Vivek and Noreen. Good luck, young friends, Godspeed, and may the future never lose the bright promise of this moment ....

****

Goa-ing Strong

Goans, like feni taken neat, surprise, delight,
invigorate and, occasionally, cause pain.

The citadel-in-siege mentality has, thank heavens, mellowed with time, but when I was a child our extended Catholic family was as insular as they come. Even our Hindu neighbours were kept at a certain distance, not in any derogatory sense, but by some unfathomable and unbridgeable dimension. Or so I believed until I eavesdropped on a proposal of matrimony.

A young man wanted to marry my sister. Monumental foolishness in my view, but my parents took the matter seriously. Mother: 'Family?' Father: 'Britto from Margao. Only son. Huge properties. Pots of money.' 'Does *he* do anything?' 'Looks after the family business.' My mother sniffed, clearly underwhelmed. 'Are they Brahmins?' 'No.' 'That's that then.' Chapter closed. Child flummoxed until, years later while researching my first book, the biography of Vasudev Salgaocar, I discovered that we were both Saraswat Brahmins. And later still, leafing through a family diary, I learned that but for a fateful twist of history, my surname would have been Naik.

Two Saraswat brothers had converted centuries earlier and Naik, by Portuguese fiat, became Simoes. Hundreds of similar transformations took place: Pai/Fernandes, Shenai/Pereira, Bhandi/Vas. And when affluence determined conversion, splendidly curlicued, potently hyphenated names – Garcia Fonseca-Ribeiro, Gozanca-Mascarenhas, Diago Soares-Ferrao – with family crests thrown in for good measure, were solemnly bestowed. Hindu to definitive Iberian Catholic. Yet, once a Saraswat, a Saraswat forever. But managing contradictions is a particular Saraswat talent and you won't find a more fervently committed Catholic this side of the Vatican.

Goa's Saraswats mingle in full strength at the Governor's Republic Day tea party. Here, the neophyte invitee is politely grilled in a sort of Masonic ritual where caste, family and origin are carefully elicited. First in neutral English, 'Where are you from?' 'Colvale.' 'Hmm … any connection with Albert Simoes, high court judge in Lisbon?' 'My father's first cousin.' The penny drops, bounces, performs joyful acrobatics. English is cast aside. Mellifluous Portuguese takes its place. 'But of course. *Simplicio*. He married Alba Gama Rose from Saligao. My dear chap, we're third cousins. Are you free for dinner Saturday?' The umbilical connections never let go. I was in Nairobi once, blissfully incognito, when the phone rang. 'Francisco?' I was last called Francisco at my christening. 'Mirabeau da Gama. We're cousins. Can you do lunch tomorrow?' It wouldn't do to say no to the government's chief legal advisor, and, yes, the clan was alive and well in Kenya, thriving, as usual, excessively.

But flip the Goan coin and there's minted gold of a different order. Our house on Candolim beach is surrounded by a fishing clan fifty families strong. All D'Souzas. In and out of each other's houses all day long. All living within hailing distance. And, at the crack of dawn, anguished by night-long separation, hail they did. With an ear-splitting enthusiasm, which stunned the hamlet's large, noisy community of cocks and dogs into instant silence. The name-calling and faces attached to them were bewilderingly interchangeable. Sylvia and Agnes and Mary. Anton and Joaquim and Dominic. Inextricably entangled in generations of D'Souzadom. Then I met a dashing iconoclast who dared to be different and answered, so help me God, to the name Archangel.

Divine providence. Angelic harbinger of the good things our village had on offer – brilliant *tiatr*, pedigreed *sorpotel* and caju feni of unimpeachable provenance. The last two essential prerequisites to the first. The *tiatr*, irrevent Konkani folk theatre on a makeshift stage under the stars, takes pointed barb to local egos urgently in need of deflation – the sarpanch, the postmaster, the fattest bhatkar, are all fair game. The humour tends to slapstick, the broad swipe and the wicked aside when, as one, the audience shouts '*Borem!*' which means 'good' but here, rudely, 'Up the sods!' Goan words are informed with a guileful elasticity.

Encouraged no end by the *tiatr* I rushed into print – unwisely – with a few words of my own, poking gentle fun at one of my family's pet foibles: ' … there are Goans and *Goans*. Goans from Salcette, an unpromising lot, tend towards parsimony. Sanguem, that luckless district, is distinctly short on couth. Marmagoa is all ships, confusion and money. How can culture flourish in such poor soil? All fair-minded Goans agree, however, that Bardez is supremely civilized (we came from Bardez) and it is common knowledge that the Saraswat Brahmin Roman Catholic Goan from Saligao (us!) is clearly without peer.' Whereupon, one of Salcette's leading literary lights, in a towering rage, sent me a very violent letter, threatening a thrashing with chappals, tar and feathers and a parade in a public square where, presumably, I would be put of my misery.

Oh well, even a Saraswat Brahmin Roman Catholic Goan can't win them all.

****

The Bimbilli Brothers

Y̲ou will not find the village of Bimbilli on a Goan map, and Anthony and Felipe are not the brothers' real names. They would be hugely embarrassed at publicity of any sort. It has never been in their nature to seek recognition; and the people among whom they live and work, and have made their names, would react at best with amused disbelief, at worst with a sense of very real disappointment at praise in print so out of character with the lives these men have led.

I have known them for ten years. We have become friends, and in the blossoming of our friendship, I have had reason to examine my own life and redefine the nature of success as I had always understood it, including my own. I had, with the world at large, associated success with the more aggressive human values: the ability to wrest money and power from a hostile environment; the speed and strength to drive lesser men to the wall; a higher order of intelligence, guile, talent, stamina; a touch of ruthlessness; above all else, a burning focus of purpose which brooked no denial. These were qualities to be admired and emulated. They were the golden touchstones of success. In their absence lay failure.

The beginning of my re-education began in the most unexpected of ways – and a beguiling synchronicity – with a mutton roll at the Friday Mapusa market, and a village *tiatr* under the stars that same night in Candolim. The mutton roll was quite simply the best I had ever eaten, while the *tiatr* – a wicked satire on Goan mores, conceived, written and performed in Konkani – by far the best of the genre I had ever seen. I was not about to let well alone. Good food and good writing are passions with me; I made swift enquiries. Goa is an extended and intimate neighbourhood and, within days, I met Anthony, the baker, and Felipe, the playwright, and discovered – to my pleasant surprise – that they were brothers.

When you seek friendship in Goa it is offered without reservation until you prove unworthy. Then you cease to exist. You also discover that reticence and discretion are the better parts of friendship. It took years before I learned that the baker's art was the least of Anthony's accomplishments, that Felipe's talents lay much farther afield than the stage, and that the inviolate bond between the brothers – never revealed by word, look or gesture, yet a palpable presence when you were with them had been forged in the fires of destitution and sacrifices.

Like so many Goan lives, their memories of early childhood were scarred by an act of treachery and dishonour. Cheated out of his inheritance and property by an elder brother – and left penniless overnight – their father died within the month ('of shock and sorrow' Felipe recalls without bitterness). The young widow and her children – Anthony was seven, Felipe one – moved from the ancestral house, now a place of shame and disgrace, to the anonymity of a village far to the north. Poverty in Goa is genteel, rarely visible, concealed from all but the most intimate. The mother took to stitching, sold fish in the local marketplace, sought any part-time employment she could find no matter how demeaning. But it was never enough to maintain her family. Anthony had to leave school. In utter despair she wrote to a distant cousin in Bombay who owned a bakery and whom she had never met. He replied by return of post. It was her first piece of good luck. They could do with a boy about the place. At the age of seven, Anthony was packed off to Bombay to begin to earn a living. His mother had to borrow the money for the bus fare from the local moneylender.

'They were kind people,' Anthony recalls, 'but the work was back-breaking. From ten in the morning till ten at night, we made the dough and shaped it. The baking began at six the next day. By seven I was delivering bread all over the neightbourhood, in a basket slung on the handlebars of a cycle. There were no holidays.'

'How long did you work there?'

Anthony smiled, 'Seven years.'

But his cousin was a just man. Within a month, Anthony was put on a monthly stipend; a year later on a salary which was increased, scrupulously – at the best market rates – every Christmas. He sent the money to his mother with a single stipulation; part of it was to be set aside for Felipe's education. She was to use the rest to run the house. She did no such thing. Without Anthony's knowing, she put the rest in a savings account in his name. He returned to Goa at the age of fourteen to a modest nest egg. 'But the best news was about Felipe,' he says, 'he was doing brilliantly at school. He led the class in every subject and even at that age, his ability to work hard was astonishing.'

In hindsight one could say the same thing about Anthony. He had learned a skill. He could make and bake bread. He withdrew all of his savings and invested them in an earthenware oven, fired by wood, in his mother's backyard. The 14-year-old baker was in business and his two major concerns were to remain with him for the rest of his life; the fledgling bakery, and Felipe's education and career.

*

While the rewards of success are there for all to see, very few of us are privy to their brutal genesis: the hard graft, the sweat and tears, the crises and heartbreak. Baking in Goa is both an art and craft, part of a glorious culinary heritage distinguished in equal parts by Portuguese and ethnic influences, and made richer by the source materials of a lush coastline – coconut, bran, unpolished rice, toddy and molasses. But every *vaddo* in a village has several bakeries. Anthony had to relearn and fight for his trade. Beginning with a single loaf, the pau made with toddy, he improvised and experimented until he was able to offer what no other baker in the village could: a daily range of fragrant, freshly baked breads and *bolos*, the delicious coconut-and-molasses sweet breads. His fifth anniversary as a baker was cause for two celebrations. He owned the largest and best bakery in the village, and Felipe at eleven, became the youngest award winner of Goa's premier high school literary prize – an essay contest where the entry had to be composed in both Konkani and Portuguese. In the retelling, I was touched by their pride in each other's accomplishments. Felipe talked endlessly about Anthony's bakery; Anthony had words only for Felipe's award.

*

Two extraordinary careers had taken wing. It is nearly twenty-five years to the day. Anthony's bakery remains in the village but it is now housed in a mint-clean concrete building standing on half an acre, with a phalanx of huge electric ovens for the baking, but the dough is still mixed and kneaded by hand. And his first earthenware oven has been lovingly preserved and is still in use. He employs fifty young people, sons and daughters of neighbours, whom he has trained personally. Six vans deliver a baker's bounty of breads and pastries each morning to his own and other stores all over north Goa, a repertoire where the contemporary is enhanced by the traditional. No other baker in Goa, to my knowledge, offers *pinaka* or *letria* and the other confections of a golden yesteryear. But all of this takes second place to the pride he tries hard to keep out of his voice when he talks of Felipe's meteoric, many-splendoured career; he never let on, but it is a career which would have ended, stillborn, were it not for his encouragement, advice and financial support.

Felipe went on to become one of the most distinguished personalities of his time: brilliant playwright, enlightened educationist and – that rare and endangered species – honest and committed politician. He took three degrees, B.Ed, B.Sc, and in 1986, while attending to the needs of 5000 villagers as sarpanch, found time to complete his M.A. He chuckles at the memory. 'Three days a week at the panchayat office, four days at lectures in Panjim. Evenings for the writing. Thank heavens for an understanding wife!' He has pursued three outstanding careers. He was the youngest headmaster in the Goa school system and today serves as principal at one of the largest schools in the state, and president of Goa's

Headmaster's Association. As playwright and poet, his position in Goa is preeminent. He had written and directed fourteen plays, published a dozen books, led a *mando* troupe to eleven consecutive first prizes at Goa's keenly contested annual competitions in Panjim.

His political career has been one of sustained endeavour. He is now in a fourth term as sarpanch of the village he has so ably and honestly led for seventeen years. And it was in this role during the last elections that his courage and integrity were put to their severest test. Neither Anthony nor Felipe will talk about those fraught weeks, but I was able to put a picture together, piece by piece, from casual encounters with village friends. Felipe was standing for a fourth five-year term and all the cards were stacked against him. A state minister with vested interests in the village, used money, muscle, influence and intimidation in support of Felipe's opponent; a whispering campaign accused Felipe of corruption and worse, calling to serious question all of an honourable political career; a national corporation with a major presence in the area, and much clout with the state government and the centre, campaigned vigorously but discreetly against him. All seemed lost. So my friend, Felipe, took to the hustings on his scooter, and on foot where there were no roads, while Anthony's fleet of vans was requisitioned by his supporters for the duration. They went from *vaddo* to *vaddo*, from house to house, putting their case to the people. Felipe's message had the clarity of truth. 'When I could help,' he told his people, 'I did so. When I could not, I told you why. I have not been able to do everything you wished, but I have done a great deal, and I will continue to do so if you place your trust in me again.'

At the victory rally held on the night the results were announced, trucks with lathi wielding goons drew up in the dark with their lights off. At Felipe's urging, his supporters dispersed and a bloody riot was barely averted.

Anthony and Felipe, brothers and friends, each first among equals. Felipe remains Goa's most honest and efficient sarpanch. And Anthony's mutton rolls are still the best in the land.

****

The Storyteller

His father emerged
inch by inch from beneath
the bed, bum first, just
as Jose's rasping cough
broke loose. He gave Jose
a murderous look and
pressed a finger to his lips.

Nine Stitches to the Inch

The pariah hawk circled high in the sky with a stealthy discretion, talons laid back, wing tips spread, great hooked beak turning swiftly this way and that like a scythe looking to reap every last tendril, whirl and eddy of wind. Then it saw Jose on the balcony, paused in mid sweep, gathered itself with leisurely grace and descended in long, spiralling arcs. It was confused. Jose, for once, was silent and the hawk was too high to see or smell the scraps of bloody gristle in the plastic mug. It was a daily ritual. Mrs MacDuff cleaned the day's raw meat with a butcher's knife, chopping, cutting, trimming with deft practised strokes. The scraps were collected. 'Jose,' she called from the kitchen, 'feed the birds.' He loved the chore. In a trice he was out on the balcony, calling to the hawks in a pale imitation of the scavenger's hunting cry when it caught sight of prey. A single high-pitched scream of rage and blood lust before the wings disappeared into the body and the hawk plummeted down like a stone only to unfold the yard-long wing-spread taut at the very last second, curved, clawing talons reaching down to break and rend.

Jose had lost his voice and he was in a quandary. The caning that lay in wait for him in Latin class later in the morning was the least of his problems. This day Father Vincenti would have cause. 'MacDuff,' the guttural voice would command, 'conjugate!' How was he to cope with Latin verbs before the class without a voice? Silence, which was construed as sullen rebellion, drove Father

Vincenti into an insensate rage. The caning took place in front of his desk in full view of the class. The sharp edge of the wooden ruler, with all of the wrathful, stocky weight of Father Vincenti's body behind it, raised painful welts on the palms of Jose's hands, six 'cuts' on the left, six on the right. He was secretly proud of the welts and at the recess break made a small production of examining them till an admiring crowd of boys gathered about him. For favours rendered – a bit of tuck, the loan of a top, a fistful of marbles – he would allow the welts to be felt, prodded, squeezed. Then, hands smarting, tucked into the pockets of his shorts, he sauntered off, whistling with feigned nonchalance, waiting for the hated taunt which never failed to be hurled at him from a safe distance across the quadrangle, 'Good for you, Onion Eyes!'

Truth will tell. Jose's head was too large for his body and his eyes were too large for his head. His mates at school had first nicknamed him 'Double Coconut Onion Eyes' and had soon abbreviated this tiresome mouthful to the crisper, more telling 'Onion Eyes' and Onion Eyes he had remained. 'Look at it this way,' his grandfather had said on the last occasion he had returned from school much the worse for wear in defence of his given name, 'they could have called you Blackie.' Point well made. His father was the colour of coffee and how he had come by the name MacDuff would forever remain one of life's perplexing mysteries. His mother, a Goan from Canacona was a toasted ivory and Jose's own genes, abandoning all further argument, had taken joyful refuge in the deeper shades of chocolate.

'If you've finished with the birds,' his mother called from the kitchen, 'give Mr Cohen his ties, then clean up and get ready for school.'

Would he ever be finished with the birds? He was entranced, as always, by their grace, precision and strength, the sheer arrogance of their easy command over wing and wind, and when he fed them, the blazing focus and purity of their deadly intent. Jose threw the scraps one after the other, in all directions, as high as he could fling them. Out of nowhere the sky filled with hawks. Screaming and plummeting. Turning and twisting. A blurred frenzy of beating wings, flashing beaks and clawing talons. The scraps were seized in mid air, torn and eaten mid flight, even as the birds twisted and plunged again and yet again. Not a scrap touched the ground. Then, as miraculously as they had appeared, they were gone, up, up and away, black specks floating high in the sky.

His mother stormed into the bedroom.

'I've called to you twice.' She was rigid with the anger that seized her ever so often, so quickly and with such little cause.

'I can't talk,' Jose said and was alarmed to hear the words come out, 'Ah garh gok.'

'Open your mouth,' his mother said, 'wide and turn your face to the light.'

His father stirred on the double bed, sat up, belched, ran a hand over his stubble and lit a Charminar.

'What's wrong with the boy?'

'A sore throat, Joe.'

'The little bugger's been stealing tamarind again,' his father said and threw Jose a glance of casual malevolence. There was little love lost between them. Jose looked his father steadily in the eye and allowed the hint of a smile to play about his lips, a conspiratorial smile. He would not be slapped today for he and his father had shared an alarming secret in the early hours of the morning. Archibald, looking to dinner, had woken Jose up where he slept on a mat on the floor. He sat on the back of Jose's right hand, fluffing up long metallic wings the colour of dark honey, his feelers delicately exploring the tips of Jose's fingers for a spot of unwashed grease or congealed gravy, his tiny mandibles extended, opening and closing in ferocious anticipation. Archibald was a gentleman; he never nibbled deeper than the last layer of epidermis and he never drew blood. But there was no joy for him tonight.

Out of the corner of his eye, Jose saw his father raise himself with exaggerated care on to his elbows and peer intently at the back of his mother's head. Then he nodded his own in a satisfied sort of way, slid off the bed backwards without a sound and crawled on all fours under it. Intrigued, now wide awake, Jose flicked Archibald off his hand and fought to contain the rising cough in his throat. He swallowed hard and the pain took him by surprise. So did his father's inexplicable contortions. Joe MacDuff began to behave in a most peculiar fashion. His bum, sticking out at an acute angle from under the bed, wiggled every which way as he groped in the spaces between the slats and the mattress. In a matter of seconds the bum ceased its agitation (it had been there before). There was a little sigh of relief and accomplishment. Jose heard a cork being teased ever so carefully, then a small pop, a series of quick, surreptitious gulps, a long pause, a stifled burp, then caution thrown to the winds, a long Herculean swallow, the cork eased back. His father emerged inch by inch from beneath the bed, bum first, just as Jose's rasping cough broke loose. He gave Jose a murderous look and pressed a finger to his lips. Too late. 'You awake Joe?' his mother called sleepily. 'Cigarette,' his father mumbled, growled, 'Can't a man enjoy a fag in peace in this house?' He padded off to the balcony. There he belched loudly. Twice. 'Come back to bed,' his mother said, 'you need to rest.' And Jose's heart shook with hate and rage.

He woke to the sound of the doorbell and his first chore of the day. It was the butter woman. She opened a huge earthenware pot filled to the brim with white, freshly churned butter and piled a heaping mound on to the saucer Jose gave her. With a theatrical flourish she produced a wooden paddle, gave Jose a toothless grin and said, 'So what will it be this morning?' and before he could choose, the gnarled old hands brought about a swift and magical transformation. The paddle made fluttery pats at the mound of butter, evoking the hint of a curve here, there, with a grand flourish, an angle and a plane; fingertips soothed an edge, worked a detail, until form and meaning took shape before Jose's wondering eyes. A series of deep verticle strokes and a tiger's fangs emerged, a tight half circle with the paddle and the head stood clear, the ears pricked up — presto! — whiskers yet. One last twist and tweak and a snarl rent the morning. She held the tiger's head to the light and grinned again, well pleased, wiped her fingers and the paddle on the palav of her sari and took the proferred rupee.

'No thank you today eh?' A bony finger poked Jose in the ribs, 'Lost your tongue?'

'Thank you,' Jose said, and all he heard was a hoarse, 'Grah groo.'

His second chore did not call for speech, which was just as well, for on the rare occasion when he had to deliver a message, usually an apology, along with the ties, he was afflicted with a sudden and prolonged stutter. Jose had to deliver six boxes of silk ties to Mr Cohen who lived a floor below the MacDuffs. Mr Cohen was a German Jew and an enigma within a paradox within a deep, dark secret. Only Mrs MacDuff was privy to the mystery and she kept very careful counsel indeed for Mr Cohen, who employed her as a seamstress, was the only regular source of the family income.

Jose could not say why he hated Mr Cohen with such a passion, but he knew very well why he loathed his father when Mr Cohen visited on business. Joe MacDuff changed character like a chameleon. He bowed and scraped; he smirked; he shuffled; he drew up the best chair for Mr Cohen; he made cups of tea; he rubbed his hands together nervously, driven distraught by his willingness to please; he behaved, in short, like a man in ceaseless terror of discovery and exposure. Guilty as charged, Jose thought. He had picked up the phrase from his latest Perry Mason and – boy! – did the shoe fit. There was cause for Jose's withering contempt. In between short, feverish bouts of doomed employment, Joe MacDuff spent most of his time seeking new and ever more ingenious hiding places all about the house for the long, slim bottles of 'tincture' he consumed with such relentless voracity and which he acquired by means unknown to anybody despite Mrs MacDuff's best sleuthing efforts. 'Bastards', was his only response when the government's prohibition policy was declared. He went about circumventing it without further ado and with considerable success until the occasional incendiary failure when Mrs MacDuff, on one of her rare dusting sprees, discovered a hidden bottle, Jose ducked for cover and all hell broke loose.

Now, as if he had read Jose's mind, Joe MacDuff chuckled and said, 'Paint his throat.' Without a word, Mrs MacDuff went to the kitchen, opened the drawer of the cabinet in which the medicines were kept and returned with the bottle of mercurochrome and a wad of cottonwool. The red liquid spread over the cotton like spilt blood. 'Open your mouth,' his mother said, 'wider.' She held Jose's tongue down with a spoon, shoved the cottonwool deep into the back of his mouth as far as she could go and scrubbed vigorously in the general vicinity of his tonsils. Mrs MacDuff believed that nothing should be done in half measure. She went at it with a will. A red hot knife sliced into Jose's throat. With a muffled scream, he struggled and pulled free. Never in his life had he known such pain.

'Stop fussing,' his mother said, 'wipe your mouth and take Mr Cohen his ties.'

'Sissy,' and his father smiled.

Jose would have protested if he could but he was quite beyond speech. He collected the six cardboard boxes of ties (they were papered over with a mottled pattern like dried snakeskin; whatever went on in Mr Cohen's head?) and prepared a face to meet Mr Cohen's. He was doomed to failure. Where Jose was a warm chocolate, Mr Cohen was a leached white; where Jose's hair fell thick and black and glossy and glinted, like his eyes, with a thousand points of dancing lights, Mr Cohen wore a pale blond monk's fringe; pale blond eyebrows disappeared without trace into a pale pink forehead; and his eyes, washed of all but the palest of blues, were strangers to all but the bleakest of feelings. Where Jose's smile gave the finger to life as it was, and celebrated the sheer joy of life as it ought to be, Mr Cohen's lips lay like a thin gash across his face, mirthless and unforgiving.

Mr Cohen had his reasons. In the great tide of human flotsam and jetsam laid to rest on distant shores by the Second World War, Mr Cohen was as weird a piece of protoplasm as was ever washed up in a Bombay working class neighbourhood. He appeared overnight, without warning, in the first floor flat at Yasdani Chambers directly below the MacDuff's. In no time at all he was at their front door, the black suit, white shirt and black tie at sinister odds with his pale blondness. Under his arms he held the boxes of hand-printed silk, light flannel interlining, cardboard forms and bobbins of matching thread which awaited Mrs MacDuff's painstaking ministrations.

'I understand,' Mr Cohen said in a voice which, like his eyes, had long forsaken all hope of human correspondence, 'that you are a seamstress looking for vurk.'

A month later Jose, with good cause, said to his mother, 'I hate Mr Cohen.'

'He puts food on the table.'

'Deepak says he's a Nazi.'

'Don't ever let me hear you say that again.'

'Sorry mother.' *Nazi monster!*

'Mr Cohen is a German Jew from Heidelberg. He lost his family in the war. They were taken away from him, every one of them, by the Gestapo and he's been trying to find them with the help of the International Refugee Commission ever since. Don't breathe a word of this to a soul. You will never understand what the poor man's been through.'

'No mother.' *Liar! Nazi monster!*

Only when he mispronounced 'W' and 'V' did Mr Cohen betray his origins. And, of course, when he sought perfection from Mrs MacDuff under pain of punishment which, Jose reflected bitterly, was just about all of the time. The ritual was precise and unfailingly surgical. Mr Cohen would raise one of the silk ties Mrs MacDuff had assembled with such care to the light, reverse it over his fingertips, examine first the stitching on the label and, if that passed muster, examine the lining under a magnifying glass until the pale blue eye, now monstrously enlarged, seemed to Jose to float about the room, disembodied and menacing. For long moments Mr Cohen would remain silent while Jose would hold his breath. Then the monk's tonsure would shake from side to side with slow deliberation. 'Eight stitches to the inch. This vill not do Mrs MacDuff. You haf contracted for nine. You vill haf to make the ties again, no?'

'Yes Mr Cohen.'

He never failed to bring the smallest imperfection to her attention. But there was no hint of censure, not the slightest suggestion of malice, not by inflection or glance. Just the measured syllables, dropping like stones into the pit of Jose's stomach.

'Send the ties down with the boy tomorrow by eight. I haf a meeting with Evans and Fraser at nine. And I vill haf to cut your fee by ten percent as usual.'

Nazi monster! Why then did his mother incline her head ever so reluctantly and lay the side of her face on the back of Mr Cohen's hand where it rested behind her on the chair? And why did Mr Cohen's index finger rise and stroke his mother's cheek?

The unshaded bulb above the heirloom Singer sewing machine was switched on. Mrs MacDuff drew up a stool. With a blade and needle she first cut, then unravelled the stitching on each tie, removed the interlining, laid ties and linings, one above the other, in a neat pile on a side table. Then she made the machine ready: inserted the bobbin, threaded the needle, folded over the edges of a tie with the greatest possible precision, and began. Bent over the machine, pedalling with her right foot, she guided the tie's lining under the needle which now rose and fell with dazzling speed, defying Jose's eye. He was afraid for her. Would the needle plunge and tear into his mother's fingers? Would the blood ruin the silk? And – God help them all! – what would Mr Cohen do if that happened? But Mrs MacDuff seemed oblivious to all possibility of disaster. The bones along her back stretched, curved, formed a long, lumpy ridge under her dress and began a rhythmic mimicry of her moving foot, riding up and down, up and down. Every so often she muttered under her breath, 'Nine stitches, nine stitches.' They remained with Jose the whole night long, echoing louder and louder yet till the moment of white hot terror when, the boxes of ties held precariously under both arms – impeccably stitched, perfectly labelled, steam-ironed with cardboard inserts so the edges would curve softly – he banged his forehead on the brass knocker on Mr Cohen's front door.

But on this morning something was amiss. The door was slightly ajar. Jose paused, then took his courage in both hands and spoke out, 'Mr Cohen?' The words rang in his head making no sound. A penitential voice, which surely could not have belonged to Mr Cohen, edged with an emotion Jose was unable to put a name to – dread? longing? despair? – answered uncertainly, 'The door, it is open.' Cautiously Jose let the boxes of ties lead the way, only to find Mr Cohen sitting on the edge of a sofa in, in … good grief … a dressing gown and bare feet! It seemed to Jose as if a giant hand had crumpled Mr Cohen's face and put it together haphazardly causing terrible hurt. Mr Cohen was there and he wasn't there: he had fled to some desolate arctic corner of his soul. A doppelganger with Mr Cohen's drained and shattered features had taken his place. Jose placed the boxes of ties on the coffee table and quickly pocketed the envelope marked 'Mrs MacDuff'. He tiptoed to the door. 'Goodbye Mr Cohen,' he said and once more his voice failed him. 'Nine stitches to the inch,' Mr Cohen mumbled. He seemed mesmerized by the telegram on the floor. 'Vithout nine stitches I will lose the business. Nine stitches ...' but his voice held no conviction.

*

Jose's first thought when he woke the next morning was, 'I am in deep shit.' His eyes burned in his head like holes with live coals in them. He tried to open his mouth and slivers of pure agony landed down his throat. His body ached deep within the bones. When the doorbell rang – the butter woman and here he was flat on his back! - and he tottered to his feet, the room made a slow, wobbly circle, his knees refused to support his body and he collapsed with a thump on his bum. 'Open the fucking door and get the butter,' his father roared. He was in a vile temper. Gainful employment was his lot this day, courtesy his blasted wife. She had spoken to that meathead of a busybody, Father Leonard who had a word with that dried up old Parsi cow, Freny Dholakiz, who ran a home for retarded children and had a fortnight's replacement vacancy for a supervisor, a position for which Joe MacDuff was supremely unqualified. Worse, he would have to live in. Worse still, he would have to play hide and seek with the tincture bottles in a strange, hostile environment with no telling if he was caught in the act.

'Open the door,' he yelled again and was about to assist vigorously with the sole of his foot on his son's bottom, when he noticed a line of white foam dribbling out of the corner of Jose's mouth. 'Dora,' he called sharply. Mrs MacDuff knelt beside Jose and felt his forehead, his throat, wiped the foam off his lips. 'He's burning,' she said. 'Can you talk Jose? Where does it hurt son?' Jose made a mighty effort to speak but now words as well were beyond him. He made a sploshy, liquid sound halfway between a gurgle and a gargle. 'Get the fucking thermometer,' Mr MacDuff snarled. 'You smashed it a month ago,' Mrs MacDuff said, 'when you were drunk and thought you were dying. Ask Mrs Kurien for hers. Go on. Quickly.'

Dire news spread in Yasdani Chambers as swiftly as it happened. Within ten minutes the thermometer arrived, en fete, with a small party in tow. Plump and lively and mysterious Mrs Kurien (no one had ever set eyes on Mr Kurien), given to scented goings and rumpled comings at all hours of the day and night, tossing her curls now and clinging quite unnecessarily to Joe MacDuff's right arm. Occupying the left flank was Major Simpson, or was it Colonel Simpson? Retired from Montgomery's Desert Rats or was it Mountbatten's Burma Corps? Awarded a meritorious OBE, then, again, perhaps a DSO with Bar? He was inordinately fond of Jose and fed him heroic quantities of Chivers Thick Cut Marmalade on toast on weekends ('I don't trust the bugger,' Mr MacDuff, seeing corrupt sexual practice where none existed, would declare darkly in his cups). Bringing up the rear was Fat Hari, called thus because he was famously thick in the head and even more so around the middle. They formed a keenly interested and voluble circle about Jose.

'Here, let me wipe your mouth darling,' Mrs Kurien went down on a dimpled knee, caressed the back of Jose's neck with her left hand, while she tenderly wiped the muck off his mouth with her right. Mrs MacDuff's lips tightened perceptibly. 'Move over,' she said brusquely, 'and let me take his temperature.' 'Under the tongue,' Major Simpson said. Dora MacDuff gave him a look. 'Open your mouth, my son.' Jose made the effort of his life. The thermometer went in. She began to count silently, one and a one, two and a two, till she reached three minutes. Then she took the thermometer to the window and squinted at it in the light. They crowded around her with the exception of Mrs Kurien, lost to all the world but for Jose, and Mr MacDuff who hovered nervously at the periphery. 'One hundred and four point five,' Mrs MacDuff announced, lips trembling, but Mrs Kurien hadn't heard. She was bent very low over Jose, making cooing noises deep in her throat and stroking his cheek. Jose was now seeing two of everything and – holy shit! – *four* of Mrs Kurien's proudest assets which she had never believed in concealing. The plunging V of her blouse revealed a pair of the most delicious breasts Jose had ever seen at such close quarters, lolloping this way and that within inches of his nose, rising and falling with every languid breath she took. Happy for once this morning, Jose wished there could have been four of Mrs Kurien, or five, or more. Mrs Kurien straightened up reluctantly and teased a curl into place with a plump little pinkie. 'What ever could it be,' she asked of no one in particular.

Major Simpson flung himself into the breach, seized the flag from a fallen comrade, won the day and gave himself a promotion on the battlefield. 'Reminds me of the Irrawady campaign,' Colonel Simpson announced, in his Field Commander's voice, a daring raid on an impregnable enemy position successfully concluded. 'Major offensive with two crack divisions, heavy artillery in the rear to soften them up, infantry up front cutting them to pieces. I was in charge of a Gurkha battalion at the time and before you could say, "Yellow peril" my boys were falling down where they stood. By the dozens. Looked very much like young Jose here. Perished like flies in a flitpit. Never did find out what the bug was. Did more damage than the Japs.' But it was Fat Hari who pointed the way. 'D-d-do you suppose,' he stuttered, as he usually did at any attempt at creative thought, 'we should send for D-d-doctor Sequeira?"' 'Splendid idea,' said Brigadier Simpson, setting the official seal of the High Command on this excellent plan. Fearful of the consequences, Joe MacDuff bestirred himself. 'Have to go,' he muttered, ' job to do. I'll be in touch, Dora. Take care of yourself, son.' He picked up his suitcase, praying that the bottles of tincture wouldn't tinkle, and made posthaste for the front door only to be stopped in his tracks by the Head of the Secret Operations Executive for South-east Asia. Eyes narrowed to slits, prepared to order termination with extreme prejudice, Major General Simpson drew himself erect and issued a curt order. 'You will stop by at Doctor Sequeira's. I want him here at once.'

Joe MacDuff made himself scarce. Mrs MacDuff sighed and hurried off to the kitchen to prepare a cold compress for Jose's head. Mrs Kurien gave it a safe minute or two, then her voice quivered with investigative zeal. 'Could it be,' she whispered, 'mumps?' 'Bumps?' Fat Hari, whose hearing was deficient in inverse proportion to his size, exclaimed loudly, 'Bumps!' 'Shh,' she gave Jose a look of melting concern, 'you never know,' and in a flash she was at his side on the mat, legs tucked demurely under her thighs and when she caught Major Simpson's eye, moustache quivering agitatedly in a most unmilitary fashion, she tucked the ends of her skirt modestly under her buttocks, fluttered her lashes and pressed hard against Jose's hip as she did so. 'Lie still, honey.' Her fingers caressed the soft places beneath the lobes of his ears and under his jaw, slipped into his pyjama bottoms, felt longer than was strictly necessary along his groin and, quite carried away by the gravity of his medical condition, gave his penis a friendly squeeze. 'Not a lump,' Mrs Kurien said regretfully, sprang to her feet and adjusted her skirt, just as Major Simpson's warning cough announced Mrs MacDuff's return.

An imperious knock on the door and Dr Sequeira's mane of white hair, shampooed and blow-dried, tossed casually hither and thither, made his presence felt at once. His unkinder critics had been known to suggest that if Dr Sequeira's errors of judgement were disinterred they would fill a good sized mortuary to overflowing. But Mrs MacDuff's faith in Dr Sequeira was unshakeable. After all, as he was at subtle pains to bring to the attention of all and sundry at the slightest opportunity, he *was* a Gaud Saraswat Roman Catholic Goan, and Mrs MacDuff knew in her bones – as all Sudras did – that this particular brand of Brahmin *never* made mistakes. Quite unimpressed by Jose's condition (Dr Sequeira saw worse every day) he palpitated Jose fore and aft, deployed his stethoscope with thumping abandon, peered briefly down Jose's throat, paused for dramatic effect and announced, 'As I suspected, the boy has the gruppe.'

'Oh no,' Mrs Kurien murmured in a despairing sort of way; she hadn't the faintest idea what that was: none of them did.

'Begins with the lungs,' Dr Sequeira explained. A touch of professional expertise was expected of him on such occasions and he never disappointed. 'Spreads through the oesophagus and trachea and attacks the throat. We shall have to cup the boy.'

Now that was something they were all familiar with. 'Just the ticket,' Major Simpson said, 'let me give you a hand, Mrs MacDuff.' 'I'll slice the onion,' Mrs Kurien offered. 'Only,' Dr Sequeira reminded her sternly, 'from the thickest part.' 'Camphor,' Fat Hari added happily, this *was* going to be his day, 'do we have c-camphor?'

'Make sure its fresh.' Dr Sequeira squiggled indecipherable hieroglyphics on a pad and gave the prescription to Mrs MacDuff. 'Four times a day for the fever. Give him plenty of fluids. Bed rest. No school.' And he gave Jose the special crocodile smile he reserved for children. 'That will be twenty rupees.' He pocketed the notes. 'Regards to Mr MacDuff. Have to dash. Busy morning. Let me know how he does.' And off he went, tossing his white mane once or twice for good measure.

Jose was laid flat on his back on the bed. Mrs Kurien declined all help when removing his pyjama top and untying the string of the bottoms. Tenderly, she massaged Jose's belly button. 'We do not cup below the navel,' Mrs MacDuff said coldly. Jose was made to lie still while the cupping took.

Bedroom slippers shuffled at the door. There was a polite, controlled rat-a-tat-tat of knuckles on wood. Oh my God, Mrs MacDuff thought, it's *him*. Mr Cohen stood in the doorway in his dressing gown. 'Vere are my ties?' he asked. Then he saw Jose lying barebodied on the bed, the wine glasses prettily catching the light. 'Make vay.' He approached gingerly and stood a good two feet away from Jose. 'Open your mouth, boy,' he ordered. 'Turn your face to the light.' Jesus H, Jose thought, and painfully did as he was told yet again. Then Mr Cohen did a very strange thing. He bent forward at the waist, handkerchief over his nose and mouth, magnifying glass in his free hand. A huge pale blue eye and its twin played tic-tac-toe in Jose's head, then dwindeled with great speed as Mr Cohen walked rapidly backwards to the door. His voice, muffled by the kerchief, filled the small room with doomsday prophecy. 'Diptheria. The boy has diptheria. You must move him at vunce to the Arthur Road hospital. At vunce or I vill inform the authorities.'

It says much for the respect in which Mr Cohen's opinions were held that no one thought to question his diagnosis. Besides, they had all heard, with half an ear, that there was an epidemic on, but then wasn't there always? Diptheria was one of a clutch of 'communicable' diseases, a term which the people of Jose's tenement had come to believe, with more than a little justification, was government gobbledygook for quick and nasty death. Once diagnosed, victims had to be moved immediately to Arthur Road, the city's only hospital for infectious diseases. Not to do so was a criminal offence. Yet to obey was almost certainly a sentence of death. The residents of Yasdani Chambers, quick to gallows humour, claimed that it was no coincidence that the Arthur Road hospital lay within a short funeral procession's walk from the Haines Road cemetery for Christians and a burning ghat for Hindus.

'Diptheria,' Mrs Kurien said, with a catch in her voice.

'The poor lad,' Major Simpson patted Mrs MacDuff on the shoulder. 'I'll go with you.'

They popped the wine glasses, leaving round, red bumps on Jose's chest, they wiped him down; it did little good; he alternated between bouts of ague and hot, sticky sweats. They put on his pyjama top, bundled him in a blanket. 'Food,' Mrs MacDuff said. There was a bruised look to her eyes. 'Will they give him food at the hospital?' 'But he c-c-can't s-s-swallow.' 'Soup then, hot soup.' 'There isn't time, Dora.' Mrs Kurien stuffed a pair of fresh pyjamas into a bag, a hand towel, toothbrush, mug, a bottle of boiled water. 'Goodbye, darling.' She was careful not to touch Jose. They carried him down the stairs, hailed a Victoria. Major Simpson was about to say, 'Arthur Road,' but caught himself in time. 'Go straight,' he ordered in his best seargent major's pidgin Hindi, 'I will direct you along the way.' Seized by an irrational panic, Mrs MacDuff said, 'Put the hood up. Somebody may see us.' With great difficulty Major Simpson did so. The horse began a leisurely amble and refused, when whipped at Major Simpson's urging, to go any faster. As if in protest, it began to fart loudly and shit – mushy, stinking plops – without breaking stride as it carried Jose away, giggling helplessly, to his destiny.

At Arthur Road hospital they were lying down and dying, in Major Simpson's evocative phrase, like flies in a flitpit. Crowds clamoured for entry at the gates and were admitted grudgingly, one victim at a time with a single companion, through a barred steel door. Disease and death were no strangers to commerce, Major Simpson noted grimly, dispensing rupee notes like confetti to the hospital guards. He carried Jose in his arms while Mrs MacDuff used her elbows and the bag to bump, shove and thrust until by brute force and bribery they came at last to the entrance. 'You need not fill the form,' the man in grey said, having observed their progress with an appreciative eye, 'sign here.' Major Simpson slid a ten-rupee note between the folds. A nod of the head and they were through. Another ward boy led them along a cobbled path to what appeared to be a cattle shed with tiny, barred windows set high in the walls. He touched finger to forelock and refused to go away. Major Simpson's last note changed hands. They passed from bright sunshine into an eerie dusk. As their eyes adjusted to the gloom, shapes emerged, formless inchoate bundles of dispossession clad in hospital issue several sizes too large, lying in neat rows on reed mats on the floor, separated from each other by two feet of space.

A young intern moved down the narrow passageways. He wore a surgical mask and carried the weight of his body like a tired old man. A ward boy followed with the biggest hypodermic syringe Jose had ever set eyes on and a bottle of dark brown fluid on a tray. From body to body the intern went, like a marionette. Two steps, down on a knee. The ward boy exposed a thigh. In with the hypodermic. Up again. Two steps, down on a knee. When the intern came to them, he looked about him vaguely and pointed to an empty mat under a window. 'Put him there,' he said. His hand fluttered in a futile gesture about the room. 'I have so many others to attend to.' They lay Jose down. The ward boy tugged at Major Simpson's sleeve. 'You must leave,' he said. 'Only one person may stay and not during the night.' Jose shivered on the mat, the white mould now welling thicker at the corners of his mouth. It oozed and clung and stuck and spread with a monstrous life of its own, fiercely resisting Mrs MacDuff's attempts to dab it off. 'Let it be,' Major Simpson said, 'the doctor will be with him soon.' He put his arm around Mrs MacDuff's shoulders and gave her a little hug. Then he looked down at Jose with tears in his eyes remembering other departures. 'Goodbye, son,' he said and gave him up forever.

The ward boy prised open Jose's jaw as brusquely as he would a goat's at a cattle fair. The intern wiped the sweat from his eyes. 'Bad case,' he said, swabbed the blood from the needle, wiped a spot on Jose's thigh with the same blood-soaked swab and plunged the hypodermic in.

'Serum,' he said briefly.

302 / The Storyteller

'When will he get better, doctor?'

'I will know by the morning,' the intern said. 'If the serum fails we must put a tube in his throat to allow him to breathe and try once more with the serum.'

'By the morning,' the ward boy said sardonically in Marathi, a language Mrs MacDuff had never acquired, 'somebody else will be lying on that mat.'

'Can I bring him food?'

'Food,' the intern repeated the word as if he had never heard of it before. 'Food? He cannot swallow and it is not allowed by the rules.'

'But he hasn't eaten all day.'

'We have a thin soup,' the intern said, 'with glucose. When they can't swallow, it is administered through a funnel and a rubber tube.'

'Can I stay the night?'

'No.' His patience was wearing thin. 'You must leave before dark.'

Jose slept no sooner his mother left and was woken by the sound of a heavy weight being trundled across the cobblestones. Figures appeared in the doorway like yellow wraiths, lit by the sulphurous glow of the gas lamp in the street. They pushed a long, high wheelbarrow between the silent bodies on the mats. An intern in a white coat led the way. He shone a torch rapidly left and right as he went along. Once in a while he paused and the wheelbarrow stopped behind him. He knelt, felt with the stethoscope at a neck, a heart, nodded. The ward boys slipped a rubber band with a tag over the head. The intern scribbled briefly on the tag. The body was lifted by the knees and armpits and put in the wheelbarrow. Body piled upon body till the wheelbarrow could take no more. A foot stuck up in the air, a hand belonging to somebody else flopped over the edge, a balding head of hair, as if taking its restful ease, reclined against a corner. Yet they came on, hesitated at Jose and moved to the man who lay at his side. Jose turned and looked at him. This, surely, could not be the posture of death. What would Mr James, the undertaker, whose tidy work Jose had witnessed with awe on more than one occasion, have had to say about this unseemly sprawl of arms and legs, all akimbo, the gaping mouth, the open and sightless eyes? *The bugger's dead*. Where had the voice come from? His father's face hovered before him, raging, cursing, hurling abuse at Jose's swollen eyes. *Dead, I tell you, the bugger's dead. Dead. Dead. Dead*. The words hammered into Jose's head as he slipped first into delirium then, exhausted, into a blessed oblivion.

'No change,' the intern said to Mrs MacDuff the next morning. 'What do you have there?'

'A hot water bottle.'

'Very well, only this once. But the rules forbid it.'

'Has he taken any nourishment?'

'No.'

'Put him on a drip then,' Mrs MacDuff said, her voice rising.

'A drip!' the intern shouted. The bodies on the mats stirred; heads turned; the ward boy looked angrily at Mrs MacDuff. 'Why not intensive care?' he screamed, 'a private room? Day and night nurses? Why don't we all live forever? We had fifteen dead here during the night.' He turned on his heel, muttering in disbelief, 'A drip ...'

Mrs MacDuff slipped the hot water bottle under Jose's pyjama top. She sat on the mat by his side, looked this way and that over her shoulders. 'Shhh,' she said to Jose, unscrewed the metal top and raised the hot water bottle to Jose's lips. 'Chicken soup,' she whispered. 'Try and drink some.' But Jose could not swallow. Hastily Mrs MacDuff screwed the cap back on, dabbed with a napkin at Jose's face and neck. A shadow fell across the mat. For a heart-wrenching moment Mrs MacDuff made ready to meet her nemesis, but the ward boy was on a familiar errand of disposal. He carried a small black child in his arms. A tube poked out of the hollow in its throat. He put the child on the empty mat beside Jose's and regarded it for a moment with an unperturbed and professional eye. Mrs MacDuff, with a visible effort, tore her eyes away from the tube.

'Tracheotomy,' the ward boy said dismissively; clearly, in his view, it was a pointless concession to what little life remained.

'Is there nobody with him?' Mrs MacDuff asked.

'He was left at the gate,' the ward boy said, 'at three in the morning. Dying. We get at least a dozen like him every night. More girls than boys.' He shook the child gently by the shoulder and its head lolled like a rag doll's from side to side, then it lay still and unmoving, the distilled embodiment of all things dark and dead. The black skin clung to the tiny mockery of a body like a shroud drawn tight over the bones. The only sign of life was the tube in his throat. Once, after long seconds, it twitched. The ward boy shook his head again. 'He will be gone before dawn,' he said. 'We must give him a name.'

'A name?'

'For the tag,' the ward boy said, 'Pandu.' He rolled the word around his tongue and chuckled. 'Yes, Pandu.'

Jose shuddered.

As the shadows lengthened across the ward and Mrs MacDuff made ready to leave, Jose took a turn for the worse. His limbs began to shake, his lips moved soundlessly, bubbles of foam gathered at the corners of his mouth as swiftly as Mrs MacDuff could wipe them off and he sank into delirium. When his mother spoke to him he could not respond. Before she knew it, the intern was at her side. He issued terse instructions to the ward boy. 'I will give him an injection,' he said, 'to stop the seizure. It will also help him breathe.' He found a vein in Jose's arm and inserted the needle with great care. 'He will sleep with that tonight,' he said. 'If he's not better tomorrow we must do the tracheotomy and give him more serum.' He touched Mrs MacDuff's arm. 'Go home,' he said with a gentleness quite at odds with the way he had been earlier in the day, 'and get some rest. There is nothing more that we can do. Your son is in God's hands.'

The wheelbarrow did not wake Jose. Nor did the yellow glow of the gas lamp which fell harshly on his face, made black, funereal hollows of his eyes and limned the skull beneath the skin. A constriction across his chest woke him. He was suffocating. With every breath he took a soft, heavy weight inched inexorably towards his throat. He opened his eyes. A small hand felt for his face. A gurgle of sheer delight as a familiar object, Jose's nose, was discovered, claimed, investigated. Pandu. He sprawled across Jose's chest and wriggled like a frisky amoeba. He made small happy noises and drooled. His eyes shone like polished black marbles; they were full of mischief. A squeal; a finger went into Jose's ear and tugged at a lobe. Suddenly then, like an exhausted puppy, he ceased all activity, made water on Jose and fell asleep in the crook of Jose's arm with his thumb in his mouth.

At first light, he sat up on his mat and bawled. He was alive and well and by some blessed alchemy Jose would never, in all the rest of his life understand, so was he. An alien emotion creased the intern's eyes above the surgical mask. They crinkled at the corners. For the first time since Jose had known him, he smiled. He examined Pandu. 'This one will live,' he said to the ward boy, lapsing into Marathi. 'We can remove the tube in a day or two. Give him some milk.' He turned to Jose who opened his mouth wide without being asked to do so and, for the first time in many days, took a deep clean breath. 'So will he,' the intern said. 'You are going to be well' – in his slow precise English – 'Your mother will be very happy.' 'Bhagwan ki kasm,' the ward boy said, confused and cross. His predictions were rarely wrong. 'It is the work of God.'

But God had still to complete a capricious morning's work and now He chose Mrs MacDuff, of all people, to be his unwitting accomplice. She had risen early, packed the ties and, crossing herself, filled Jose's hot water bottle with chicken soup. The door of Mr Cohen's flat was ajar, as usual and this, like his dressing gown and bare feet, had ceased to be cause for surprise. But today Mr Cohen had dressed for a very special occasion. The black shoes were polished to a brilliance; the seams on the black socks were perfectly straight; the pants were pressed to a fine crease. Then Mrs MacDuff noticed, with utter disbelief, that the shoes with Mr Cohen's limp feet in them were suspended a foot above the floor. They rotated slowly now to one side, now to the other, as did Mr Cohen hanging with a broken neck from the ceiling fan at the end of a knotted rope of Evans and Frazer's ties.

Mrs MacDuff held Jose tight and rocked on her heels. She felt her son's heart beating strongly against hers. She tried to hold the engulfing tide of horror and loss at bay and failed. 'Mr Cohen,' she said. Her voice broke and she began to sob. 'Mr Cohen is no more ...'

****

Bernie Finklebaum Jr.
Learns a New Word

Whenever I hear the nasal twang of the American abroad, raised in adenoidal protest at some real or imagined outrage, I am reminded of the hapless Bernie Finklebaum Jr. A couple of Colonel Jeremiah Saldanha's gentle lessons in Goan etymology; a Christmas drink with Gerson and Jude, the redoubtable public prosecutor and inspector general of police whom I came to regard with awe as The Two Just Men; a working partnership with those geniuses of the perfect car wash, Tweedledum and Tweedledee; and Bernie would have emerged a wiser and better man, equipped to confront life's small injustices with a wink and a smile. Did he learn anything from his bruising encounter with Aloysius, the master carpenter of Siridao? I doubt it. The Finklebaum Jrs. of this world hurtle on regardless; they will never understand that one man's carved chest can well turn out to be another man's folly.

The only folly in sight this fine Christmas Eve morning was the third caju feni that Gerson was urging upon me with the commanding authority that only the law can bring to bear.

'That'll be my third before noon,' I protested.

Gerson was not impressed. 'The law is never an ass,' he pronounced grandly, 'when it comes to drinking before lunch on Christmas Eve. Drink up, it's going to be a long weekend.'

Jude, the inspector general of police, poured me three fingers of caju, added a splash of cold water as an afterthought, and said, 'How else will you keep your strength up?'

Gerson's is the final legal word in sixty thousand kilometres of Goan territory; it does not, however, extend to the kitchen. His wife Anna's voice rose above the clatter of pots and pans. 'Not a drop more unless you eat something. Won't be a minute.' And true to her word, in moments large platters of fried prawns and Goa sausage turnovers appeared. We ate as Goans do when they enjoy their nosh, in reverential silence. And Jude had a point; it was wise, if not imperative, to keep one's strength up.

In Goa the Christmas spirit begins to shake a glad leg, quite literally, at brunch on the twenty-fourth and proceeds, in ever swifter good cheer, to the early hours of the twenty-sixth. In between there are lunches which begin at three in the afternoon and end weightily at seven, and dinners which commence alcoholically at one in the morning and seem to go on forever. A pause for midnight mass (sung – the strength now well and truly up – vigorously off-key) and on to the first Christmas party of the day. A refreshing catnap as dawn breaks, then up and stirringly about at ten when the day really begins with a round of visits to friends and distant branches of the family, a lunch to test strong men to their limits, a grand ball that night at the Club National, and home to bed as dawn nuzzles the night. Everybody collapses on Boxing Day.

I raised my glass, 'Down with law and order.'

Jude chuckled. 'There's not much of that about over Christmas. Crime seems to take a holiday.'

'Strange, I should have thought just the opposite.'

'Soused,' Jude said, 'out of their minds. Thieves break into empty houses; pickpockets try it on with police inspectors; smugglers land contraband at customs' wharves. Very few arrests though.'

'Why is that?'

'The forces of law and order,' Jude sighed, 'are as human as the rest of us. Let's be charitable and say that the spirit of peace and · goodwill reigns.'

'Except,' Gerson said cryptically, 'when it comes to pigs.'

They exchanged mischievous glances and laughed. I had known them for ten years; one would, I reflected, be hard put to find two more good-tempered, mild-mannered and heartily feared men in all of Goa. Now they were agreeably relaxed, feet up, toasting the yuletide spirit, and inclined to frivolity.

'Pigs?' I repeated, intrigued. A Tall Tale was in the offing. 'Tell me more.'

Gerson turned to Jude. 'Tell Frank,' he said, 'about the case of the purloined pig.'

'That shouldn't count really. It happened on December 23.'

'Near enough,' Gerson said.

'Despite the forensic abilities of the best minds in the business,' Jude said, 'the case of the purloined pig remains stubbornly unresolved.'

'We strongly suspect,' Gerson added, 'that one man's purloined pig become another man's *sorpotel*, but there isn't a shred of evidence to prove it.'

'As these things go,' Jude said, 'a tragic ending.'

'A grave miscarriage of justice,' Gerson agreed, 'yet not without drama. Like all sensational crimes, it has everything. Grand larceny, hot pursuit, violence, lynch law and, at the end of it all, a mystery that has never been solved.'

They were beginning to enjoy themselves.

'The suspense,' I said, 'is giving me a thirst.'

I helped myself to a jumbo feni; so did they; then Jude settled back and told us the tale of the purloined pig.

Two days before Christmas, seized by one of those inexplicable impulses that only occur at this time of peace and goodwill to all men (and women!), Jude decided to be nice to his wife. He would shoulder the burden of the day's household chores and buy the fish himself. He met his wife's solicitous suggestion that he lie down till the urge went away with dignified silence and, feeling particularly virtuous, he walked to the village *tinto*. It was a morning to lark about without a care, a nip in the air, a gentle breeze from the sea and a sky which would remain a clear blue forever. The village was making ready for Christmas. Red and green buntings adorned front porches; holly and mistletoe set the sophisticates apart from the hoi polloi who made do, poor things, with Chinese lanterns and intricately wrought Stars of Bethlehem. But social distinctions seemed not to matter; there was an energetic bustle wherever you looked, much excited to-ing and fro-ing, a glad and generous feeling to the day.

The village square was in the process of waking, a scene of positively bucolic arousal which unfolded each morning in movements so slow as to induce mesmerized slumber. The exquisite reluctance with which Da Silva the Grocer, put his shutters up evoked a sleepy sympathy; the achingly ponderous movements of Barboza the Baker as he placed loaf after loaf resentfully on the counter touched one to the drowsy core; the morose resignation of Mendonca the Cold Storage Merchant as he put down the Kwality Icecream sign struck dreamy chords of fluffy fellow-feeling. The thought of a day's work – the last, thank God, before Christmas – lay heavily upon the morning.

As if on cue, the Holiest Family in the Village, led by a Pious Elder, eyes averted from all of this irreligious disorder, disdain for lesser mortals in every stride, made its way to the church for mass, pointedly ignoring the day's first drunks, quenching unquenchable thirsts on the steps of the *tinto's* taverna. The drunks couldn't have cared less. They exchanged ribald sallies with the fisherwomen, bright as peacocks, exchanging colourful and inventive oaths, as they pushed, shoved and jostled for the best sales positions. Looking on in various attitudes of imminent collapse, propping up walls, tree trunks, roadsigns and shop fronts, was that energetic component of the village youth which laboured diligently every morning at its favourite activity: standing and staring. Bullock carts trundled by; motor cycles ridden by murderously dangerous young men skidded and zoomed about the square. Cyclists rode and chatted amiably, four abreast, blocking everyone's right of passage. Then a young boy, no more than thirteen, made an appearance on a bicycle. He rode alone, with a pig lashed to the carrier, taking the animal to the Mapusa bazaar.

There are only a few sounds capable of penetrating the noisy hubbub of a village *tinto*: the first is the squealing of a pig being taken to market; the pig knows that no good is going to come of it and protests mightily with squeal after porcine squeal of doomsday anguish; the only other sound to equal, indeed surpass by several decibels those of the hapless porker, are the bellows of rage when a pig is found to be purloined. They now rent the air in a frenzied torrent from a very fat, very old woman who rushed into the centre of the *tinto*, stopping the traffic, glaring wild-eyed this way and that, brandishing a club and screaming at the top of her voice, 'WHERE IS HE? WHERE IS HE? THE FATHERLESS MALCREADO! HE'S STOLEN MY PIG! THE MISBEGGOTEN SON OF A SOW HAS STOLEN MY PIG!'

Nothing arouses the native ire like the theft of a pig. Breaking and entering is considered a minor peccadillo, more so as the only houses worth breaking and entering into are owned by extortionist landlords who eminently deserve and can amply afford to be parted from some of their ill-gotten gains. Crimes of passion are discussed philosophically, with a world-weary resignation: such things will happen; the heart has its reasons; Cupid does not discriminate with his thunderbolts. The surreptious shifting of a boundary stone by the dark of the moon prompts sage and legally inclined debate, when the merits or otherwise of the shifting are seen in proper ancestral and historical perspective: past injustices, unrepaid loans, mortal insults, an unlikely pregnancy, the disappearance of mangoes and coconuts, and suchlike. But steal a pig and passions are set violently aflame: rough justice is the order of the moment, and woe to the thief!

Like the Keystone Kops in fast forward, every single mother's soul in the *tinto* leaped up and rushed about in different directions, shouting all at once as loudly as they could. 'I have never seen such chaos,' Jude recalled happily, 'not even at a bull fight when the favourite bull loses.' The chaos was showing signs of developing into a small but moderately violent riot when Barboza the Baker, showing unexpected and commendable qualities of leadership, grabbed hold of Mendonca, the Cold Storage Merchant's Kwality Icecream sign and waving it above his head like colours retrieved in battle, charged to the aid of the Victim, with Mendonca and Da Silva the Grocer, all thought of work gratefully abandoned, close at his heels. The layabouts and the fisherwomen brought up the rear (while the *tinto's* cats made hay among the fish) and the drunks, pausing for quick refills, sought, however unsteadily, to aid and abet.

They gathered supportively around the old woman, patting her shoulder, making sympathetic noises, looking around, about, under, above as though the pig might have taken wing, but she would not be consoled. The first rush of rage was replaced by wailing grief. She sobbed hysterically, tore at her hair, beat her breast with clenched fist, called upon the Saints to witness her plight, beseeched the heavens. Was she not a virtuous woman? Had she not lived a God-fearing life? Did her neighbours not know her as the very soul of honesty? Had there been a day, a single day, when her life had been anything less than pure and blameless? What had she ever done to deserve such a calamity? Never in her life had she reared a sow of this stature, *madre de deus*, with her own two hands like a child! And the way her pig had bred! Litter after litter popping out like peas. What could a poor widow like her do now?

Heart-rending wails, sorrow to make strong men weep, a soaring grief which only immediate and vengeful action could put to rest. Find the thief! Bring the rascal to justice!

There was an investigative quiver in the air, a sense of urgent, manic enquiry. Barboza the Baker, now a fearless leader unafraid of the odds, led the way.

'How big was the pig?'

Quick to grasp the general trend, Mendonca the Cold Storage Merchant, asked, 'Was she black, white or spotted?'

'She might,' Barboza said shortly, 'have been brown. It's been known to happen.'

But, as any fool could tell, there was more to a purloined pig than its colour. Da Silva the Grocer went off at a clever deductive tangent, 'When did you last see her?'

One moment snuffling happily, as only a well-beloved pig can, the next gone, vanished into thin air, not a hint of hair nor hide, gone, gone without trace. The old woman crossed herself. The largest of the fisherwomen, moved as fisherwomen rarely are, to tearful sentimentality, enquired with great tenderness, 'Was she an amiable pig? Warm-hearted? Affectionate? A member of the family?'

A tactical error. The past tense prompted a fresh outburst of wails, lamentation, gasping sobs and wringing of hands.

The investigation was getting rapidly nowhere until one of the drunks, with a leap of inspired lateral thinking, showed the way.

'The boy on the bicycle,' he shouted, waving his glass about triumphantly and spilling the contents down the shirtfront of Barboza, who seemed, for a moment or two, to be less of a Man Among Men than a very wet and angry baker. Heedless, seized with the joy of revelation, the drunk shouted again, 'The boy with the pig on the bicycle. There he goes, the swine!' As one, the crowd looked up the road. A few hundred yards ahead, pedalling calmly and leisurely, as though without a care in the world, the wicked boy, the brazen felon, the ... the stealer of sows – was making off with the old woman's purloined pig!

'AFTER HIM!'

'I have never in my life,' said Jude admiringly, the recollection mint-bright as the day, 'seen such a swift and purposeful pursuit of a villain. Well worth writing up in the training manual. Before you could say, "Save the sow" they were off in a howling mob, some on cycles, others on foot, picking up sticks, bricks, anything they could lay their hands on as they went. The boy on the cycle with the pig at the back was a bit thick. He heard the commotion, turned, looked back, thought nothing of it, pedalled along whistling, heard the baying behind him get louder by the minute, looked over his shoulder again, realized with horror it was *him* they were after, shot up straight in the saddle as if he had sat on a live wire and hared off down the road. Big mistake. Here was guilt, no question about it, with a capital 'G'. Would an innocent man flee in this fashion? Howling lustfully, like a pack of hounds closing in on a fox, the mob went after him.'

A simmering shoot-when-you-see-the-whites-of-his-eyes excitement descended on the *tinto*. There were oaths in the air and blood in every eye. Weapons were being assembled. The old woman sat against a wall, grief replaced by quivering intensity. She held the club in her right hand, in a grip of iron, testing its weight, heft, balance, smacking it thoughtfully into the palm of her left hand every so often. The fisherwomen had removed their chappals and placed them within easy arm's reach, ready to leap up and belabour the stealer of pigs at the first opportunity. The drunks were stocking up on Dutch courage with the urgency that comes over men about to enter into battle.

They heard the moans of the villain well before the mob reached the *tinto*. At first all was a babble of confusion, and cries of pain to the sound of crisp thwacks, and 'Take that you rascal', 'Break his head!', 'Rub his nose in dung.' And other equally inventive suggestions. Then the voice of those in command could be heard above the din.

'To the police station with him' – Barboza the Baker leading, as always, from the front.

'Take him to the church. Let the padre pass judgement' – the Pious Elder, conscience troubled no doubt at having forsaken early morning mass for a spot of mayhem.

'He would have made five hundred rupees on this pig' – Da Silva the Grocer, deductive to the bitter end.

'It's a black pig,' Mendonca the Cold Storage Merchant who, once he got his teeth into an issue, never let go.

And then a small voice, touched with tears, bewildered and – good for the rascal! – edged with terror, pleaded to no avail, 'It wasn't me. I haven't stolen anybody's pig.'

'Liar!' And he was cuffed about the ears.

'Turn him upside down and beat the soles of his feet!'

'Throw him into the well!'

'IT WASN'T ME! IT WASN'T ME!'

The fisherwomen had risen as one, ominously, scowling, muttering vile abuse, chappals clutched, ready for action. The old woman stood four-square, holding the club with both hands over her shoulder, head lowered, shuffling her feet like a bull about to charge. The layabouts were rolling up their sleeves dramatically, massaging their biceps and taking deep, significant breaths. The drunks focused carefully on the centre of the mob, rushed forward, lurched this way and that, caromed into each other, tripped over the fisherwomen's baskets and their own feet, then, overcome with the confusion of it all, rushed back to the taverna to top up one last time before the fray.

Jude sighed; in seconds he had ceased to be the father of a family of four doing his good deed for the day, and become Goa's inspector general of police at the scene of a pignapping, the only cop present at the caper. Duty called. He climbed on to a convenient beer barrel, rolled the day's *O Heraldo* he was carrying in to a makeshift megaphone and issued a command, crisp and compelling, 'Police. Stop this nonsense at once!' He was immediately recognized. Nobody would look him in the eye. Feet were shuffled. Throats were cleared. The layabouts sought urgent flight. The drunks fled into the darkest recesses of the taverna.

Holding the old woman firmly above the elbow ('She seemed quite demented by now,' Jude said, 'and capable of anything') he led her to the edge of the mob. It fell apart hastily. Only the baker, the grocer and the cold storage merchant stood their ground. They held the boy by his wrists, the back of his trousers and the scruff of his neck. He had been in the wars; the bruise on his cheek was a promising purple; the black eye was well on its way to an early ripening; the shirt had been torn off his back; he had been rolled several times in the mud which, for good measure, had been liberally applied all over his hair. The pig, stricken dumb by the drama of the past hour, now remembered the purpose of its journey, raised its snout to the sky and squealed to high heaven, as if stuck prematurely in a tender part. The old woman took one look at it, shook her head in disbelief, smacked her palm against her forehead, sat down on the road, stood up, pointed at the pig and whispered, 'That's not my pig ...'

'Not your pig?' – Barboza.

'THAT'S NOT MY PIG!'

'How could it not be your pig?' – Da Silva.

'It's a black pig, anybody can see that' – Mendonca, obsessed to the point of no return.

'My Esmeralda' – sobs, wails, fresh heights of biblical grief – 'is pink and white, with a black patch over her left eye.'

For long moments, there was a guilt-stricken silence. Then the Pious Elder turned an inquisitor's relentless eye on the boy, 'God will punish you for this, you scoundrel!'

'Why did you run off in the first place?' Da Silva wanted to know.

'Leading us on, eh?' Barboza accused.

'Your idea of a joke, you wicked boy!' – Mendonca fumed. 'We'll teach you a joke!'

'*MALCREADO*!' The mob, furious at the injustice of it all, was once more in full cry. Jude's patience was at an end. He threatened mass arrests on the spot, incarceration and bread-and-water over the Christmas holidays. The mob fled. Jude led the boy off, reflecting on the impossibility of reconciling justice with the law, and walked him home, a good half hour to the *vaddo* where he lived. The pig, saved to squeal another day, and quite undone by all the excitement, fell asleep, the boy's family and friends – a clan of *ramponkar* Figuerados – swore vengeance and sought to assemble a war party and plunge into battle with the louts at the *tinto*. Jude calmed them down. This took another hour. Then as gallant saviour of an innocent young life, a drink or two was pressed upon him. It would have been ungracious to refuse, or to say no to one for the road. By the time he got back to the *tinto*, all the fish had been sold. The cats were licking their chops.

'My wife,' Jude concluded ruefully, 'was not best pleased.'

'Did they ever find the old woman's pig?' I asked.

'Fat chance,' Gerson said.

'You'd be surprised at the number of pigs reported missing in Goa every week,' Jude said, 'and never recovered.'

'Perhaps,' Gerson suggested, 'you could consider a Missing Pigs Bureau. Identity cards for pigs, at five rupees a pig, a snip. From this day on, nobody will own a porker without its picture. I can see the posters up, Jude, in every *tinto* in the land. Missing porker. Answer to the name of Percy. Beloved member of the Fonseca household. Black wart above left eye. One cauliflower ear. Imperious snort. Engaging smile. Last seen midnight November fifth in lustful pursuit of Angela, the next door neighbour's sow. Finder will be handsomely rewarded with a virile pigling from Percy's next litter.'

Gerson was in full, hilarious flight. He would have gone on in this inventive vein till inspiration collapsed, but the doorbell rang, an unwelcome interruption. It rang insistently. Once, twice, thrice. 'Who's it Anna?' Gerson called. Anna answered in a troubled voice, 'Raoul Pimenta's wife dear, with the children' – a pause – 'she wants to meet you. Shall I send her in?'

'No,' Gerson said, banter forgotten, a slight edge of regret in his voice, 'I'll be out in a moment.'

Jude went with him. I was intrigued. I heard a woman's voice, speaking rapidly in Konkani, the emotion barely in control, rising in pitch and intensity, breaking into muffled sobs. Anna consoling her. Gerson calm, patient, comforting, Jude adding a sentence or two with a gentleness quite at odds with his reputation and position. The front door was at the end of a long corridor and it was difficult to hear what was being said, more so as the woman spoke very rapidly, in obvious distress, and was answered in low tones. Every time she raised her voice, Anna shushed her as one would a child. Then I heard one of the children cry out, 'Please *patrao*, please. Only for Christmas day.' Footsteps returning down the corridor. Gerson's voice in English, 'Take them to the kitchen, Anna and give them something to eat.' Jude popped his head through the doorway. 'We won't be more than five minutes, Frank, help yourself to a drink.' He disappeared into the corridor. Serious conversation again. Measured, objective tones. Long, thoughtful pauses. A sense of debate on issues of consequence. Gerson's voice rose unwittingly, gladly, 'All right, let's do it. You tell her Jude.'

'Public prosecutors aren't expected to shirk their responsibilities,' Jude said, 'Go on, set a good example. *You* tell her.'

'I suppose I'd better,' Gerson's voice faded towards the kitchen.

Jude came in and made straight for the feni, poured himself a large drink and said, 'This one I've earned.'

'What's going on?' I asked.

Gerson came in just then, sighed mightily, attacked the bottle, did himself generously and collapsed into an easy chair. He raised his glass and said, 'Merry Christmas, Raoul Pimenta.'

'This is no way to treat a guest on Christmas Eve,' I said, 'what was that all about?'

'Raoul Pimenta,' Gerson said, 'is in the Fort Aguada jail serving a fifteen-year term for manslaughter.'

'It's a mandatory sentence,' Jude explained, 'for the crime.'

'But the man is not a criminal,' Gerson said, 'no criminal record, not even a misdemeanour. A *ramponkar*, liked by the other fishermen in the *vaddo*. Happily married. Two kids. He was young when it happened, twenty-nine or thirty I think, and even with time off for good conduct he's going to be locked up for ten years.'

'It's not too bad a place,' Jude said, 'the villains call it the user-friendly jail.'

'The guards and jailors are both there for the long haul. They strike up friendships. Small favours are exchanged. The guards fetch and carry. Hot meals are smuggled in on weekends, with a bottle or two of feni. They borrow from each other when they're short. And conspire when they think no one's looking. It's not entirely unknown for prisoners to disappear from their cells at lights out and reappear mysteriously when the morning gong goes.'

'What's the punishment for that?'

'Oh, they are never caught. A blind eye, a long rein, larger purposes, and all the rest of it.'

'How,' I asked, 'did Pimenta get into trouble?'

'A nasty piece of luck,' Gerson said, 'and on the one occasion, poor devil, when he had every reason to celebrate. After six months of the old run around, he had finally managed to get a loan from the village co-operative bank for an outboard motor. He and his crew heard the good news one morning while bringing the boat in from a night's fishing. Excited, they rushed off to the bank, as they were, bare-bodied, in langotes, to confirm that the loan had been cleared. A celebration, quite naturally, seemed called for. No sooner said than done. They descended, en masse, at the local taverna, and went at it with a vengeance.'

'Seems perfectly reasonable to me,' I said, remembering Joaquim and his merry gang, the catamaran which grew up to become a motor boat, and the monumental binge that followed masquerading as breakfast.

'It wasn't his day,' Gerson continued, 'as luck would have it, a gang of out of state labourers were knocking it back at the next table. Surly bunch. Everybody seems to have drunk too much too quickly. One of the labourers poked fun at Raoul's langote. Hot words were exchanged and they came to blows. The *ramponkars* are a tough lot and once the blood's up, difficult to control. Raoul hit the man on the temple. His skull cracked. He went into a coma and never regained consciousness. Died three days later. There was a post mortem. The blow had caused a blood clot in the brain, and that led to a stroke. Death by cerebral haemorrhage. In a word, manslaughter. Fifteen years in the slammer, without benefit of parole, but with time off for good behaviour. He's just about completed a year.'

'Was that his family?'

'His wife,' Jude said, 'a gem, and two lovely children. But the boat's in his name and his crew work it. They are well provided for. Still, it just doesn't do for a family not to have a man about the house.'

Two plus two made a golden four fit for Christmas.

'I suspect,' I said dryly, 'that there will be, shall we say, a temporary alleviation of the situation?'

'What on earth are you talking about?' Jude threw his hands up in mock horror; Gerson rolled his eyes heavenwards.

'Only for Christmas day, *patrao*,' I said.

'How could we ever do a thing like that?' Gerson said gravely.

'It would be against the law,' Jude added.

I laughed out loud. 'Since when,' I asked, 'has the law had anything to do with justice?'

'If even a hint of this slanderous accusation got out,' Gerson said, 'it would be as much as our jobs are worth.'

'However,' Jude chortled, 'the law is not without compassion.'

'Particularly,' Gerson said, in his I-will-not-be-trifled-with public prosecutor's voice, 'if a prisoner is deemed to be critically ill. It is then left to the discretion of the authorities concerned whether or not he is granted temporary leave of absence – strict vigilance of course – to spend a day or two with his loved ones.'

'Who's discretion?'

'Ours,' they said.

Just then a young woman and two children, radiant as rainbows, rushed in breathlessly, exclaimed, 'Happy Christmas, *patrao*!' – in English yet. The woman went on her knees to touch Gerson's feet. He would have none of it; he pulled her up gently and said, 'Merry Christmas. Off you go now.' And off they went, on winged feet, feisty as angels, straight up to Cloud Nine.

Simpatico!

Here is a Christmas tale, I thought, to save for my children's children!

Embarrassment was writ large in Gerson's small, self-deprecatory smile, and Jude's eyes refused to catch mine. They were trying hard to appear modest and nonchalant, going off on all sorts of unnecessary tangents in order to put Raoul Pimenta behind them. But I was without mercy this Xmas Eve.

'Love's word, *simpatico*,' I said, 'one can't have too much of it.'

'Where do you plan to go on the twenty-fifth,' Gerson asked Jude.

'The Clube Nacional,' Jude said, 'they have two new bands on for Christmas.'

'From the big, bad city,' Gerson's eyes lit up, 'and a genuine Egyptian belly dancer. That should stir up the city fathers.'

'Not I hope,' Jude added chuckling, 'our old friend, Isabella from Porvoreim.'

Tsk, tsk, pale pink herrings. Did they really think I'd take a rain check on my very own true tall tale?

'Did Mrs G,' I said, 'have any belly dancers on The List?'

Gerson scratched his head and looked vaguely troubled. 'You shouldn't believe everything you hear,' he said.

'Rumours,' Jude admonished, 'will be the ruination of Goa.'

'After this morning's work,' I said, 'what's left of your reputations is in shreds. It's time to come clean, but I must admit, from what I've heard, your handling of The List was a neat piece of action. Very nifty indeed. Warms the cockles of one's heart. Courage beyond the call of duty, etc.'

Jude glanced at his watch. 'Must rush,' he said, 'early lunch. Wife will be furious if I'm late …'

'You did say Frank,' Gerson glanced at his watch, 'that you were expected home by one.'

'Not,' I said, 'before I get to the bottom of this. I want the truth mind, nothing but …' And I launched into my own True Tall Tale.

*

If Mrs G hadn't existed, it would have been necessary to invent her. Illustrious daughter of one of the nation's Founding Fathers, she walked tall in his footsteps, took up the political inheritance like a duck takes to water (or, as her unkinder critics would have it, as a shark to a feeding frenzy) and ruled the land with an iron hand in an executioner's glove. Cabinet ministers trembled in her presence and were dismissed from office in the time it took for their knees to knock; chief secretaries fell by the wayside in droves; state governors found themselves roofless between breakfast and lunch; civil servants were decapitated by the trainload. When Mrs. G said, 'Jump!' you did not simply say, 'Yes, ma'am,' you did a triple-somersault and said, 'How high?' twice, the second time on the way down. But Mrs G GOT THINGS DONE. It was not as if she was a dragon lady, she was a perfectly reasonable prime minister so long as you did it her way.

But, as we all know, the processes of a democracy are maddeningly irresolute: opposition parties are cussed beyond belief; the press, when it is not illiterate and misinformed, is up to all sorts of mischief and rabble-rousing, being polite only to its proprietors; that seditious bunch of no-gooders, the civil libertarians, may not be locked up without due process of the law and one could grow old waiting for justice to appear to be done; criminals who should be hanged, drawn and quartered at public celebrations, are let off for *lack of evidence*! A disgraceful situation, fraught with peril for the nation. One morning, Mrs G, all patience exhausted, stamped an imperious foot and declared, 'Let there be a National Emergency.'

The black shadow of dictatorship had fallen like a shroud over eight hundred million Indians. They were the lucky ones. The thousands who had the misfortune to incur the wrath of the dragon lady and her minions were hauled off in black Marias in the dark hours of the morning and deposited in the nearest jail without benefit of chargesheet or trial, there to languish till Mrs G decided on their future. No bets were being laid. As with everything she did, Mrs G went about the Emergency with ruthless efficiency and astonishing speed. Lists of enemies of the state -- real, imagined, notional, marginal -- were drawn up for immediate arrest and incarceration, with a fine disregard for the niceties of cause, proof, bail, trial, defence, prosecution, and all of the unessential impedimenta which, until then, had come in the way of true and radical patriotic action.

Indeed, a fine democracy was very much in evidence. The List was wholly without bias or discrimination: members of Mrs G's own party shared cells with communists and other subversives; captains of industry rubbed shoulders behind bars with leader writers; smugglers found themselves sharing bed and board with members of Parliament; film stars and bureaucrats were forced into reluctant intimacy; contract killers sent delicate shivers down the spines of couturiers. Judges were jailed; maharajahs and maharanis showed no clemency; prelates put away without a thought. Mrs G was nothing if not thorough in all of this spring cleansing; it could hardly be helped if a few babies went out with the bathwater. The blameless, the innocuous, the merely idiosyncratic, they too, in fear and trembling, awaited the rumble of the tumbrils.

As we all know, in operations of this nature, conducted on such a dramatic and operatic scale, swift timing is of the essence. Mrs G, who didn't miss a trick, had decreed that the Emergency must not just happen, it must clearly be seen to happen all over the country, all at once! Thus it came to pass that at noon on the morning of that fateful day, a thick manila envelope, marked, 'HIGHLY CONFIDENTIAL & TOP PRIORITY' arrived in Goa by special aircraft, was rushed from the airport by motorcycle courier, and placed on the desk of the public prosecutor. At exactly the same time, a copy was handed over to the inspector general of police.

The conversation which followed between the two has not, so far as I know, been officially minuted, but the gist, I believe, is faithful to the spirit of the exchange:

Gerson	: 'Did you get it?'
Jude	: 'Just this moment.'
Gerson	: 'Daft.'
Jude	: 'Bonkers.'
Gerson	: 'Certifiable. Have you gone through it?'
Jude	: 'You must be joking. There are hundreds of names here. Alphabetically. Neat. Just like the telephone directory.'
Gerson	: 'A regular Who's Who.'
Jude	: 'A regular Who's Hit.'

Gerson	: 'Is this an open line?'
Jude	: 'Which planet are you on?'
Gerson	: 'We'd better meet.'
Jude	: 'Right on. If I'm not with you in ten minutes, you'll know I'm behind bars.'
Gerson	: 'Very funny!'

They pored over the lists in a silence broken only by exclamations of wonder, awe, bewilderment, disbelief.

'Everybody who's anybody is in here.'

'Except the village idiot.'

'They've gone haywire,' Jude said. 'Why on earth do they have Julian Fernandes down. He's in the organic manure business.'

'Creates a stink!'

'Good grief. Umberto Miranda. But he's a pig farmer.'

'And about as political as a peanut.'

'The Count of Asagao.'

'Mistaken identity. It's the great, great grandfather they want. He was put away for sedition by the Portuguese.'

'Perhaps it's the bloodline they're worried about.'

They scanned page two.

'No more mando festivals. They've put the finger on Victor Coehlo.'

'Dilip Kamat as well.'

'But he's in trucks and barges.'

'Strategic transport I imagine.'

'The director of the Carnival? Subversive?'

'You think that's odd. Here's the harbour master.'

Jude chuckled. 'Alberto Figuerado. They *have* got something right.'

'Since when has owning a restaurant been a political crime?'

'Have you eaten there lately?'

They leaned back. Thirsty work this. Two more large fenis to get the incarcerationary zeal going. No such luck.

'This,' Gerson said, 'is going to be difficult.'

'Can you see Lousito Braganza in the Aguada lock-up without four-course meals and a wine list twice a day?'

'Or Aloysius Sequeira without his guitar and his girlfriend?'

'Utterly fiendish,' Jude said, quoting from the Most Urgent memorandum attached to the list, 'ARREST AND IMPRISION IMMEDIATELY. REPRESENT GRAVE THREAT TO NATION. NOT TO BE RELEASED UNDER ANY CIRCUMSTANCES. STAND BY FOR FURTHER INSTRUCTIONS.'

'They haven't left us much choice.'

'Still, we can do the decent thing.'

'It would be inhuman to arrest them before lunch,' Gerson said.

'Or without warning,' Jude said.

'Perhaps if each of us phoned ten of them...'

'... and asked each of them to call ten others. Brilliant.'

'Give them time to put some decent food together, pack a toothbrush, light reading, a bottle or two, that sort of thing ...'

'And at a civilized hour.'

'Certainly *not* during the siesta.'

'Unthinkable!'

While chauvinist historians are strident in their claims that the Portuguese legacy is corrupt beyond hope of redemption, and point to the evidence – a subservient and, in unfortunate areas, a quisling population which still yearns for the bad old days; the unshakeable belief that hard labour is inimical to good health and well-being; the illusion that life should consist of uninterrupted wassail and song; an unhealthy preoccupation with the pernicious influences of good food and much drink – it must be said that in the matter of the siesta, the Portuguese knew their onions. There is no more civilized and rejuvenating preparation for sunset and evening star. The length of the siesta is fair measure of the generosity of the meal which precedes it, and it is not unusual for the siesta to extend from two hours to four or five in the afternoon. You disturb the Goan in his siesta at your peril. Goa slumbers and may not, short of natural calamities and Acts of God, be stirred. Judges take to bed; politicians snooze; tycoons take their restful ease; carpenters down tools and assume horizontal positions; prelates put their feet up; even the pigs get in forty winks.

Gerson and Jude made their phone calls before lunch. Goa's telephone system was exercised as never before. One hundred and fifty would-be arrestees sat down philosophically, and with whetted appetites, to groaning boards (how soon would they see another?) which the women of the household had put together with exemplary speed and inspiration. Would the Emergency disturb their siesta? Perish the thought. They slept the sleep of the just, the innocent, and the magnificently fed.

One may only speculate on the high drama of the actual arrests, but I like to think that it was a friendly and relaxed scenario, unfolding with courtesy and good grace. A uniformed figure ambles up to the house, pauses to admire the bougainvillea, knocks gently at the door. It is opened without undue haste. Pereira, the Harbour Master, well rested and in excellent humour, stands in the doorway.

'Good evening officer. There you are then. Do come in. Take a seat.'

'Packed and ready are we? Bit of a nuisance this.'

'Can't be helped I suppose.'

'Out in no time I expect.'

'Can't take any chances though. The wife's got a small hamper going. Won't be a minute. You in a hurry?'

'Not at all. Take your time.'

'One for the road?'

'Sounds like a *very* good idea.'

'There you go.'

'Great stuff. Where do you get it from?'

'Arpora.'

'Thought as much. Well, cheers.'

'Mud in your eye!'

*

'Well?' I said.

Gerson and Jude did not quite writhe, but it was a near thing.

'Outright slander,' Gerson said.

'The very stuff of libel,' Jude said.

'Dare breathe a word of this nonsense to anyone,' Gerson promised, 'and you'll face charges.'

'It should be fun to arrest you,' Jude said.

'I shall thoroughly enjoy the prosecution,' Gerson said.

'The selection of a judge will be a matter of some delicacy.'

'Judge Saldanha?'

'Judge Saldanha will do nicely.'

'He owes us one.'

'A hanging judge, but there ...'

'Who cares,' I said, 'so long as he's *simpatico!*'

Then, for no reason at all, I thought of Bernie Finklebaum Jr. There were three words in this delightful morality play that Bernie would have done well to take to his acquisitive little heart; three words doing yeoman service – *susegade, alegria, simpatico* – come gloriously together in common cause. And, I suppose, yes, stretching a definition by a siesta, you could include that most generous of nouns, *phale*, as well ...

*

Why is Goa so unfortunate in its American visitors? At a distance they seem harmless enough, a bit too large for my liking perhaps, with the avoirdupois thoughtlessly distributed, and the accent – somewhere between a whine and a twang – doing nasty things to the inner ear. The uniforms put me off as well. While I appreciated the fact that Bermuda shorts had been invented for the Budweiser boyo – the six-pack/Big Mac folk hero of all those depressing TV commercials – it must be said that having seen one pair, one has seen them all. And were Hawaiian shirts really necessary when all about you lay a world created by Gaugin and commissioned by God? All, however, was not lost. The horizon, as far as the eye could reach, was serenely unafflicted by a MacDonalds sign and Coke had yet to insult the fragrant purity of a great caju feni. But I was less sanguine after my encounter with the Finklebaum Jrs. With Bernie and Babs trampling about ham-footed in a faraway hamlet like Siridao, could the New World Order be far behind?

Every couple of weeks I make the hour-long journey to Siridao, much in the manner of an indefatigable prospector in search of a lost motherlode. Hope springs eternal. Perhaps, who knows, this day is The Day and I will have the stupendous good fortune to return with The Chest. Aloysius, the master craftsman, who has a fine sense of humour and appreciates a good joke when he sees one, smiles broadly no sooner he catches sight of me, draws up two packing cases, produces a bottle and glasses like a magician. And then, with dramatic flair, he explains why his art has failed, yet again, to reach an exquisite consummation. I sympathize with great sincerity. Art must await inspiration. Even if the surroundings fail to inspire boundless confidence; indeed, they prompt grave misgivings. Lathes of venerable provenance lie about at odd angles; saws, which, like their owner, have said farewell to the odd incisor years earlier, prop up a wall; flat stones and pieces of wood encourage antique planes to find a level; araldite and scotch tape keep heirloom chisels from falling apart. Distinctly unpromising: one's faith in Aloysius begins to falter until one catches a glimpse, in dark corners, of carved chests of utterly preposterous beauty and elegance awaiting, alas, other owners.

I arrived to find two outsize pairs of Bermuda shorts, stretched tight over rumps of heroic heft and thrust, bent over a chest, while their owners examined the intricate carving with growing confusion and unease. A piercing twang rent the air. Aloysius winced.

'Is this our chest, hon?'

'I'm not sure Bernie. They all look the same to me.'

'Hey, what's your name, bud?'

Aloysius looked over his shoulder, caught my eye, shrugged, sighed, shook his head. Bernie poked him in the chest with a hard forefinger.

'I'm talking to you fella. This guy talk English, Babs?'

'He did, hon, the last time I was here.'

Aloysius looked at the forefinger. He would have liked to do it grievous harm, but desisted. What was the protocol in America? Should he stroke it? Shake it? Poke back at its owner?

'He wants to know your name,' I said in Konkani.

'My name?' This was easy. Aloysius produced his best English, short on articles and pronouns, long on consonants, lingering lovingly on vowels; it took time, like his chests, but was well worth waiting for.

'Name Aloysius Braganza,' he said.

'Right Al, now we're getting somewhere.'

'No Al. Aloysius.'

'Al's good enough for me.'

'You better call the man by his full name, hon.'

'You ever hear anybody call me Bernard. Al's good enough for me.'

Bernie Finklebaum held out a hand the size of a baseball glove. Aloysius, alarmed, took a quick step back; Bernie took a quick step forward. Aloysius, retreat cut off by a lathe, offered two fingers and a thumb. Bernie seized them with a glad cry and thumped them up and down vigorously.

'Bernie Finklebaum Jr,' he boomed.

'Aloysius Braganza.'

'I know that Al, you tole me. How you doing?'

Ask a Goan how he feels and you can write off half an hour of your life. Aloysius massaged his stomach and groaned.

'Loose motions,' he said, and groaned again.

'What did the guy say, Babs?'

'I think he's got the runs, Bernie.'

'See what I mean, Babs. You drink the water, you're dead.'

At the word 'drink' Aloysius perked up. Out came the bottle. Dusty. Cobwebbed. Infectiously corked. Glasses, liberally finger-printed, which hadn't been near water for a week.

Mrs Finkebaum Jr. shuddered.

'I'm a Budweiser man myself, Al,' Bernie said.

'Good feni,' Aloysius urged, 'Have drink, Mr Flickinbim.'

'Finklebaum.'

'I understand sah. Fickle ... bum.'

'FINK – LE – BAUM!'

'Bum?'

'Baum!'

Was there a wicked glint in Aloysius's eye? They widened as understanding dawned, then closed briefly in gratitude. The frown disappeared; an expression of ineffable beatitude took its place.

'I call you Fink,' he said happily. 'Have drink, Fink.'

'Enough already,' Bernie muttered through clenched teeth. 'My wife ordered a carved chest from you three weeks ago. You promised it in two. I take off from this burg Toosday, not too soon for me, if you get the drift. Where's my chest?'

'What chest?'

'The chest, dummy, my wife ordered three weeks ago.'

'Oh, *that* chest.'

'Yeah, that chest.'

'Why you don't take this chest. It's a nice chest.'

'That's not the chest I ordered, hon. I wanted the fleur-de-lis. I lurv fleur-de-lis.'

'You hear that Al. Fleur-de-lis. Babs here lurvs fleur-de-lis.'

'I made this chest for German hippie, live in Anjuna. It's very good chest.'

'How come you wanna sell it?'

'The German is always drunk.'

Bernie Finklebaum Jr. took his wife aside. In a loud whisper that set the thatch quivering, he said, 'I'm gonna kill this guy.'

'Bernie, hon, you know what Doc Horowitz said about your BP.'

Bernie took a deep breath.

'You guys drive me up a wall,' he said, 'but I'm not gonna lose my cool, bud. You got a problem with my chest?'

Aloysius buried his head in his hands for a moment, then raised tragic eyes. The pity and the sorrow of it all ...

'You think, Fink, I no have problems. I go Cuncolim buy wood for Mrs Fink's chest on Saturday. No, no, no, stupido! Not Saturday. Saturday I spend in Saligao with cousin brother Vincent. It was his wife's sister's daughter's birthday. First baby, first year. How we celebrate. We all got very drunk. So I sleep Saligao two days and by the time I get to Cuncolim, what to tell, man, that rascal Fernando has gone to Dona Paula for feast of St. Theresa. Proper dumbbell. Thick in head. Like plank. He takes key of woodshed with him. The wood for Mrs Fink's chest is in woodshed. I stay two days in Cuncolim with my cousin Raul. No, no, stupido! Pedro. I eat too much prawn *balchao*. Arre! What to tell! Three days I make loose motions. Such motions, *madre de deus*, every hour, run! You never know what you are eating in Cuncolim. You take life in hands. That's Goa for you. Gone to dogs. Feni not fit for pig. Nobody cares. Bad prawns! Can you imagine, bad prawns in Goa.

Then Fernando turns up, rolling drunk, and loads wood into cart pulled by cow in full heat, I swear by my mother, and at the creek, D'Souza's bull smells the cow, breaks the fence and tries to mount her, and the cow and the cart and the bull and Fernando and Mrs Fink's wood all end up in the creek. Dear God, now Anton my brother arrive from Saudi with family and new dog. We all going Calangute for week on beach. The children like the sea and ...'

Would Bernie Finklebaum Jr. bite his tongue?

'JESUS H. CHRIST. WHEN YOU GONNA DO MY CHEST?'

Aloysius looked thoughtful, riffling no doubt through the rich lexicon at his command, but I knew, even before he uttered the magic word, that there would be joy this morning but not, sadly, for Bernie Finklebaum Jr.

'Phale!'

****

The Cobra That Nearly Never Was

Now that we have a snake stick in the house, I shall never (fingers crossed) need the services of Eurico's old friend from Mapusa, Felix Xavier Furtado, with his coil rope, bag of rice, marigold flowers, agarbatti, and jumbo-sized tin of Nescafe. The snake stick was given to me by a forestry officer who had spent years in the jungles of Tamil Nadu where the Irula tribe of snake hunters swore by its prophylactic value. No viper worthy of its venom would come within miles of the snake tree. It repelled all manner of crawling beastie and, after Radhika's close encounter with the black cobra, I was taking no chances. My snake stick was planted firmly in the centre of our largest flower bed, clearly visible to anything that crawled, slithered, hissed or went about without legs. And while I am by no means a blind convert to snake mythology, it has to be said that we have never had a snake on our property since the stick was planted into the earth.

My own close call took place two hundred metres off the beach in front of our house. I came up from a dive, shook the water from my eyes, and there, a foot in front of my face, was a small and erect periscope. It began to undulate, spade-shaped head held forward, tongue flickering. For a second or two we stared at each other in utter horror. Then, as one, we flipped over backwards never to meet again. I learned later that the venom of the sea snake is tenfold more poisonous than the cobra's. It feeds on small fish. A lightening-swift bite. Within moments, the fish has no future and the snake has lunch. But it is timid, avoids human contact and, in living memory, has never been known to strike at a person. There is a moral to be discovered in this: when swimming off a Goan beach the morning after the night before, even if you feel like a dog's breakfast, it's best to pretend you're a person.

Snakes abound in Goa. 'Part of the ecology,' my forestry officer friend had said cheerfully. 'We need them more than they need us. Poor devils, ever since Eve they've had a bad press. My son keeps a grass snake as a pet, friendly little fellow.' Give me a Cocker Spaniel, thank you very much, but the point was well taken. Visitors to Goa need not pack the anti-venom with the sun block. I suspect there is more snake lore about than snakes, and in twenty-five years I couldn't have set eyes on more than half a dozen. There are, however a few things that the budding herpetologist should know about Goan snakes. They come in two varieties: harmless and lethal. Alas, hundreds of the former are mistakenly slaughtered for the latter. These are four in number, distinct in appearance and, for all practical purposes, invisible: the cobra, the Russell's viper, the krait and the saw-scaled viper. The first three are large nocturnal hunters, acutely sensitive to ground vibrations, and flee silently at the most distant sound of a human footstep. The saw-scaled viper is bad news – a foot in length, no thicker than a thumb, sand-coloured and stupid, it is difficult to detect underfoot and strikes in a fast blur at the slightest provocation. The good news: it is rarely found where lots of people live.

Snakes figure prominently in the Goan Tall Tale. As the feni goes down, inspiration takes wing. You will hear of cobras seeking vengeance after weeks or months at some real or imagined slight; snakes with two heads; rat snakes the size of young pythons breaking legs and arms with careless abandon and the swish of a tail; mating vipers disturbed in their dalliance, forsaking pleasure for hot pursuit; and so on. The truth of the matter is, happily, far less dramatic. There is nothing snakes abhor more than a fang to face confrontation with a person. They are shy and self-effacing though, on the rare occasion, as we shall see, they can be foolish. They pay dearly for the lapse. When a poisonous snake is cornered, it is set upon with savage cries and heavy sticks by strong men bent on murderous annihilation. Rat snakes are put down without thought or care (though, at six feet, thick as a man's upper arm, swift, agile and generously fanged, one would think that discretion would be the better part of valour). The Russell's viper is dispatched ignominiously. Kraits are beaten over the head and incinerated. But the cobra is sacrosanct. It is worshipped as a living deity and never harmed. What then does one do with a cornered cobra? The Cobra That Nearly Never Was, my own true snake story, offers one possible solution.

A pleasant way to spend a crisp winter morning in Goa is to visit my cousin Eurico Ribiero's antique shop situated on one of the most charming lanes in the village. Lined on either side by flowering gulmohur trees, it ambles up a hillside to the Fort Aguada Beach Resort, dropping sheer on the right to the ruins of a moat, and cresting gently hundreds of feet on the left to the ramparts of the fort, the old Portuguese lighthouse, and the plateau which boasts two distinctive features: a fabulous view of bay and beach; and a fertile breeding ground for snakes of all kinds, sizes and proclivities. These, at times, pay unannounced and unwelcome visits to the traditional Goan cottages which follow the lane, gardens overrun with bouganvillea, mango and chickoo trees, coconut palms and ornamental hedges. They are built in an age-old fashion with amber, laterite brick, dressed by hand and open-faced, and Mangalore tiles and the beams contain innumerable nooks, crannies and dark, concealed corners impossible to get at, where pigeons nest, lizards, rats and bats make homes, and the odd rat snake may be glimpsed at night trying to organize a warm supper.

Eurico had converted one such cottage into his shop, going to elaborate lengths to maintain its original architecture and character, right down to the easy chairs on the wide verandah, the carved side tables, the pewter beer mugs from Macao and the chilled Arlem lager, frosting even now in an ancient ice box, a bottle or two of which we proposed to consume on this fine December morning. Nothing ever disturbs the tranquillity of Eurico's approach to life, not even a Californian tourist brandishing a thousand-dollar traveller's cheque. He greets customers horizontally, feet crossed on one arm of the easy chair, offers a mug of the finest, a languid hand, and a smile that says, pleasure, my dear fellow, before any talk of business. It is an amiable philosophy and has served him well.

We were at the cottage gate when a piercing cry shattered the pastoral calm. I heard the crash of a table overturned, the sound of glass shattering on tile (oh dear, I thought, not the Macao mug.). A figure came hurtling down the verandah steps, shirt tails flapping behind it, a long-handled broom clutched aloft, covered in cobweb and old dust. Eurico. Pale beneath the tan. Violently agitated. 'There's a cobra in my roof,' he shouted, 'a cobra! A cobra!' for all the world to hear. The announcement took immediate effect. In minutes, out of airy nothingness, a truly rural crowd of villagers materialized. The word 'saap' passed in a horrified whisper from lip to lip. 'Cobra'. There is no more chilling noun in the reptile lexicon in Goa, but these were stout-hearted sons of the soil, and it just wouldn't do for a fellow Goan to have a cobra about the house. A solution must be found. The crowd broke up into small animated groups. Earnest conclave ensued, heated discussion, nervous wit. Opinion was sharply divided. 'Smoke it out,' suggested a young firebrand. His friends, instantly enthused, chorused, 'Yes, yes.' 'No, no,' Eurico was now as close to wringing his hands as I have ever seen him. 'No smoke without fire eh?' said an old wag, and the crowd, jolly and feisty at the prospect of an entertaining morning's work, guffawed noisily. Eurico was not amused. I took him aside. He had the look of a man who has plumbed the very depths. Would he ever be the same again? 'Firecrackers!' a voice bellowed, 'that's what we need, firecrackers!' Eurico twitched. I sat him down under the shade of a gulmohur. 'Tell me all about it,' I said soothingly.

The morning had held out the promise of a truly lovely day even for December. A cool breeze brought the scent of marigolds wafting into the verandah. Pigeons cooed in the eaves. Fluffy white clouds chased each other in a clear blue sky. Puppies played with their shadows on the lawn. God was out on a Goan ramble this day, well pleased with his work. Eurico poured the perfect head of beer into the Macao mug, raised it to his lips, and was about to give silent thanks for small blessings when, out of the corner of his eye, he thought he saw a shadow move on a beam above his head where the tiles rested on the rafters. It moved again, sinuously. A rat snake, Eurico thought, and rushed fearlessly to the store room for a long broom and a torch. He shone the one and prodded vigorously with the other, bringing a shower of cobwebs and ancient dust down on his head. The snake refused to budge. Then a thought struck Eurico. He turned the broom upside down and banged on the rafter with the hard end, hard enough to rattle the tiles. He heard an angry hiss, saw the spectacled, spreading hood, yelled, and ran for his life. The cobra moved swiftly up and away, disappeared into a cranny, and there it hid, reflecting no doubt on the injustices of life.

'I cannot have a cobra in the rafters,' Eurico said wanly, 'suppose he falls on the head of an American tourist?' I had to admit that it was not an encouraging prospect. Then a village elder laid his hand on Eurico's shoulder and said, 'You will have to send for Felix Xavier Furtado.' 'Felix,' Eurico repeated, eyes alight with remembrance and hope, 'Yes, we will have to send for Felix at once.' A motor cycle taxi was summoned. A young man, in a crimson vest and a bikini arrived astride a racing Enfield, grinning from ear to ear, flexing his biceps and scattering the crowd. Given instruction and payment in advance, he shot off, revving his engine as though at the start of a 500 cc grand prix. The crowd ducked for cover. The village elder said, 'It will be a good hour before Felix gets here. He will travel on nothing except his Raleigh bicycle.'

'Who,' I asked unwisely, 'is Felix Xavier Furtado?'

The village elder gave me an icy look.

'He has a way with cobras,' he said, appalled at my ignorance.

It proved to be an eventful hour. A few of the braver young spirits decided to enter the house. A brown bottle had appeared mysteriously among them. It was passed from hand to hand. Generous swigs were taken. Fortified, armed with long bamboo poles and flashlights, they charged up the verandah steps. Eurico and I followed cautiously behind. From room to room they went, banging on walls and floors and rafters. The beams of their torchlights crisscrossed the ceiling. They shouted; they drummed on empty kerosene tins with coconut ladles; they careened into each other around blind corners to muffled curses. The youngest of the lot, inflamed with Dutch courage, climbed on to the shoulders of the tallest, leaped for the nearest rafter, missed, fell to the floor in a crumpled heap and dusted himself off sheepishly. The din should have brought the house down, let alone a cobra. Now, terrified out of its wits, the snake had probably decided to hibernate for the rest of the winter.

Undeterred by their lack of success, the young villagers rushed out of the house. We followed, gladly. One of them went off and returned with a long wooden ladder, a bamboo pole, and – Eurico gasped and clutched at my arm – a string of firecrackers. They brushed off his protests (the second bottle was making the rounds with much greater urgency than the first). Eager hands tied the string of firecrackers to the end of the pole. The ladder was propped up against the roof. The young lad who had challenged the rafter with such unsuccess now redeemed himself. He scampered to the top, set the crackers alight, and waved the pole above the tiles. The noise was deafening. Showers of sparks descended on Eurico's roof. A great cheer went up from the crowd. All the cocks in the neighbourhood began to crow. But not a hint of a speckled scale, not a slither, not the faintest suggestion of a hiss.

The bedlam died down. A disappointed silence took its place only to be replaced moments later by growling suspicion. A voice was raised, 'Had there ever been a cobra?' Another, rudely, 'Does my aunt have balls?' A third, 'Probably drunk and imagined it all' … 'A waste of good time' … 'Does he think we have nothing better to do.' 'It was a cobra,' Eurico said in a small voice lacking in conviction. The tinkling of a bell intervened bringing a sudden hush to the crowd. A brass bell, the kind one found on the handlebars of bicycles fifty years ago, with a small metal thingummyjig sticking out at the side which one pushed rapidly this way and that with a thumb. The bell was attached to a Raleigh pedal-pusher of magnificent vintage, clearly a family heirloom, lovingly handed down from father to son; the thumb belonged to a weathered old party who wore broken horn-rims tied with string and a pork-pie hat. He pedalled furiously towards us. The crowd made way respectfully. The old man came to a racing stop and leaped lithely off the saddle. Eurico embraced him with a grateful cry, 'Felix!'

336 / The Storyteller

It has been ten years to the day, but what happened next remains as vivid for me as this morning's news. Felix Xavier Furtado wasted few words. With an equal economy of movement, he untied a large tin of Nescafe from the carrier of the Raleigh, a jute bag and a coil of thick, rough coir rope. These he took to a coconut tree nearest to the roof of Eurico's shop. He tied one end of the rope to the trunk of the tree, a foot and a half from the base, uncoiling the rest as he walked to the house and climbed up the ladder to the roof. There, negotiating the tiles with nimble ease, he tied the other end of the rope tightly to the cornice. The rope now stretched taut and firm from the top of the roof down to the tree trunk.

He clambered down the ladder, returned to the coconut palm and took the lotus position, legs crossed, squatting before the trunk. He placed a clean white handkerchief on the ground before him. From the jute bag he removed a handful of marigold flowers, three sticks of agarbatti and a small brown paper bag of raw rice. He arranged the flowers and a handful of rice on the handkerchief, stuck the agarbatti upright into the soil and lit them. The pungent incense spiralled around the tree, made a wreath about his head and settled on the rope passing a foot above the porkpie hat. Then Felix Xavier Furtado did a very strange thing. He extended his arms, palms open, facing towards the earth, and began chanting a mantra in a low, pure, lilting cadence. The mantra rose and fell, rose and fell, a mesmerizing chant. It travelled barely a quarter of an octave. It had no beginning and no end, each phrase dissolved into the next, yet it seemed informed with an arcane and wistful yearning.

Suddenly there was a quick, collective drawing of breath. Heads turned towards the roof. A black cobra, in full grown prime, was making its leisurely way along the tiles towards the cornice. There it paused, lifted its head, and aligned its body with the angle of the rope. Then it began a gingerly descent. I held my breath. Surely it would lose its balance and fall right into the crowd, angry, writhing, striking. But, if anything, it moved more quickly as it descended finding secure purchase on the rough coir strand, passed over Felix's head, slid down the tree and coiled before him. The ribcage expanded; the hood spread to its full terrible oval, the tongue flickered inches from Felix's eyes which were now open and wonderfully calm. The mantra rose to a warmer pitch, then fell, softer, softer yet to a whisper. Felix lowered his palms above the cobra's hood, and as his hands and the mantra fell, the hood slowly retracted. The cobra lowered its upper body and lay its head between Felix's knees while the mantra faded into the magic of the day.

Felix opened the Nescafe tin, stuffed the docile cobra in like so much soft plasticine, put the lid back, thumped it down, and dusted his hands off. He smiled. It had been a good morning's work. He accepted no payment and was never offered any. He gave Eurico a hug and off he went on the ancient Raleigh, rope, bag and Nescafe tin securely fastened to the carrier. The cobra would be released later in the day in the rain forest of Valpoi.

Commit the name to memory as I have: Felix Xavier Furtado. On those awkward occasions when a cobra drops in for a chat and a quick bite, he is a good man to know!

****

A Christmas Tale

'**T**was the night before Christmas
And alone on a dune
The fisherman Kaitan
Gazed at the moon.

Inspiration had fled
Not a sign from on high
That the pigling he coveted
Baked fatly would lie

On the small dining table
At a grand Xmas lunch
Alas poor Kaitan
Could just afford brunch.

His problem was one
That all of us know
The fish weren't biting
The wolf howled at the door

A family of seven
And that was no joke
A wife, five girls, a boy
Is a lot for one bloke

Priscilla, Jacinta, Assunta …
Then push came to shove
Maria, Theresa, Pedro …
Oh the complications of love!

Two ten-rupee notes
And a paisa or two
Tucked under the mattress
It just wouldn't do …

To buy a young pigling
Three months and no more
Stuffed, trussed and made ready
Just the day before …

… Christmas, he sighed
Oh where would we be
Without a baked pigling
For you, thee and me?

Would twenty rupees stretch
To a trotter? An ear?
A spare rib? A shank?
Fat chance! Oh dear …

I've got it! I've got it!
I'll buy the worst one
A snip for two tenners
Kaitan, well done!

The disgrace of the litter
Cross-eyed and knock-kneed
All bones and no bottom
Snuffles and greed

An ugly, tiny, scrawny runt
Sad, sorry and meek
I'll feed him up and down the clock
Till he's round, fat and sleek

Pedro will be put in charge
Shall we call the pig Freddy?
Perhaps not. We may miss him
When he's stuffed, baked and ready

Two tenners changed hands
For a pig in a poke
Mrs Kaitan was furious
Is this some kind of joke?

Pedro, little Pedro
The apple of my eye
Will you fatten up the pigling
Till the day it has to die?

Oh Dad, yes Dad
You bet I will
He's cute. He's cuddly.
I shall call him Skinny Bill

The naming of a pigling
Is no time for kerfuffle
You may, said Mrs Kaitan
Call him Snuffle

Seven days, seven nights
Till the moment of dread
How was a young pigling
To keep his head?

That night Snuffle lay
With his nose on Pedro's arm
And prayed to the heavens
Please don't let me come to harm

Make friends with young Pedro
Said a voice from above
He can't grunt. He's ungainly.
Offer him love

He has only two feet
Forgive him for that
He can't root. He can't grub.
And to you that's old hat

Despite his ten fingers
And ten useless toes
He has a kind heart
And believe me it shows

Do your hot hoof shuffle
And tricks with your tail
Turn a cartwheel or two
And try not to fail!

Teach him that piglings
Are more than just lunch
They clown, dance and giggle
When it comes to the crunch

It worked like a charm
And before you knew it
Pedro and Snuffle
Had become a duet

They made friends with a mongoose
Hissed at a snake
And when life got too boring
Jumped in the lake

They shared the same pillow
Built castles in the sand
Chased chickens, stole chikoos
And went hand in hand

Isn't it odd
They heard someone say
That a pig and a boy
Should behave in this way?

Snuffle snorted
Pedro wrote in the sand
With one little finger
Isn't life grand?

But Christmas was just
two days away
And Snuffle began to cry
Pedro was torn asunder
Why oh why?

Dad! You can't cook Snuffle
Pedro cried out
It's cruel. I won't let you!
What was that all about?

Snuffle laughs
I hear him cry
Snuffle dreams
Why must he die?

I love Snuffle
And Snuffle loves me
Please Daddy please
Let him be

There are seven of us
And on Christmas day
We shall stuff and eat Snuffle
I don't care what you say!
The next day Snuffle vanished
The sun had yet to rise
And Pedro's heart broke
Into a million shards of ice

Snuffle dear Snuffle
Where have you gone?
I am alone and lost
And quite forlorn …

Not a sniffle. Not a giggle
Nor hide nor hair
Snuffle had vanished
Into thin air!

Pedro sat dressed
In his Christmas best
He had no appetite
For the fest

Priscilla laid the table
Assunta brought the forks
And all that wretched Kaitan did
Was pop a lot of corks

How could Theresa giggle
At a time like this?
Maria all a-simper
While Jacinta blew a kiss

Then his mother made an entry
With a huge covered platter
Pedro's eyes grew round as saucers
Whatever was the matter?

The platter wiggled
all over the place
This way and that
While the cover bounced
up and down
Like a daft hat

His mother placed the platter
Right on the floor
And with a flourish Kaitan threw
The cover through the door

Snuffle! Clean as a whistle
Groomed nose to toe
With a pink ribbon
Tied up in a bow!

Snuffle wiggled
And did a hot hoof shuffle
Snuffle chuckled
And turned a cartwheel
Snuffle giggled
And did tricks with his tail
And best of all
He had brought Pedro some mail
Pedro's smile
Lit up the day
He opened the card
What would it say?

There is only one gift
For someone you love
The gift from the heart
That lasts forever

Merry Christmas

Epilogue: The Red Typewriter

The quick brown fox jumped over the lazy dogs'. That was always the first line typed, before the start of an article or book, on the old red Underwood that sits on my dad's heavy oak wood desk. It was to test the ink and to make sure no keys had fallen off. (One could never be sure what to expect from an antique!) It needed a lot of looking after. We had to keep it covered and clean it almost every day. Touch wood, it hadn't needed any repairing in years, even though it had been carried on a Japanese freighter, seen the Taj Mahal and backpacked around various parts of Europe.

My dad would type every day, starting around eight in the morning. His cat, O'Cat, as he was referred to, would sit by him and stare at the Underwood transfixed as he typed. Around noon, after having received no attention, not even a pat, O'Cat would rise and with one quick swish of his paw, rip the paper from the carriage and dart out of the room like a bat out of hell. On Sunday mornings I would sneak up on my dad, jump on to his lap, and sit there bobbing on his knee as he tried to type. I would watch with astonishment the speed at which he typed. The poor Underwood, already staggering, had to go on. After he was done I had to have a go, and he had no choice but to let me. I'd jab at the keys with my little fingers, and my dad could only grin as he watched his precious typewriter being mauled. Our beach house in Goa was my dad's favourite working place. We would go there ever so often as it was only a few hours away from home. My dad would religiously carry his Underwood with him. When he was working on his book, there was no place for any distractions. We would all be thrown out of the hall. The Underwood and my dad were the only two allowed to remain. He would clear the dining table, place the Underwood on a clean mat and begin typing. This daily ritual lasted from about nine in the morning till five in the evening. He only took a break for a quick lunch, but dinner was a family event. Obviously, the Underwood attended. As time went by, I begun to understand the passion he had for the machine. He told me how he'd had it for twenty years. It had always been loyal. It had never given up. It had helped him produce countless articles and books. He stressed how strong the Underwood was and how he couldn't imagine the day when it would need repairing.

But, one fine day, it needed to be repaired. While the Underwood was taken from place to place to get mended, my dad was in depression. No one in India could seem to figure out the problem. The future of the Underwood seemed grim, its little life hanging by a thread. We had begun to believe a solution would be impossible to find, until ... A phone call from my dad's brother in England. There was an Englishman in London who said he might be able to bring it back to health. On our next trip to London, off we went, my father clutching his Underwood in his arms. Mr Fison, an old doddering man in his late seventies, lived in a typical English mansion. My dad talked with him over tea and biscuits while my mother and I looked on. My dad told him about how he had been gifted this first love by his sister on his twenty-fifth birthday. They went on to share more stories and the abundant love and admiration they had for Underwoods. Mr Fison talked about the many he had seen in his time, and the number of lives he wasn't able to save. He always found it terribly hard to break the news to the owners. Some broke down, while others just thanked him and left.

After what seemed like hours, we were led (Underwood still clutched tightly in hand) to a humongous garage in his backyard. An enormous brass lock held the two large doors firmly together. Out came an equally large key, which was used carefully to unlock it. The doors creaked open, allowing us to enter. The room we walked into was poorly lit, but that didn't allow you to miss the graveyard of typewriters! The odds and ends of various kinds of 'dead' typewriters were piled almost to the roof. Mr Fison took us past this room to a smaller room adjoining this one. The 'graveyard' now seemed almost like a transition space, preparing you for what came next. This was a brightly lit room, carpeted unlike the first. But what caught your attention was on the left wall.

A row of shining Underwoods. It seemed as though they were revered by this man. Mr Fison told us we were the first customers he had brought into his work space. He had never met anyone who shared the same kind of love for Underwoods as he did. And so he wanted us to see these.

As we stood there in stunned silence, Mr Fison slowly pried away the Underwood from my dad and doddered off to the desk on the right. He placed it down as though its life depended on him. He put on another pair of glasses and started his examination through a magnifying glass. A few minutes later, he turned to us (still standing open-mouthed, staring at his collection) and smiled at my dad. `It can be fixed!' were his words.

His hand reached into a drawer and, slowly, out came the parts that were needed. I still remember the grin on my dad's face. I don't think he could have been happier. The precious life of his Underwood would be saved. I think Mr Fison was equally pleased. He couldn't stop smiling as he healed the Underwood.

Mr Fison gave my dad a huge black steel box in which to keep the Underwood. He said it would protect it from any danger. My dad is no longer with us. But the old red Underwood still lives on, on his heavy oak wood desk.

Chicago　　　　　　　RADHIKA ELIZABETH SIMOES
September, 2003

Chronology

Index